Mike Gold: A Literary Anthology

MIKE GOLD:

A Literary Anthology

Edited, With an Introduction
by MICHAEL FOLSOM

International Publishers
New York

Library of Congress Catalog Card Number: 79-184672

ISBN: (Hardback) 0-7178-0344-9; (paperback) 0-7178-0346-5

Printed in the United States of America

Contents

The Pariah of American Letters

MIKE GOLD's is a legendary life. For many years he was the best known literary Communist in the United States. He was the initiator of the so-called "proletarian" movement in American literature. His essay, "Towards Proletarian Art," which appeared in the February 1921 *Liberator*, was virtually the first call for the creation of a literature distinctly by and for and about the American working class. His *Jews Without Money* in 1930 was the first popular success of that remarkable movement. The bitter wit and polemic high dudgeon of his literary criticism and journalism helped define the "proletarian" sensibility.

For his efforts, Gold earned the love of many, and also abiding notoriety. Some genteel critics and lofty scholars vigorously calumniate his memory. Others ignore him wholly, or reduce him to a grudging footnote—as befits what they consider a wart on the buttocks of American literature. Gold died perhaps the most detested writer in our history, the very pariah of American letters, and that was his accomplishment. Most of the people who determine official literary judgments in our society Gold took for or turned into chosen enemies. Characteristically, he once so nettled one great American author with repeated broadside denunciations in his *Daily Worker* column that the great man stormed into the paper's office and demanded to confront the offender. Gold was out, and the receptionist asked if there were a message. "OK," said the famous author, "tell Mike Gold that Ernest Hemingway says he should go fuck himself."*

Such were the tributes accumulated by a man who spent his literary life, as a Communist and a revolutionary, working to build socialism in America. There were lots of people who did that, once upon a time. But Gold stuck it out. He died a little

---

* This anecdote is told by Carlos Baker in his *Ernest Hemingway: A Life Story* (Scribners: New York, 1969), page 459.

tired after the ravages of the McCarthy period, and a little cynical after many a disappointment, like the truth about Stalin, the "Moscow trials," the defection of so many old comrades. But he died still holding to the dream of his youth. That dream, Gold had written in 1921, was of a time "when there is singing and music rising in every American street, when in every American factory there is a drama-group of the workers, when mechanics paint in their leisure, and farmers write sonnets. . . ." And, Gold argued then, the only way to realize that dream was "the revolutionary method—from the deepest depths upward."

Now, any Ph.D. in English Literature can tell you that academics consider such talk, at best, simplistic romanticism, and, at worst, a dangerous delusion which threatens the very integrity and existence of literature. (It is perfectly reputable to devote academic passions to the study of aristocratic poems about shepherd poets, but the very suggestion of farmers writing sonnets elicits snickers.) For such views, Gold will never be forgiven by the literary establishment, as many of his one-time comrades have been of late. But the humble and the defiant cherish his vision, and that is all he would have asked of posterity.

Gold is a kind of legend now—a devil or a saint, depending on your point of view—and all the more legendary because his memory is obscured by fond rumor, ill will, and ignorance. Aside from *Jews Without Money,* almost none of his voluminous works is available in print, and many who have strong opinions about Gold and his work (pro and con) really know little about either. This anthology returns to print the most important of his writings.

A ponderous critical introduction to these selected works would betray Mike Gold's blithe spirits and suffer his revenge. He never had much use for the professorial way, and his works defy the professorial touch. A couple of brief quotations will help suggest the nature of the man's gifts and limitations.

Gold once described a new kind of writer who was appearing in America:

> . . . a wild youth of about twenty-two, the son of working-class parents, who himself works in the lumber camps, coal mines, steel mills, harvest fields and mountain camps of America. He is sensitive and impatient. He writes in jets of exasperated feeling and has no time to polish his work. He is violent and sentimental by turns. He

lacks self-confidence but writes because he must—and because he has real talent.

He is a Red but has few theories. It is all instinct with him. His writing is no conscious straining after proletarian art, but the natural flower of his environment. He writes that way because that is the only way for him. His "spiritual" attitudes are all mixed up with tenements, factories, lumber camps and steel mills, because that is his life.

Gold was always best when he was writing veiled autobiography, and, in this passage, he was describing himself as much as anyone else. Certainly, no more precise or penetrating word has been written about his own style and temperament and literary situation. If anyone else ever came close to catching his spirit, it was Walt Whitman—Whitman the dirty, disreputable, and democratic, whom Gold loved above all other poets, and who wrote in *Democratic Vistas:*

. . . We presume to write, as it were, upon things that exist not, and travel by maps yet unmade, and a blank. But the throes of birth are upon us; . . . hot from surrounding war and revolution, our speech, though without polish'd coherence, and a failure by the standard called criticism, comes forth, real at least as the lightenings.

That lightening in Gold's best work is a stark vision of both the grotesquery and the humanity of life at the bottom of what used to be called "the social pit." The childhood discovery of grassblades growing underfoot through cracks in sidewalk cement always stuck in Gold's imagination as an apt semblance of the life he knew. On the one hand there were all the gargoyles of the slums haunting his memory and filling his fiction—the deformed, degraded, degenerate, all carved by poverty and greed in the workers' quarters of capitalist America. On the other hand there were heroism, self-sacrifice, and struggle to give life and hope of greater life. And especially there was *community*—the community of boys banded together for adventure and defense in the jungle of streets, the community of women (whores and wives, Jew and gentile) coming to each other's aid in times of domestic crisis, the communities of the theater, the cafe, the job. And then there was the vision of triumph, the hope of destroying these foul slums, and building there, as Gold called it at the end of *Jews Without Money*, a "garden for the human spirit."

Explicit politics played very little part in Gold's fiction. His unfinished works, the novels he started unsuccessfully after *Jews*

Without Money, try to get into political issues, situations, stories. But that appears to be one reason they never were finished. When Gold did try to introduce politics into his world of fiction, he was often clumsy. The political ideas seemed "tacked on"—as at the end of *Jews Without Money,* or at the end of "Faster, America, Faster" in this collection. But in the journalism and the literary criticism, Gold's politics is up front, clear and strong. And politics was always there behind the fiction, beneath it for foundation, even working against it sometimes. One cannot grasp exactly what Gold was getting at in his stories without understanding that he conceived them in the context of his own daily work to change beyond recognition the world he represented in art.

If there was a difficult contradiction in Gold's consciousness, then let him again account for himself. In his peculiarly brave, prescient, callow, "mystic" essay, "Towards Proletarian Art," in 1921, Gold spoke—almost chanted—of the relations between the dying of capitalism and the soul of poets like himself:

> We rebel instinctively against that change. We have been bred in the old capitalist planet, and its stuff is in our very bones. Its ideals, mutilated and poor, were yet the precious stays of our lives. Its art, its science, its philosophy and metaphysics are deeper in us than logic or will. . . . We cling to the old culture, and fight for it against ourselves. But it must die. The old ideals must die. . . . Let us fling all we are into the cauldron of the Revolution. For out of our death shall arise glories. . . .

Itzok Isaac Granich was born April 12, 1893,* in New York's East Side ghetto to Jewish immigrant parents, the first of three sons. Early in life, he adopted Irwin for a Christian name, and his first writings were signed that way. During the Palmer Raids of 1919–1920, he took "Michael Gold" for a protective pseudonym, and it stuck. (The "real" Michael Gold was an old man who endeared himself to the young revolutionary by having fought in Abe Lincoln's war to free the black people, and who didn't seem to mind having his name stolen for a good cause.)

Gold has accounted for his first twenty-one years in *Jews Without Money.* The book is not factual autobiography, but, in most respects, it catches the essence of the life lived in the ghetto

---

* The correct year of Gold's birth is 1893, not 1894 or 1896 as Gold and others have, on occasion, variously indicated.

and on the fringes of Christian America just before and after the turn of this century. *Jews Without Money* explains much about the shorter works collected here.

One telling liberty which Gold took with his experience in that book emphasizes a central fact of his life and literary/political motivations. He was not, properly speaking, a "child of the proletariat." The father in the book is a housepainter and peddler; the real Pop Granich was a capitalist of sorts. He was the very poorest and most dependent of entrepreneurs, to be sure—a store-front suspenders-fixture manufacturer who often brought home at week's end as little as his several employees did. His sons were early driven out of school and into the lowest ranks of the proletariat, because Pop's health and business failed. But they were reared on aspiration, on the hope of making it in the New World—as was every impoverished immigrant's child.

The point is not that Gold was really a bourgeois, but that his bitterness was the bitterness of disappointment as well as the bitterness of the oppressed and exploited. When Pop Granich emigrated from Rumania in the 1880s, America promised to reward an eager newcomer's industry with the good life, and America defaulted. Gold was a precocious child who wanted nothing more than to go to college. America promised him an education, then forced him to drop out and sweat for pennies instead of finishing high school.

America even had a self-exonerating legend which it taught its victims. Abe Lincoln educated himself by firelight, and, if young Isaac Granich couldn't do the same by gaslight after twelve hours of work in a sweatshop, well, it was his own fault, his lack of grit and fortitude. At least that is the way it often seemed to him. His moody temperament was prey to self-hatred and self-pity, which were added to resentment and deprivation to produce a troublesome complex of angry motives and disadvantages.

But Gold inherited a zealous Jew's fierce hope for justice and retribution, as well as a romantic Jew's love of high culture, and that sustained him. Desperate adolescent hope in a Jewish Messiah—who would look like Buffalo Bill and slaughter the *goyim* and *gonefs*—gave way to commitment to revolutionary working-class politics:

> O workers' Revolution, you brought hope to me, a lonely suicidal boy. You are the true Messiah. You will destroy the East Side when you come, and build there a garden for the human spirit.

These familiar words from the closing of *Jews Without Money* are an epitome of Gold's temperament and spiritual career. Anger and organization overcame self-pity; violence strove for tenderest conclusions. The story, "Love on a Garbage Dump," which is reprinted in this collection, confirms this pattern in Gold's thought and spirit. Equanimity was never his portion. The road of excess was, in William Blake's good proverb, Mike Gold's way to the palace of wisdom.

In a sense, Gold's life really began with the event which ends *Jews Without Money*. At that unemployed demonstration in Union Square in April 1914 which apparently decided his commitment to revolutionary politics, he bought his first copy of the revolutionary *Masses* magazine. He had been writing verse and stories for a while, but without hope that anyone would print what a poor kid had to say about poverty. The *Masses* would and did. Four months later a poem of his appeared in its pages. It was a eulogy to three anarchist terrorists who had just been killed, so it appeared, by their own bomb. That was the beginning.

The *Masses* was Gold's schoolhouse—the *Masses* and the Provincetown Theatre, which was the dramatic wing of revolutionary Bohemia around the time of the First World War, and which produced Gold's first one-act plays, along with those of Eugene O'Neill. Gold's great teachers were Max Eastman and Floyd Dell of the *Masses,* who curried the poet and hopeful novelist, and George Cram ("Jig") Cook of the Provincetown, who made him a dramatist. Brave John Reed was his hero in those chaotic years of war and revolution. No lost rebel poet ever found more congenial mentors or a better time to bloom than did Mike Gold in Greenwich Village on the eve of the first world holocaust, at the dawn of Soviet power.

In the years just after 1914, Gold moved out of the ghetto and into the Village. He gave up manual labor when he discovered he could earn his keep at newspaper work. Radical politics proved to be no such pat solution to his problems as the conclusion to *Jews Without Money* suggests, nor was the life of art an especially comforting one. In rebellious Bohemia, the Revolution was less a political discipline than a lifestyle and a good-natured posture. Gold foundered and quested and ran with the reddest of the red—the Wobblies and anarchists and the first liberated children of the middle class who practised free love and free

verse in equally studied and gawky fashion. It was a heady, ec-
static life, and a desperate one. Gold was often on the verge of
nervous breakdown during these early years, and several times
over the brink.

The Russian Revolution, the formation of the Communist
Party in the United States in 1919, and a little reading of Lenin
put some structure and spine into Gold's politics. But it was a *little* reading. Gold admitted that he never had a head for theories,
but his hurts and his heart kept him true, and far truer than
many a once radical intellectual who scoffed at Gold's impul-
siveness and sentimentality.

Just before the World War, Gold spent a lot of time in Boston,
first trying to pick up his education at Harvard (he dropped out
after less than a semester, when his money and spirits failed),
then bumming around, working as a reporter and in a Fabian
bookshop, joining the anarchist leaders of the cordage workers'
strike down in Plymouth. Another stint in New York, working
on the Socialist daily *Call,* then Gold was off again, this time to
Mexico (1918–1919) to avoid being drafted.

In January 1921, Gold became an editor of the *Liberator,*
which had succeeded the suppressed *Masses.* He was one of the
younger generation of literary radicals (Joseph Freeman was another) who began to take over leadership of the movement from
the tiring Eastmans and Dells just as prosperity and red scares
were decimating the Left. "Thoughts of a Great Thinker," reprinted here, suggests the hectic pace of editorial responsibility
which Gold couldn't take for long, and by the end of 1922 he
was ready to take off once again—this time for California.

While the *Liberator* was gradually turning into a political
journal under Robert Minor's editorship and dying (it merged
into the *Worker's Monthly* at the end of 1924), Gold was working as a journalist in Oakland and on Fremont Older's San Francisco *Call.* For two years in the Bay Area he sniffed Jack London's air, consorted with working-class Reds and upper-class
poets, and sweated over the novel about his childhood which had
been a long time brewing (see "Birth," reprinted in this collection), and which would take the rest of the decade to distill into
Jews Without Money (1930).

In 1925, Gold got the chance to tour Europe and visit the
young Soviet Union, where he had his first book published, a
collection of his stories, with an introduction by Big Bill Hay-

wood. He came back enthusiastic for the brand new "construc-
tivist" theater of Meyerhold, which he had seen in Moscow, and
took up his dormant dramatic career. Quickly he knocked out
two full-length plays (his first and virtually his only), and in
1926 and 1927 was instrumental in setting up radical theatrical
groups.

One of these ventures, the New Playwrights' Theatre, produced Gold's *Hoboken Blues* (about the black poor of Harlem
in the Jazz Age), along with works by John Dos Passos, John
Howard Lawson, and others. In 1929, a revived and commercialized Provincetown Playhouse produced his *Fiesta*, which was
an attempt at a Broadway musical about the peons and patri-
cians of rural Mexico. Neither play was much of a success. Gold
had a sympathetic hankering for the poor of other cultures, but
not the intimate feel which he did have of his own culture in the
Jewish ghetto.

Gold had been troubled by the turning of the *Liberator* into a
wholly political magazine, and, even before its death, he was
urging the creation of a new radical literary periodical. In 1926,
his desire bore fruit in the establishment of the *New Masses*. The
first issues of the new magazine were a self-conscious imitation
of its namesake, an attempt to revive the brilliant spirit of the old
Bohemian-left-liberal alliance. But what had been a force and a
possibility when the old *Masses* lived was no longer, and, after a
fat subsidy from a liberal foundation ran out, the new magazine
faltered. In 1928, Gold and a few other of the Communists
among the original *New Masses* editors picked up the pieces and
set out on a new tack. Humble in its format and virtuous in its
poverty, Gold's new *New Masses* was "a magazine of workers'
art and literature." For four years, it conducted an experiment in
creating an actual "proletarian" literature in the United States,
attempting to rely upon the contributions of working men and
women, rather than on those of professional writers with radical
sympathies. The experiment was no great success. The magazine
did gather a cadre of real worker-poets with now-forgotten
names like H. H. Lewis and Martin Russak, but circulation daw-
dled and influence drooped. At least, however, Gold was instrumental in sustaining the impulse of radical literature. As the Depression deepened and radicalism became imperative once again
and a new crop of professional writers came leftward, the *New
Masses* was ready to hand, a vehicle for the expression of a re-
born leftwing literary movement.

Gold was thirty-seven years old in 1930, already an "old man" of Left letters. In that year, events conspired with his dec-ade-and-a-half of dogged commitment to make him famous. In February, *Jews Without Money* appeared, and it went through eleven printings by October. In September, the liberal literary es-tablishment was distressed to read in the *New Republic* Gold's attack on the novels of Thornton Wilder. The time and the place were just right. A year earlier, at the height of the Boom, there would have been no audience for a book about poverty. In the *New Masses,* where Gold had been writing for years, his attack on Wilder would have echoed ineffectually. But the *New Repub-lic*'s polite readers' outraged answers set Gold at the center of the new decade's first big public literary brawl.

Gold was a national figure now, the budding "Gorky" of American literature. In that good year of 1930, he attended the first of the decade's big international leftwing writers' confer-ences (at Kharkov, the Ukraine), and he was lionized. But he paid a price for success: the early termination of his career as a novelist and playwright. He published nothing of consequence in the line of imaginative literature after 1930, though he tried and tried. His papers contain innumerable manuscript beginnings of plays and novels, but none ever came close to completion.

A part of the problem was Gold's constitutional aversion to sustained effort. His brilliance was always erratic. But the hectic events of war and revolution and the responsibilities of a radical with an influential name bore upon him also. In 1933, he deter-mined to employ his talents and repute for the most popular, im-mediate benefit, and he became a columnist for the *Daily Worker*. He continued as a journalist for the Communist press on and off for the next thirty-three years, almost up to his death.

Gold was an asset. Many readers took the paper first or mainly for his columns in which they found the gut responses of a tender and angry man, the "human side" of the Revolution. Many an older radical today recalls that he or she was brought into the movement by Gold's hot words and simple stories about the daily fight—words and stories which lived in a way that deadly political harangues and hair-splitting argument never did, and never will. But the grind of a daily column, plus constant speaking engagements, demonstrations, and picketlines, told on his time and talent. He never did get around to finishing those books and plays he was going to write.

At the end of his life, Gold looked back on all that with some bitterness—not against the movement which took him from his heart's desire, but against the times which seemed to demand that he desire to give himself away so urgently to the movement. Obituaries which reported that he had become "disillusioned" and had left the Communist Party in his last years were either mischievous or ill-informed. To the end, he would have repeated what he said in 1932 at the full height of his literary career: "I want Socialism so much that I accept this fierce, crude struggle as my fate in time; I accept its disciplines and necessities; I become as practical and realistic as is possible for me; I want victory." Still, Gold knew how much he had sacrificed for the sweets of a victory he never tasted.

Gold became the Jimmy Higgins of literary radicalism in the 1930s. He shied from leadership in literary organizations like the John Reed Clubs early in the decade and the League of American Writers later on. Asset that he was in writing for the other Jimmy Higginses of the world, who were always his best and favorite audience, he was sometimes considered a liability among the literati. During the "United Front" period of the later 1930s, when just about every writer of note in America was openly willing to work with the Communist Party in the fight against fascism, Gold's gruff opinions and rude manners embarrassed people who were afraid of losing influential allies.

From his very earliest commitment to the radical movement, Gold had been deeply upset by philistine attitudes he came across, even on the Left, about how poetry was a waste of time and art was the dalliance of sissies. He never got over his chagrin at Robert Minor's decision to give up his incomparable gift with a crayon in favor of a strictly political career. John Reed was Gold's hero, among other reasons, because he was a revolutionary *and* an intellectual. In "John Reed and the Real Thing," Gold observed:

> In the I.W.W. the fellow workers would tar and feather (almost) any intellectual who appeared among them. The word "intellectual" became a synonym for the word "bastard," and in the American Communist movement there is some of this feeling.

Gold had little patience with self-conscious craftsmanship, and he talked down "style." Truth, he argued, was enough in art. He himself could use the terms "intellectual" and "college" invidiously. And, like the black militant today who is so intent on building the dignity of his own people that he denies the white race any gift or virtue, Gold at times insisted that his people, the poor and the working class and their writers, had nothing to learn from studying the great literature of the "bourgeois" past —even though he himself had been weaned on Schiller and Shakespeare and Tolstoy, and his reverence for them never flagged.

All during the 1930s, Gold was feverishly active, but, in the much larger stage of radical literature, he played nothing like the central role that had been his in the lonesome 1920s. He addressed none of the first three American Writers' Congresses (1935, 1937, 1939), and, when he spoke before the fourth (1941), he had become prominent again in a dwindling field. In that 1941 speech (printed for the first time in this collection), Gold stressed the contribution of the "proletarian" phase in the literature of the decade, and he generously acknowledged his own "fate in time." He compared the "proletarian" literary pioneering, which he led, to the winning of the American West. The pioneers prepared the way for the planting of civilization. When the cities grew, "some of the pioneers then moved on to other virgin soil; others were swallowed up in the new civilization. Many were crowded out, and even forgotten. But still, they had planted something; it was enough of a reward for a pioneer."

After the "Moscow Trials," the Finnish War, and the Molotov-Ribbentrop Pact, the literary Left disintegrated, and to Gold fell the task of defending what remained, and of spiking the "renegades" who had followed Roosevelt into the "Phoney War." His main blast was a series of articles in the *Worker* which were reprinted as *The Hollow Men* in 1941, just before the Nazi invasion of the Soviet Union. Gold's survey of the silliness of a generation of middle-class, sometime-radical writers, like his psychological analysis of their motives, still has much to recommend it, but there is a bitter constriction of the heart in that document which speaks of Gold's terrible disappointment at the end of a decade of high hopes. The "renegades" chapter from *The Hollow Men* is the most painful piece to reprint in this volume. It is reprinted because its difficulties must be dealt with, especially since they were representative of a major passage in the intellectual history of the American Left. The essay on the "renegades" is overlong and might easily be edited. But the point is that, for instance, Gold did feel called upon to quote at length from the then current version of the *History of the Communist Party of the Soviet Union* as a way of trying to deal with American problems, and that he, like many, many others, did find himself trapped into taking a monstrous fraud, the "Moscow Trials," as a justification for his attack on ex-Communist writers in the United States. Gold's argument only makes full sense when we understand the ancillary "evidence" he brought to bear. One way to avoid the repetition of error is to admit it. This unwieldy, but important, essay remains as it appeared in *The Hollow Men*.

In the 1940s there were more bitter fights. Though he considered it necessary, Gold had never felt at ease with "United Front" policy which stressed alliance with middle-class liberals over revolutionary working-class consciousness and activity. Fighting fascism was one thing, but forgetting about revolution was quite another, and after the War he was one of the first Communists to take a public stand against long-time party head, Earl Browder, who had liquidated the party as such. In 1946, Gold was among the most uncompromising "old-line" stalwarts in "the storm over Maltz," the last of the major "Old Left" literary squabbles. (Gold's articles on Albert Maltz's literary "revisionism" are reprinted in this collection.)

Gold and his family spent the late 1940s and early 1950s in France, returning to the States in the McCarthy time to find his movement in disarray and his nation hysterical. He made one last effort, a national speaking tour in 1954. Terribly the times and their disasters had outstripped him. His report of that tour, aptly titled "The Troubled Land" and published in *Masses & Mainstream* (July 1954), concluded with desperate assurance that a new "People's Front" against reaction was gathering in the land. But that was buncombe, and Gold knew it. Audience after audience had been made up of old folks. Much as Gold loved his old comrades, he saw little use in the public life of a talker if he couldn't talk to the young.

In 1957, Gold retired to San Francisco, away from the battle and heartbreak of mother New York, back to the golden land of his youthful adventures. (New York, he had written in 1928, "is a machine that grinds the mind to powder.") He picked up his column again in the weekly *People's World,* and kept at it through failing eyesight and health until just before his death in April of 1967, reluctantly giving up the last of a half-century in the radical press to devote his energies to his memoirs.

When the country began stirring again in the 1960s, Gold had trouble appreciating the style of the new young politics of alienation and dissent, and many of the few young who read him in the *People's World* had a hard time figuring him out. But when Gold came home from his walks down past the corner of Haight and Ashbury streets, he came back sure that something—something crazy, like when he was a kid in Greenwich Village, lost and rebellious and pulling pranks to shock the bourgeoisie, and hailing in the Soviets—something *real,* was afoot, and there was still hope, to be sure.

This is primarily a *literary* anthology, because Gold's aspirations, gifts, and achievements were primarily literary, though arithmetically, perhaps, the bulk of his writing was political journalism. Gold put more art in his politics and more politics in his art than most, but still there is a distinction to be made. Readers who came to know him through his "Change the World!" column may be puzzled to find the writer in this book rather different from the one they remember; others who now meet Gold for the first time should know that they meet only part of the man, even if it is the most important part. But neither Gold nor history would be served by an attempt, in a small anthology of the essential works, to be pedantically representative and mechanically balanced. Rather, there is something here to offend every taste and opinion, my own included, and that is how it should be.

This anthology contains no excerpts from *Jews Without Money,* because that book is now available in paperback (Avon), and none of Gold's dramas, because they wouldn't fit. Otherwise it contains the best stuff he wrote. Also some which is obviously bad. I have chosen some materials strictly because of their historical importance, regardless of their eternal merit. One will find here all of Gold's writings which are frequently referred to in historical discussions of American literary radicalism, almost all of which have never been reprinted.

All of the works, except those which are undatable, are printed in chronological order. The few footnotes are Gold's own; information which might be found in editorial footnotes is included in the headnotes to each piece.

Any attempt to be punctiliously faithful in the transcription of Gold's writings must be frustrated by Gold's devil-may-care approach to the mechanics of English. Niggling accuracy would

only reproduce chaos. I have taken the liberty to correct typo
graphical errors and to regularize spelling and mechanics silently
—and occasionally to revise other minor haphazardry in Gold's
practice, especially practice dictated by the conventions of journalism. But the texts appear here virtually as they were first published. This point should be stressed because Gold made a number of revisions in some of his best pieces when he prepared
them for previous anthologies, among other things cutting out
the most militant references to communism and revolution.
While such changes are an author's prerogative and may have
seemed appropriate in other times, they are unnecessary now,
and the restitution of the original texts was Gold's wish.

    I collaborated with Mike Gold on this anthology until Gold's
death in the spring of 1967. The contents remain pretty much as
Gold intended; the editing, introduction, and notes are solely my
responsibility.

MICHAEL FOLSOM

Boston
May Day, 1971

Bucket of Blood

And now a toast to my city
I'll drink in a bucket of blood
Viva! the blackjacks and roses
Hurrah for the glory and mud!

This untitled and undated manuscript fragment was found in Gold's papers. There was a saloon on the Bowery, around the corner from where he grew up, called The Bucket of Blood.

Three Whose Hatred Killed Them

These wild, bitter men, whose iron hatred burst too soon,
Judge them not harshly, O comrades.
Forgive them their sin, for they loved much.
They hated, but it was the enemy of man they hated.
They lusted for man's blood, but it was the blood of those who
shed man's blood they lusted for.
They thought to spoil God's clay, but it was to save much more
of that sacred stuff that they thought this.

Think of them, dear comrades, as fellow soldiers too impatient to
await the signal.
Undisciplined warriors, aflame for battle and loath to bide the
issue
Until came reinforcements, fresh troops by love and reason re-
cruited,
Singing as they came to join us, the Army of the Brotherhood of
Man.

This is the first piece Gold had published in the regular press (he recalled that an East Side settlement house newsletter printed a couple of his poems or stories earlier). On July 4, 1914, Arthur Caron, Charles Berg, and Karl Hanson, who had been active in the anarchist movement, and who were about to go on trial in connection with a protest demonstration against the "Ludlow Massacre" in Colorado, were killed by a bomb in their tenement apartment on upper Lexington Avenue, New York City. As Gold's poem suggests, it was generally assumed—on the Left as well as in hysterical newspaper accounts—that the petard which hoisted these men was, indeed, their own. John D. Rockefeller, who owned the bloody mines in Colorado where the massacre had taken place, may or may not have been their intended victim. Irwin Granich, Masses, August 1914.

MacDougal Street

Bill, pipe all these cute little red doll's houses
They are jammed full of people with cold noses
   And bad livers
Who look out of their windows as we go roaring by
   Under the stars
Disgustingly drunk with the wine of life
And write us up for the magazines—

MacDougal Street was the main thoroughfare of Greenwich Village in Gold's youth, as it is today. Irwin Granich, Masses, *May 1916.*

A Damned Agitator

THE STRIKE was now smoldering into its seventh week, and, perhaps, it would soon be a bitter ash in the mouths of the men. For funds were at an ebb, scabs were coming in like a locust plague, the company officials were growing more and more militant in their self-righteousness, and the strikers themselves were drifting into a settled state of depression and dangerous self-distrust. Their solidarity was beginning to show fissures and aching cracks.

All these woeful conditions beat in like a winter sea on the tired brain of Kurelovitch with the bleak morning light that waked him. He lifted his throbbing head from the pillow, looked about the dingy bedroom with his bleary, sleep-glazed eyes, and heaved a long, troubled sigh out of his pain.

At a meeting of company executives once Kurelovitch had been denounced as a dangerous agitator, whose pathological thirst for violence had created and sustained the strike.

"A Damned Agitator" was one of Gold's earliest published and most popular stories. It was one of a number of short fictions he contributed to the New York Call, the Socialist daily, in 1916–1917, and became the title story of two early collections of his work. The Damned Agitator and Other Stories was number seven in the Daily Worker's "Little Red Library" series (around 1924). In 1925 a larger collection of the same name appeared in Russian in Moscow with an introduction by Big Bill Haywood. A very heavily reworked version appeared in 120 Million in 1929. The changes were not in structure or argument, but in tone mostly. Gold quieted things a bit, slightly softened his representation of the brutal and grotesque. The one major change he made was to shift the nationality of the group of workers who waver and want to break the strike. In the earlier version they were Russians, in the later French Canadians. In small ways the 1929 version has things to recommend it, but 120 Million is much easier to find than the New York Call Sunday supplement, and, in keeping with the policy of this anthology, the text here is the earlier version. Irwin Granich, New York Call, March 4, 1917.

"The man is a menace, a mad dog, whose career ought to be stopped before he does more mischief," said one venerable director, his kind, blue eyes developing a pinkish glare that would have horrified the women folk of his family.

"The scoundrel's probably pocketing half of the strike funds," declared another director with plump, rosy gills and a full, bald head that glittered like a sunset cloud, as he stunned the long table with a blow of his balled fist.

But Kurelovitch was not a mad dog, and he was not waxing fat with industrial spoils, as so many of the directors had. He was really a tall, tragic, rough-hewn Pole, who had been suddenly hammered into leadership by the crisis of the strike, by reason of his unquenchable integrity and social fire. He had deep, blue, burning eyes, a rugged nose and moustaches, and his hands and form were ungainly, work-twisted symbols of the life of drudgery he had led.

Now he was thinking wearily of all the thorny problems that would be heaped upon him that day in the course of the strike. As he extricated himself from the bedclothes and sat up to dress, the problems writhed and clamored in his jaded brain for solution. For seven weeks now he had risen almost at dawn and had labored till midnight at the Titan task of wringing a fifteen per cent increase out of capitalism for his fellow workers. He had grown gaunt and somber and wise in the process; skeptical of man and of God. He had seen plans collapse, heads broken unjustly, sentences inflicted by corrupt judges, babies and women starving. He had heard himself assailed as a monster by the other camp and as a weakling and tool by the more embittered of his own side.

His wife heard him sigh, and she called from the kitchen, where she was already stirring.

"There ain't no coffee for you this morning, Stanislaw," she announced in a sullen voice, in which there was also anger and scorn. "And there ain't no nothin' else to eat, only a few hunks of old bread."

Kurelovitch stumbled wearily to his feet and entered the malodorous kitchen. Greasy pans and platters and sour garbage were strewn about, and in an opaque cloud of smoke his wife was hovering over the stove, their fourth child mewing in the nest of her arms. She was heating all the milk she had for the infant, and

when her husband came in she turned on him with swift viru-
lence.

"No, not a taste of food in the house, damn you," she spat.
"And the kids went to bed last night without hardly any supper."

"But it's not my fault now, is it, Annie?" the big man returned
humbly as he went over to her and put an arm over her shoulder. She cast it off with fierce contempt, and stood him off with
a volley of words that were like poisoned arrows, each piercing
straight to his vital parts.

"It is your fault, you clumsy fool, you," she screamed out of
her over-laden heart. "You were one of the first men to go out
on strike, even though we hadn't a penny in the house at the
time. And last week when the company wanted the men to come
back you talked them out of it, and so we're all still starving,
thanks to you."

"But, Annie—" the tall man attempted gently.

"Don't Annie me, or try to fool me with one of your speeches.
You know the strike's lost as well as I do, and that after it you'll
be blacklisted in every mill town in New England. But you don't
care if your children starve, do you? You'd be glad to see us all
dead wouldn't you?"

The man had crumpled under the attack, and he seemed as
small almost as his infuriated wife. But then he straightened in
the dusty pallor of the kitchen, and moved to the door.

"I'll see that you get a lot of groceries and things from headquarters this morning," he said huskily, as he went out into the
dark, bitter streets.

Kurelovitch shivered at his contact with the gray, sharp air. A
thin ash of snow had fallen through the night, and was now a
noisome slush, after its brief experience with the mill town,
which degraded everything it touched. The muddy ooze
squirmed through the vulnerable spots in his shoes, and started
the gooseflesh along Kurelovitch's spine. Across the river in the
drab morning he could see the residential heights where the rich
dwelt, and they reminded him of the village of his youth, with its
girdle of snow-crowned hills and peaceful cottages. He remembered a Polish lullaby his mother used to sing to him, and shivered the more.

From the rough bridge which bound the split halves of the
town he could see the mill, glowering and blocking shadows deep
as ignorance on the rotting ice of the river. The resplendent em-

blem of America gleamed and waved from a staff on the low, sprawling structure as if to sanctify all that went on beneath. And now Kurelovitch had traversed a morass of decaying huts and offal-strewn streets and was directly within the massive shadow of the mill. Two or three of his fellow-workers recognized him, and came hurrying forward from the picket line. Kurelovitch's day had begun.

"The damned gunmen are out for fight this morning," said a sombre, chunky Pole, swathed in old burlap and a tremendous fur cap that had come from Europe.

"Yes, they must have gotten more booze than usual last night," said another striker between his chattering teeth.

A young picket with brooding, dark eyes burst out with a hot voice, "Well, we'll give them any fight they want, the dirty lice. We're not afraid." Kurelovitch put his hand on the young chap, and then the three went with him to where about fifty or more of the strikers were shifting slowly up and down the length of the wide mill gate.

There were men and women in the line, all dark and silent and seeming more like a host of mourners than anything else in the world of bitter sky and slush-laden earth. They were muffled to the chins in grotesque rags, and their breaths went up like incense in the chill morning. A mood of sadness and suspense hung about them, and whenever they passed the knot of gunmen at the gate they turned their eyes away almost in grief.

Two of the gunmen had detached themselves from the evil-eyed mob huddled, like a curse, at the gate. They carried clubs in their hands, and at their hips could be seen bulging the badges of their mission in life, which was to break strikes and to murder.

They came up to Kurelovitch and sneered at him with sadistic eyes. As he walked up and down in the sluggish picket line, they dogged him and used their vilest art to taunt him into resistance.

About an hour later, as he was departing from the line, the two gunmen still followed him. A little group of pickets, therefore, formed themselves in a cordon about Kurelovitch and escorted him to the strike headquarters, burning all the way with repressed rage. Kurelovitch was a marked man in the strike zone, and his maiming was a subject of much yearning and planning by the gunmen.

The daily meetings of the strikers were held in a great barn-like structure in the center of the tangled streets and alleys of the mill-workers' quarter. A burst of oratory smote Kurelovitch as he entered the great room and a thousand faces, staring row on row, orientated to the leader as he marched in.

"Kurelovitch, Kurelovitch has come," ran a murmur like wind through a forest.

Kurelovitch leaped on the rough stage, where others of the strike committee were sitting, and whispered in consultation with a fellow Pole. He learned that there was nothing of moment that day—no sign from the bosses nor funds from sympathizers. It was merely another of the dark days of the strike.

"But many of the Russians are getting restless," the man whispered. "Raviloff has been at them, and yesterday their priest told them to go back. Give 'em hell, Kurelovitch!"

Kurelovitch came to the edge of the platform in a hush like that of an operating room, looking out over a foam of varied faces. They were faces that had blown into the golden land on the 12 winds of the world, though about nine-tenths of the faces were the broad-boned, earthy, beautiful faces of mystic Slavdom. Daylight struggled through large, smutty windows and dusted the heads and shoulders of the strikers with a white, transcendent powder. A huge oilcloth behind Kurelovitch proclaimed in big, battering letters, "We Average $9 a Week and We Are Demanding 15 Per Cent More. Are You With Us?"

The air tightened as Kurelovitch loomed there, a sad hero, stooped and gaunt with many cares. Finger-deep hollows were in his cheeks, and, with his blazing eyes and strong mouth, he seemed like some ascetic follower of the warrior Mohammed.

"Fellow workers . . ."

In low, thrilling Polish he began by disposing of the secular details of the strike, as on every day. Then something would come over Kurelovitch, a strange feeling of automatism, as if he were indeed only the voice that this simple-hearted horde had created out of their woe. The searing phrases would rush from his lips in a wild, stormy music, like the voice of a gale, and as mystic and powerful.

With both hands holding his breast, as if it were bursting with passionate vision, Kurelovitch lifted his face in one of his superb moments and flamed up like an Isaiah.

"Fellow workers," he chanted, giving the words a value such as cannot be transmitted by mere writing, "we can never be beaten, for we are the workers on whose shoulders rest the pillars of the world and in whose hands are the tools by which life is carried on. Life, liberty and happiness—let us not rest till we have gotten these for ourselves and our children's children! Let us not permit the accidents of a strike to stay us on our journey toward the beautiful city of freedom, whose grace is one day to shine on all the world.

"We are beginning to starve, some of us, but let us starve bravely, for we are soldiers in a greater and nobler war than that which is bleeding Europe. We are soldiers in the class war which is finally to set mankind free of all war and all poverty, all bosses and hate. Workingmen of the world, unite; we have nothing to lose but our chains; we have a world to gain!"

Kurelovitch ended in a great shout, and then the handclapping and whistles rose to him in turbulent swirls. He found himself suddenly weary and limp and melancholy, and his deepest wish was to go off somewhere alone to wait until the hollow places inside were refilled. . . .

But, with the others of the strike committee, he left the platform and fused into the discussions that were raging everywhere. Everybody tried to come near Kurelovitch, to speak to him. He was a common hearth at which his people crowded and shouldered for warmth, his starving, wistful people who believed him when he said they could wipe out the accumulated woe of humanity. . . .

He was treated to long recitals of the workings of the proletarian soul in this time of want and panic and anger. He heard a hundred tales of temptation, of desperate hunger, of outrages at the hands of gunmen. Kurelovitch listened to it all like a grave, kind father confessor, untying many a Gordian knot with his clear-eyed strength and understanding.

And then came to him Raviloff, the leader of the Russians, a short, black, wrinkled man, with slow eyes that became living coals of fire when passion breathed on them.

He was angry to impotence now. "You said in your speech that I was a traitor, Kurelovitch," he shouted fiercely. "You lie; I am not. But we Russians think this strike is lost, and that we'd all better go back before it's too late."

"It's not lost," Kurelovitch replied slowly. "The mills can't work full time until we choose to go back. And, Raviloff, I say again that you're a scab and traitor if you go back now."

Raviloff flushed purple with wrath, and rushed upon the tall

Pole as if to devour him. But Kurelovitch did not lift his stern, calm gaze from the other's face, and a light like that of swords came and went in his blue eyes. The Russian surged up and touched him, chest to chest, and then Kurelovitch intrigued the other into a sensible discussion that served to keep the Russian on the firing line. . . .

And thus it went. So Kurelovitch passed his day, moving from the swooning brink of one crisis to another. He sat with the strike committee for many hours in a smoky room and agonized over ways and means. He addressed another large meeting at headquarters in the afternoon. He went out on the picket line and was singled out for threats and taunts again by the gunmen, so that he felt murder boiling in his deeps and left. Then he had to return later to the picket line because word was rushed to him that five of the pickets had been arrested in a fight finally precipitated by the gunmen. Kurelovitch spent the rest of the afternoon scurrying about and finding bail for the five.

Toward night he had a supper of ham sandwiches and coffee, and then he and three of the strike committee went to a meeting of sympathizers about 15 miles away. Kurelovitch made his third passioned address of the day, and stirred up a large collection. The long, dull, wrenching ride home followed.

He got off the trolley car near his house about midnight, his brain whirling and hot, his heart acrid and despairing. The urgency of the fight was passed, and nothing was lift to buoy him against his weariness. He walked in a stupor; the day had sucked every atom of his valor and strength. He wished dumbly for death; he was the cold ashes of the flaming Kurelovitch of the day. Had gunmen come now and threatened him he would have cringed and then wept.

There was a feeble light waning and wavering in the window of his little three-room flat, and when he had fumbled with the lock and opened the dilapidated door he found someone brooding with folded arms near the stove. It stood up awfully and turned on him with baleful eyes, like a wild beast in its cave.

"You rotten dog!" his wife screamed at Kurelovitch in the vast quiet of the night. "You mean and dirty pig!"

"Annie, dear—"

"To go away in the morning and leave us to starve! To send food to other's families and then to forget us! Oh, you'd be glad if we all died of starvation! You'd laugh to see us all dead, you murderer!"

Kurelovitch was too sorrowful to attempt an answer. He went to the bedroom where he and two of the children slept and shut the door behind him. His wife took this for a gesture of contempt, and her frenzy mounted to a blood-curdling crescendo that ran up and down the neighborhood like a ravaging blight. Heads popped out of windows and bawled to her to cease for Christ's sake. And, finally she broke down of sheer exhaustion and Kurelovitch heard her shuffling into bed.

There was anguished silence, and then Kurelovitch heard his poor, overburdened drudge of a wife weeping terribly, with gulping sobs that hurt him like knives. . . .

And now he could not sleep at all, even after her sobbing had merged into ugly snoring. He tossed as in a fever, as he had on so many other nights of the seven frantic weeks of the strike.

He went blindly for relief to the window, beyond which reigned the cold, inimical night. The shabby slum street dwindled to an obscure horizon, and the mass of the mill building could be seen dominating over the ragged houses. No being was abroad in the desolate dark; he saw a chain of weak lanterns casting morbid shadows, and the vicious wind whipping up the litter of the streets. The stars were white and high overhead, as distant as beauty from the place where Kurelovitch burned with sleeplessness. He heard the rattling, gurgling snore of his wife.

Kurelovitch ached with his great need of forgetfulness. As he twitched on his humid bed the days that had gone and the darker days to come ranged about and taunted him like fiends. The feeling that he held the fate of the strike in his hand rested on him monstrously, and his starving children made him gasp and cry like one drowning.

In dumb anguish he prayed unconsciously to the power of the righteousness, to God or whatever fate it was that had brought him into the world. But no relief came that way, and, finally, after a struggle, he groped with all his pangs to a little dresser in the room, where he searched out a brandy bottle. This he took to bed with him, and drank and drank and drank again, till the past and the more terrible future were blurred in kindly night, and the great dark wings of peace folded over him and he sank into the maternal arms of oblivion.

On the morrow he would wake and find the ring of problems haunting him again, and he would grapple them again in his big, tragic fashion till his soul bled with many fresh wounds as he stumbled home in the night. And thus he would go on and on till he was broken or dead, for Kurelovitch had dared to spit into the face of the beast that reigns mankind, and never for this sin would he be permitted to know sweetness or rest under the wide shining range of the heavens.

God Is Love

Poverty had imprisoned nine old men in a shaky loft down-town, and had sentenced them to addressing envelopes forever. Endless, sickening envelopes they were, white and flat and inane, to be addressed with squeaky pens in the fierce and gloomy si-lence which attends all piece work.

A perpetual grimy twilight hung to the old loft. Brownish air and light came from a mouldering air-shaft; the walls were once white; spider-webs floated like banners of evil from the dusty rafters. Sometimes it rained or snowed in the strange world out-side, and then the stale-green old ceiling ran with great, blistery drops.

The pens squealed, often one of the old men broke into a fit of spitting, the spiders wove and plotted their malicious snares in the caverns of the room. And this is all that ever happened in the old loft. It was a horrible cell for innocent "lifers."

Seven of the old men had adapted themselves to this trap pov-erty had set for their old age. They had always been meek, and so now they found nothing new to revolt against. But the other two old men possessed what are commonly termed souls, and therefore they were unhappy.

One of these two was a fine, red-cheeked old oak of a man, who had once been a sailor. Rheumatism had cheated him out of an honorable death on the waves, and here he was now, diddling with pen and ink for a livelihood.

He was huge and strong, with great tatooed fists and arms, and a head like one of those giant crags that are lifted in defense by the land against avaricious surfs. His mass of hair was white and wild as spray, and he had blue, far-seeing eyes, colored deep by the skies and seas they had known.

He was a heavy drinker, because he needed something in which to plunge the hate he had for the loft and its fungus at-mosphere. For he had been fashioned for heroism and deeds, for

Irwin Granich, Masses, *August 1917.*

the open air. He grew sick for the swing of a deck under his feet, for the sharp kiss of brine on his face, for the free winds, tremendous skies, all the drama and strife of the great seas.

Sundays he would sit on a bench at the Battery and look out to the Atlantic with the eyes of a lover, his heart big with loneliness for the deep, broken waters. In the loft he never spoke to the others, but dreamed as he scribbled of strange ports lying in exotic sunshine, of gales and the rank songs of sailormen, of women and fierce moonlight, of the creaking perfumed cordage of a tops'l schooner. . . . He hated the loft and the city with the consuming hate of a caged lion. He was drunk every night, and some of the days. . . .

The other old man dreamed of God. . . . At one time he had been a minister, and what is more, a minister who truly sought God. He had been unfrocked many years back after a lascivious woman of his congregation had snared him into "sin," he never knew how. He had been glad to find refuge in the bleak fog of New York's underworld after the scandal. The shameful lot of dishwashing and porter jobs and begging he had regarded as a penance and cross, and he had hugged his sorrows to him in an ecstasy of atonement.

But latterly he was beginning to doubt. The exaltation was leaving him, and the chill of reality was settling down. He sometimes dared to imagine that he had long since expiated his crime, and he wondered why God demanded more of him.

Some nights he would wake and sweat with terror to think that perhaps there was no God of justice. He would reach out as if to catch something that was slipping from him. . . .

"My God, my God, why art Thou forsaking me?" he would weep into his hard, lousy pillow at the lodging house. And there would be only the nauseous smell of the bedbugs and the swinish snores of the men in the silence. . . .

Yet all things are finally answered, and it was through the other old man with a soul that the minister got his own terrible reply and sign from the heavens. He was going home in the enfolding gloom and scarlet of an October twilight, a little, round-shouldered old man in a flappy old suit, an umbrella and reading matter in his embarrassed clutch. . . . One knew him for the typical failure of the cities, the amiable, unmilitant kind of a man who has love for man and beast in his watery blue eyes, and is so social that there is no place for him in society. . . .

The other old man with a soul, the sailor, had not come to work that day. . . . He was probably on another spree, and the minister got to thinking wistfully of him. He also thought of God, and this with the dim, cool mystic autumn winds in the twilight conspired to make him very melancholy. . . . It was all so sad, the huge, cryptic sky, the winds out of nowhere, the dying summer and the purposeless throngs of workers. The great tenements hung black and solemn against the last silver stains of light, and somebody was singing in a window. . . .

And then the old minister suddenly befell his fellow-toiler at the loft. The sailor was staggering out of a glaring, hiving saloon, his head lolling and his brave old eyes blurred with drink. He was very drunk and very helpless, and the old minister grew tender for him, and came up and touched him.

"Good evening, brother," he said, taking the other's loose hand in his own. The sailor looked at him stupidly and muttered, "Hello."

"I missed you at the loft today," the minister said, gradually edging the other away from the saloon door.

"Yeh, I wasn't feeling so good," the sailor mumbled out of his confused mind. He swayed a little, and hiccoughed. "Come an' have a drink," he stammered thickly.

The minister did not answer, but took a bolder grip on the other's arm, and insinuated him down the street. The old sailor had lost his hat, and his beautiful pure white head was like a kingly plume against the somber night. His clothes were dusty, and he had also been stripped of his collar and tie. All the fools of the city turned and looked after the two old men as they trod a complicated way through the traffic. The fools wagged their heads sagely, and clacked their tongues.

A hurdy-gurdy shot the night through with music, and the old sailor broke into a few flinging bars of the hornpipe, moving with that mechanical gaiety which is so pitiful in old drunkards. He meekly stopped when the minister begged him to, and was meek until the two came to the next corner, where another teeming saloon gave off a great glitter.

Here he balked flatly, and would go no further. He wormed himself stubbornly out of the clutch of the frail little minister, and dragged to the door.

"Must have a drink," he repeated again and again in a sullen passion. He shook the minister's appealing grasp off him, and stumbled violently through the saloon door. There was a hum of raucous voices, the swift, hot breath of whiskey, sour beer and tobacco, the bluff welcome of the bartender.

Then the little minister was alone. He grew very sad again, for he had dreamed of rescuing the other from a night of degradation. He wandered vaguely down Ninth Avenue, wondering whether he ought to go home now and leave the sailor to his chances. And the life of the city night smote in on his thoughts and submerged them in its great surf of movement.

The sound and fury of the city night! The elevated roared like an aroused monster overhead; the people stirred and sifted in black masses on the sidewalks; peddlers barked, pianos jangled, light flowed in golden sheets from gaudy store windows; three young girls fled with locked arms down the street, laughing and screaming with joy as three lads pursued them. Chatter, gabble, laughter, hardness, fluidity, on and on the hosts poured, as if this were all of life, raising their complex and titanic anthem of nothingness to the sky!

The old minister looked at the sky and fell to thinking of God again, and so grew sadder and sadder. He thought how alien the sky was over this brick and mortar, how intrusive the stars in the lives of these pushing, screaming people. There was no God of justice, for there was no justice. There was only pain and futility. The sky was a pitiless, needless mystery. There was a void behind its curtain, but no God. What sign was there of a God in the world?

The old man moved in the city night, his soul falling endlessly in bottomless gulfs of negation. And then, fevered and overwrought, he almost fainted when there came to his simple imagination what seemed to him a miraculous answer to his questions.

Sitting on the garbage-laden step of a tenement he beheld a slum mother nursing her infant. There was a light on her face from a nearby store window, but to the old minister it was divinity. His heart melted for love of them both—the famished, ground-down mother, the helpless, trusting child. . . .

"Love," murmured the old minister ecstatically. "God is Love!"

He stood and looked at them long and long, his eyes great and shining. He thought of the life of the mother—how her days were a cycle of woes, and her moments breathed in constant pain. She lived in a pit of despair, and yet she loved. She loved and sacrificed because something moved in her that was divine —something that was God.

It was God. In the life of man God has ever been, even as He was here now on this ash-heap of poverty. God was wherever men died for an ideal, wherever mothers hovered over the babes for whom they had paid in blood and agony.

God was strong. He lived where all else seemed to have died. He stirred men to deeds that were superhuman; he gave weak women a power that was above empires. Yes, God was in the world! He was a flame that lit up the dark marshes of poverty, oppression, pain. God was love!

It was clear now. And one must love in order to know God.

So the old minister searched his heart, and found that he had not loved the world and his fellow men for many a month. He had almost come to hate, and that was why God had seemed to fail him. He must love again! He must love his fellow men at the lodging house, the bestial, rum-soaked men who swore so terribly! He must love the silent and soulless men who worked with him at the addressing loft! He must love the fate which had thrust him into these sordid, foul-smelling scenes, for this was his cross, and he must learn to love even his cross!

Love! He would go back to the old sailor and rescue that other drifting life by the power of love. He would go back to the saloon and convince the men there of God, convince them by the love overflowing from his heart and eyes.

So he went back under the bellowing elevated to the saloon. Squalling with light, it was the brightest, most beckoning spot in the dark wilderness of the streets. But its confident hard glare brought all his ingrained shyness up to defeat him. He walked timidly up to the doors and peeped into the noisy stew of the saloon. Dim in a bank of tobacco smoke he could see the great white head of his sailor friend, also the rough, cruel faces of a rout of other men. Suddenly he knew that he could not go in there and speak of love and so he went back to the sidewalk and waited for the sailor to come out.

The city night closed in and owned him again. It moved fitfully about him with its turmoil, with its cats and babies and sweaty, hard-bitten men and women. He studied a fly-specked whiskey advertisement in the saloon window for more than fifteen minutes. It pictured in poisonous green and blue "The Old Kentucky Home." The old man thought it beautiful, and it made him homesick for the soft fields of Ohio from whence he had been exiled.

A foul old woman came up and talked to him. She was dirty and leering, and she proposed a horrible thing to him. But he could almost kiss her for love, for as he noted her smirched dress and repulsive, smutty face there came to him the thought of his dear, new-found God of love. . . . How beautiful He made everything. . . .

Then the old man grew lonely for a while. He read a newspaper by the saloon's brilliant glow. An hour passed, and the old sailor did not appear. . . . The old man paced the street in front of the saloon restlessly, almost impatiently, but could not bring himself to the point of going away. . . . Something stronger than himself held him there. . . . God. . . .

And then finally the old sailor did come. The saloon doors opened outward with a crash, and through them lurched the impotent hulk of the befuddled old sailor. He could hardly stand, and a mean, city-faced bartender stood behind him and pushed the big, unyielding form with contempt and righteous exasperation.

"Out of here, you old bum," he sneered, shoving. "Out before I clip ye one. . . . Ye've made enough gab tonight for such an old son-of-a-bitch. We run a decent, respectable saloon, we do, and I'll have ye know it. . . . Out!"

The sailor looked at him glazy-eyed and unknowing. He resisted automatically, only because he was stubborn of temperament. Dully he would try again and again to push back into the barroom, and every time he did the bartender would kick him in the stomach and send him sodden to the sidewalk. Four times this happened, the old man muttering stupidly all the while. Once in the four times he hit the side of his cheek on the pavement, and it burst open, bleeding copiously.

The minister wrung his hands and tried to interfere, but the sailor thrust him aside. A group of people gathered, but none of them tried to stop the spectacle. Then at last the old sailor was too weak to get up, and lay writhing in the street.

The bartender cast a last withering look at him, and spat with slow scorn at the twisted form.

"It's guys like you what gives a black eye to the saloon business," he said bitterly as he went inside.

Then the old minister elbowed forward and bent over his friend. With difficulty he lifted the heavy body to its feet, while everyone eyed him curiously and even cynically. His meagre muscles strained as he supported the old sailor, but his heart was torn even more for the other's humiliation. . . . The old sailor went with him feebly, like a sick child, mumbling weak complaints. . . .

He would take him to his room, and let him sleep there while he himself walked the streets for the night. . . . In the morning he would come back and talk to him, and help him. . . . The old minister went out in a great flood of pity to the other. . . . The sailor must be given Love. . . . He must be taught of God. . . .

They walked a few blocks in this nightmare fashion, in the hum of the avenue. Then the old sailor drew a little out of his stupor, and all the evil of the alcohol in him began to speak. He stopped flat in his tracks before a garish window in which candies and fruits were displayed, and made as if to punch the glass in with his hand, shouting.

The old minister pulled him insistently away, saying gentle, soothing things all the while. But the old sailor was half-crazy now and he tried to shake himself free of the other again and again. He grew impatient and querulous with the minister.

"Who in hell are you anyway?" he demanded. "I don't know you. Lemme go."

"I am your brother," the old minister would say gently. "I want to take you to my room where you can be safe and sleep till morning."

And over and over again with sickening insistency the old sailor would answer, "You ain't my brother. You're a thief, that's what you are. You want to rob me."

He had fallen upon this crazy suspicion in his ramblings, and it gave him a peculiar delight to repeat it over and over. He leered shrewdly and cruelly as he said it, and the minister's heart broke within him. But his kindness did not leave him, nor his great love for the other helpless old man. . . .

The old sailor particularly delighted in shouting his insane charges when he felt people staring at him. . . . They would invariably cast suspicious eyes at the minister . . . and one or two strangers spoke reprovingly to him, and looking for a policeman, could not find him, and so did not interfere. . . .

And then the two old men, in their difficult passage of the rushing, noisy avenue, came again within the bold illumination of a saloon. Hordes moved before and around it, and its hot, strong breath came out in an assault upon the sweetness of the October wind. The old sailor's eyes kindled as he saw it, and he shook himself like a big dog in the grip of the other.

"I'm going in there," he muttered, struggling to be free. "Lemme alone."

"Brother—" the minister pleaded, holding as tightly as his strength let him.

"Lemme go. I want to go in there."

"Brother, there is nothing in there for you," the old minister said.

"Lemme go, I tell ye. I want to go in and lick that bartender."

"That's not the place," the minister cried. "Don't go in. Come home with me."

"Lemme alone, you thief, you. I'm not going with you, you thief."

The old sailor tried to wrench himself from the other's grasp and was too successful, for he toppled into a bleary heap on the pavement. The minister bent over him sadly, and lifted him to his feet again. A little stunned, the sailor walked a few steps in a docile daze. Then the alcohol madness fell upon him again, and he began his muttering and struggle.

"Lemme go, you thief!" he said more violently than before. "LEMME GO!"

He gave a sudden shout, and made a great muscular twist which almost threw the minister to the ground.

"Thief, thief," the old sailor shouted rabidly in his huge voice. One of his big whirling fists caught the feeble little minister square on the mouth, and the blood spat out. Sick and dizzy, the old minister clung to the other still, with the hope in his mind that the sailor would soon tire.

But the old sailor lashed himself into a greater fury, as the blind fighting devils in him woke in his brain.

"Thief! Thief!" and he mauled the other with great vicious blows, leaving marks wherever he struck. The two wrestled to the pavement, and black flowing waves of people turned aside from their usual channels along the avenue and foamed about as about the center of a whirlpool. There were wits in the crowd. One cried out above the dinning of the street noises. "Go it, you old roosters!" Another shouted, "My bet on the big guy," after the sailor had pounded his iron fist into the other's eye with a distinct crash. Everybody laughed at these witticisms; everyone in the crowd was in fine humor. The crowd spread and grew constantly, grew to sudden feverish immensity with curious men and boys, and pale, pitying and amused women. The antics and ridiculous contortions of the old men brought forth gales of laughter, cheers and hootings.

The little minister yielded to it all with a sick sorrow, taking the beating as he lay in the dirt without an ounce of resistance. He was too broken-hearted to fight, but shut his eyes and suffered each blow in silence, only groaning a little and weeping weakly through it all. . . . It was as if he did not care any more. . . .

The elevated stormed overhead, the streetcars clanked by, wagon wheels rattled, the peddlers barked hoarsely, the young girls still screamed joyously as they ran from pursuant lovers. Beyond the hanging dark, the sky watched as stonily as before. . . .

And a hurdy-gurdy rang out. The two old men thrashed about in the swill of the street, bruising themselves terribly. And the crowd stood about and sucked Olympian bliss out of the farce. Then a wide form in blue battered through the crowd and loomed over the two old men.

"A cop, a cop," rustled the crowd with respect. It hushed before authority, and in the silence could be heard the repeated cracks of the policeman's loaded club on the poor sides of the old men. . . . He began hitting instantly. . . .

And soon the sailor collapsed, and lay limp on the limper form of the other. The policeman lifted both of them by the scruff of the neck and held their swaying forms steady with each of his big hands.

"You bastards, you!" he spat with loathing, as he regained his breath. . . . He hated them, for they had given him work to do. . . .

"You bastards!" . . . He hauled them to a telephone, and the old minister heard through a red daze the patrol wagon clattering up a few minutes later. . . . He wondered what they would do with him, and did not care. . . . He felt hollow and dark within, and his body was a hammer that beat endlessly against itself. . . . He wept. . . .

And then they threw the two old men with souls into the depths of the van. And the crowd ebbed away grinning, chewing the happy cud of reminiscence.

The hardy old sailor slept as the wagon bounced over the cobblestones, snoring away all his aches and pains. But the old minister could do nothing but weep, holding his shredded face in his hands and weeping sorely.

One of the policemen pulled away his hands and asked, "What's the idea?" not unkindly.

But the old man did not answer, for he really did not know why he wept so terribly. He could only feel his agonized, welted body, and more terribly he could feel a quivering void within him, from whence something had become uprooted. . . .

There was a recurring, overmastering, soul-shaking sense of desolation which came over him like a darkness, the feeling that Someone or Something had tricked him. . . . He wept and wept. . . .

He wept as the sergeant at the desk took his name and charged him on the books with having been drunk and disorderly. He wept as he was led into the dark basement of the station house where the cells were.

In the sickly gaslight a keeper came forward rattling great keys. He had a bristling, round head, and narrow, cold eyes, and he stared at the two old men with hard and blasé impersonality.

"We're all filled up tonight, John." he said to the officer. "I guess we'll have to put these two in with crazy Billy-Sunday nigger."

A cell was unlocked, and the old minister felt himself jammed into it by a single positive push of the keeper's hand. The sailor fell into a grotesque heap on the boards of the cell, and sprawled there, snoring almost immediately. But the other man leaned against the bars, his face in his hands, weeping.

He could do nothing but weep. There was no light in his brain; and he had lost all he had ever owned. He was all alone at the bottom of a black sea of pain; alone. He sobbed and sobbed. And then through his pain he heard a singing and a muttering from the obscure part of the cell. He put his hands away and looked there, and saw strange, burning eyes. And in a shrill, inhuman and piercing strange voice he heard sung a hymn he had loved—

Abide with me, fast falls the eventide.
The darkness deepens, Lord with me abide—

The minister shuddered. He sobbed. He felt he could not suffer much more. "Hallelujah praise the Lord" burst out from the corner of the cell. Then the insane Negro sang again the hymn with its burden of trust and yearning and love of God:

When other helpers fail and comforts flee.
O Thou who changest not, abide with me.

He sang it again with hysterical fervency. Chaos, despair, inextinguishable loneliness fell upon the old minister. . . . The disastrous, whirling sense of having been betrayed returned to him . . . the stifling void . . . the sense of having been betrayed by One he had loved.

Abide with me, fast falls. . . .

The words twisted like inquisitorial screws into the brain of the old man. Their significance made him writhe. He could not bear this hurt any longer. It was as if the whole night had conspired to torture him. Something must snap. It was his soul which suddenly broke with a great shudder and spilled like poison through his blood. At the fifth time the Negro sang his hymn the old minister gave out a great cry of madness. He flung himself fully and madly at the face and chest of the insane Negro.

"Don't, don't, don't, don't," he sobbed fiercely. But the Negro gave a queer scream like that of some night-prowling carnivore. He turned on the old minister and tore at him with teeth, claws and feet . . . hungrily. . . . Blood spurted on the dark cell air. . . . And nobody heard or came to rescue the gentle old man who had sought God all his days. . . .

Birth

A PROLOGUE TO A TENTATIVE EAST SIDE NOVEL

I WAS born (so my mother once told me), on a certain dim day of April, about seven in a morning wrapped in fog. The streets of the East Side were dark with grey, wet gloom; the boats of the harbor cried constantly, like great, bewildered gulls, like deep, booming voices of calamity. The day was somber and heavy and unavoidable, like the walls of a prison about the city. And in the same hour and the same tenement that bore me, Rosie Hyman the prostitute died, and the pale ear of the same doctor heard my first wails and the last quiverings of her sore heart.

I saw it all afterward through the simple words of my mother, a strange and mournful picture. The doctor had stayed at my mother's bedside all through the night, for her labors had come on her soon after she had disposed of the supper dishes, suddenly, dreadfully.

"Ay, ay, when does it end, dear doctor?" she had moaned all night, while the newly-bearded young practitioner rested his tired, anemic face on his hand and stole moments of sleep.

He would flutter his eyelids to show her he was alert and sympathetic.

"Patience, only patience!" he mumbled over and over in Yiddish, as he pressed her hand. He was not long out of school, and had not grown too professionally familiar with the vast misery which is the physician's East Side.

All through my mother's travail my father sat under a jaundiced gas-jet in the kitchen, drinking *schnapps* and weeping; this was all he was fit for in time of strain or sorrow. My father was a slim, cleanshaven, unusual kind of Jew, who had been the gay

---

After thirteen more years and many false starts, Gold's intended "East Side novel" appeared as Jews Without Money *(1930). Irwin Granich, Masses, November-December 1917.*

blacksheep of his family in Rumania, loving joy and laughter as only young thoughtless people can love them. He had capped a career of escapades by running away to America and freedom at the age of nineteen, and had struggled unhappily since then. He had a broad nose, cheek bones wide as twin hills, and black proud eyes. He must have been a dancing flame of life in his youth, for once I saw him at a wedding where he shook off the years and flashed with a glad, wild, imaginative revelry such as I had never beheld in him. The poverty of the golden, promised land had eaten his joy, however, and mostly I knew him as a sad, irritable, weakly sort of father, who drank in the troubled times when the family needed him, and who loved us all to maudlinity.

"And now how is she, Herr Docktor?" my father whispered anxiously every fifteen minutes through the door, for the doctor had detected his fundamental pessimism and had barred him from the sick room.

"She is well, she is all right, please go away!" the doctor would call back impatiently. My father would wring his hands, and would creep back like a doleful, homeless dog to his vigil by the stove in the kitchen. All night he sat there like a mourner at an orthodox funeral, weeping and drinking and despairing of the harshness of life, and the pain God had put into the world for reasons unknown.

"It is so hard to live, so hard!" my father would sigh in his sad, tearful voice. He was always saying this, I remember, and in a hurt, wondering voice, as if it were a fresh discovery with him every day. My father was never anything but a child, and hunger and pain and toil and meanness he never grew accustomed to, as grown men must. He hated them without understanding them, as a child hates the rod.

The night ebbed away slowly, the hours moving over the East Side with the solemn pace of a funeral cortege. Dawn came on. It grew like a pallid mushroom in the spaces between the tenements, the great heads of the houses lifting themselves languorously in the light, like monstrous vegetation, and a few early men and women hurrying in the shadows as the white lances pricked them. Bakers' wagons lumbered through the fog; there were throaty grumblings of distant elevated trains, gongs, a horn, and other strange, cloaked morning sounds. The light spread like an infection; ashy clouds of it rolled through the windows and lay on my tortured mother, and the leaden-eyed doctor, and my father with his *weltschmerz* and brandy under the gas flame.

My mother breathed easier with the dawn, and she stirred in her humid bed and called through the door, "Rueben, you are sleeping?"

My father sprang up theatrically. "No, no, how could I?" he cried with passion. "You are feeling better, my dear little heart? Soon it will be over, my sweet little bird?"

"Yes, yes," was my mother's impatient reply. "And now get some coffee and rolls for the poor doctor here!"

So my father puttered about with various utensils in his vague way, till the brown coffee was bubbling like a happy fountain on the stove, and rich, odorous steam filled all the air with promise.

"I can find no milk!" my father wailed after one of his puerile searches. "Where is the milk, Yettala?"

"One goes out and gets it at the grocery, fool!" my mother said. "I think you would starve to death if there was no one near to tell you the simplest things, Rueben. And get some rolls; *Wiener* rolls, tell them!"

So my father threw his musty old coat over his shoulders, peasant-wise, and stamped out into the unwholesome dark of the tenement. There must have been tiny gems of gaslight glowing on every floor, as there still are in early dawn on the East Side, and strange shadows must have brooded in every corner and risen and followed him as he moved through the queer gloom, his nostrils filled with the packed odors of crowded bedrooms, old cooking, garbage and faulty sanitation, the immemorial mingled smell of poverty.

On the stoop of our tenement (so my mother told me), my father stumbled on a huddled thing that rose and accosted him. There was the dingy morning light to see by, and under an enfolding shawl my father beheld the great, sad, bewildered eyes of Rosie Hyman, the prostitute.

The East Side was rampant with prostitution then; Jewish "daughters of joy" beckoned openly from every tenement doorway during all the hours of day and night. So numerous were they that they did not even lose caste with their more respectable and hard-working neighbors; for their way of life was charged to the general corrupting influence of America, where the children of Israel break the Sabbath, eat of the unholy pig, and otherwise neglect the God of their fathers. My mother was one of Rosie Hyman's best friends.

"Rosie, you are up too early! What is wrong?" my father exclaimed, seeing some tragedy in her brooding eyes.

"I could not sleep," the girl answered, almost painfully. "It is too warm in my room."

"Too warm?" my father cried. "When everyone is shivering in this devil's weather?"

"Yes," the girl said shortly. "How is Mrs. Gottlieb now?"

"Ach, the same," my father sighed, shaking his head piteously. "It is so terrible to bring a child into the world! All night I have been weeping for my Yettala!"

"It *is* terrible," the girl said, her face darkening. "Why did you do it, then?"

My father's cheeks ran with tears. "Because I am weak, God curse me! Am I not weak, Rosie, say? Already I have two children, and here is another who will have to suffer with them. Am I not a murderer?"

Rosie had always been kind, and now she tried to comfort my father. She raised a hand through her great, red shawl and touched his shoulder.

"We are all weak before love," she said softly. "And it is not our fault, Mr. Gottlieb. God made us so."

My father wept on. "God made us so, and then He punishes us for it," he uttered with choked voice.

"Yes, that is life," the girl said. "And we poor will only be happy in the grave, Mr. Gottlieb."

"Yes, yes, yes," my father sighed, moving away as he remembered his errand. "And now go back to bed and snatch a little sleep, Rosala."

She did not answer, but stood looking after him with great, sad eyes, like a dying thing taking its last fill of vision.

When my father returned from the grocery he found her a twisted heap on the stoop, writhing like a cut worm when he reached down and touched her.

"Rosala, Rosala, what is the matter?"

Nothing coherent came from her, and my father sped and brought back the sleepy doctor. Now she was stark and silent. The doctor put down her wrist with an air of finality.

"She is dead," he announced in his young and pompous way, fingering an empty phial he had found near her. "Why do you think she did it?"

"The man she loved left her, I think," my father said. "Doctor, it is very hard to live!"

"Um-m," the doctor muttered, and went back to my mother. The news could not be kept from her, and she wept and lamented in the heart-rending Jewish manner for more than half an hour.

Then I was born.

My father hurried to tell all the neighbors, and brought back some of the women to act as nurses. It was about noon when the doctor was finally able to leave.

My father offered him three shabby one-dollar bills for his fee.

"And is this all?" the young man cried fiercely, waving the green, ragged things in a gloved hand.

"It is all we have, Herr Docktor," my father said feebly, with a shamed, red face.

"Beggars!" the doctor stormed, throwing the poor bills on the table contemptuously, and sweeping out of the door. "Buy food with it!" he shouted over his shoulder on the landing.

My father picked the bills up and regarded them long and sadly. Then he shrugged his shoulders, and went into the room where my mother was still weeping with pain.

Two Mexicos: A Story

THE WORLD was beautiful as we rode out from Guadalajara in the golden morning light. The broad Mexican spaces were blazing with color, with the glistening green of new corn and the dull green of cactus, with the fire of yellow sands and the slow, blue radiance of meadows thronged with trees. Nothing seemed solid; all was radiance; the world was the heart of a crystal ball of radiance.

Far off on the horizon loomed the mountains—the grand, savage, naked hills of Mexico, that stand everywhere like the visible passion of the land—great, glorious masses of rock cut in fantastic patterns, all barren of vegetation like jewels, and shining like them in purple, amber and rose.

The air sparkled. From the blue perfect sky winds came against our faces, intoxicating as flowers. The horses sniffed the freshness of the morning, and stepped springily over the gaps in the road, and down the rocky inclines on our way to Don Felipe's ranch, thirty miles from the city.

Don Felipe was gay, and we, too, were gayer than careless birds as we jogged through that thrilling Mexican countryside, that is always like some melodrama of color and form planned by a wild young master. We drank the winds greedily, and filled our eyes with the pageant about us, and felt strongly the mad joy of living. Don Felipe burst into song, and, clapping spurs to his horse, went roaring down the road for a few hundred yards. Then he wheeled violently and came charging back at us in a spectacular cloud of dust.

This story is loosely based on Gold's experience in Mexico (1918–1919), where he, like many other young North American radicals, went to escape the wartime draft. The background of revolution and the central conflict between the most rapacious and the most idealistically humanitarian elements of the Mexican ruling class on which this story is based, also served Gold as the material for his musical drama, Fiesta, *which was produced in 1929. Irwin Granich,* Liberator, *May 1920.*

"*Viva Mejico!*" he shouted, swinging his fringed sombrero about his head, and whooping like an Indian. "Have you anything so wonderful as this in the United States?"

"No, no!" we cried, carried away by the high, reckless romantic mood that the Mexican landscape induces in the beholder.

Felipe reined his horse in beside ours, and, digging into his saddlebag, brought out a bottle of the white, incandescent liquor named "*tequila.*" We accepted a pull at the stuff, and Felipe gurgled a great mouthful of the flaming mixture himself, his tanned face red as a poppy when the *tequila* entered his veins.

Felipe was a friend of three days' acquaintance. Phillips and I had fallen in with him while lounging about the Fama Italiana, the only good cafe in the sunlit, sweet-smelling, church-ridden city of Guadalajara. He could speak a choppy and slangy English he had picked up in one of the American border towns, and his ancestry was undoubtedly Spanish, for he had blue, bulging eyes, a tawny moustache and crop of hair, and a big, curved, Oriental nose, tenderly pink at the tip and unlike the sharp, razor noses that mark the Aztec strain. He was short and natty and slender, and unbelievably wiry, like a young tiger. He had come into town on business, and had spent almost a week on the spree that accompanied every transaction of his. Now, when he was returning to the ranch, he had insisted that we go with him for a visit.

"You will like our ranch!" he said, as he trotted his horse beside us, sitting lightly in the high, elaborate saddle, a dazzling figure in the *charro* costume he changed to from the neat Chicago business suit he had worn in the city.

"It's not a large ranch, as Mexican estates go, but we have everything for your entertainment—wild deer to shoot, a mountain pool always cold as ice, horses to ride, and many near-by places you will enjoy seeing. You will like it, I know. We employ about a hundred *peones* on the ranch, and raise corn, wheat, maguey and cattle. You will see how we lasso steers and brand them, and we will give a fiesta in your honor, and you will have many pretty girls to dance with. What more do you want? You have but to say it, and it is yours!"

He waved his hand in a large, free flourish, and we thanked him for his hospitality.

"I and my brother Enrique own the ranch—our father left it to us, and I am the elder brother. You will like my brother Enrique. He is a strong, fearless, honest man—much better than I am, but too serious. He takes life as if it were a religion, but to me, *Carramba!* it is one great joke, and I laugh at it. That is the right way, no?"

He fished out the *tequila* bottle and slapped it fondly, then offered us another draught of the liquor.

"No, thank you!" we cried. "We have just had some, and the American stomach isn't strong enough to hold your Mexican firewater and ride a Mexican horse at the same time."

Felipe laughed uproariously. "Ha, ha, ha!" he shouted, hitting his thigh, "that is true, that is true! I have seen many Gringos put under the table by our *tequila!* That is one point where we Mexicans will always have the better of you!" He swallowed another long drink, and wiping his lips, put the bottle away.

"Would you believe it," he said earnestly, leaning forward to us from his saddle, "my brother Enrique will not touch a drop of alcohol—not a drop. He is a fanatic on the subject. He goes so far that he has wished to give up our *maguey* fields, from which the *pulque* is made that the poor people drink. But I would not let him do this, and he can do nothing without my consent. If I let him have his way, we would be ruined in a year, he has such fantastical ideas on everything. Just the same, he is a good man, a real man—and the best rider and lassoer on the ranch; better even than I!"

A shade of almost somber intensity had crossed his face, to be immediately followed by the mood of bold, reckless laughter—violent mirth playing scornfully with life and death, and heedless of a single human value. That was how we found Felipe—there were depths in him, some chords that could be touched, but dominant was the full tide of his barbarianism, his strange lack of the sense of good and evil, his paganism stained with the blood of a creed that makes manslaughter a trifle, light as love.

Felipe lived but to drink, to win women, to ride horses and to prove his personal valor in contest with other strong barbarians. He was proud and sensitive; and as unconsciously cruel as an animal. He told stories of his exploits on the ride through that glowing, great scene, and we listened to him in fascinated amazement, as to some dark man from the Middle Ages.

"Once," he said, "we had a peon on the ranch who had fierce hatred for me. He was a steady, hard-working fellow, living with his parents, and in love with one of the peon girls for whom I had taken a fancy, and whom I managed to seduce. The fellow heard of this, and it made him begin to hate me.

"You must understand that in the old days the peons on the ranch were really our slaves. They owned nothing of their own, and they had to take what we gave them. They could not leave the estates of their masters, for they were always in debt to us. We did anything we pleased with them—there was no law. When they approached us on business they first had to kiss our hands.

"Now it is different. Now the peons live on our property, rent free, and work for us by the day. We pay them about 35 cents daily when they work, and on this they manage to even save a little and buy fancy revolvers and sewing machines and other luxuries that turn their heads. It is the result of the revolution that upset everything.

"My brother, you must understand, has even tried to go out of his way to turn the heads of the peasants. He gives them a bonus out of the profits at the end of the year, and he gives them little fields where they can cultivate their own produce. He is mad on the subject. He treats them almost like equals, and once he wanted to turn our entire ranch over to them, with himself as mere manager and servant to them. I came to blows with him almost before I could drive this mad notion out of his head. He fought in the revolution, you see—he was one of the first to risk his life for it, and one of the few who really believed in it, and who did not try to grab a fat political job for his services. He is a good man, my brother, but a little mad.

"Well, this peon, a tall, dark, silent fellow, began showing his hatred for me soon after he learned I had had his girl. He would scowl at me when I passed, and refused to take off his hat to salute me, as every peon on our ranch must when I go by. Once I sprang off my horse and tore his hat from his head, and flung it on the ground.

" 'You must never fail to salute your betters!' I cried, sticking my revolver under his nose. 'Do you understant that?'

" 'Yes!' he said quietly, turning on his heel, and leaving the hat there in the road.

"His bravado and insolence maddened me, and I wanted to shoot him in the back as he walked away. Perhaps I would have done so, but the thought came to me it would be better to let the beast live and to make his life a misery for him. Thus I would show him who the better man was, and at the same time give a practical lesson to the other peons, who were quite as bad as he was. It is the only method, my friend; you must daily show these cattle of the fields that you are their master; you must do it frankly and harshly; they do not understand other methods. Ah, if my brother were not only my brother, I could show the way to keep these dogs down!

"Well, to make a long story short, this Pedro meekly bore all the insults and hardships I put upon him. I once lashed him with my whip across the face, while he was working in the fields with the other peasants. I came to his cottage one day and took five of his chickens and wrung their necks before him, and walked away. We needed meat for dinner that day, you see; I did other things to humiliate him, but he said nothing. Perhaps he found it inconvenient to move with his parents from the ranch, I do not know. It may be he was making up with the girl again, and thought of marrying her before he left.

"Anyway, I came across the two one Sunday, talking in front of the church at Tomala, where we go for mass. There was a group of the peons from our ranch there, lounging about under the trees and waiting for the services to begin. I dashed up to the two lovers, and seizing the girl around the waist, swung her on my horse and rode off with her. Pedro stood looking after me with the most stupid eyes you ever saw.

"The next day he did not come to work. I was passing his cottage in the morning on my way to the wheat fields, when he sprang out from behind a stone wall and fired a revolver at me. His face was white with anger, and he did not speak a word. The shot grazed my shoulder, and I leaped on him, and dug my knife into his ribs and killed him. Then I found a rope and hung him to a tree, where every one could see him as an example. All on the ranch, when they saw him later, knew I had killed him, but no one dared to lay the case before the officials at Tomala, who are my friends. Ah, but my brother was angry with me then! We almost fought with guns that time!"

He laughed reminiscently, and spurred his horse into a proud, slow trot, with the foam coming from the checked animal's mouth. We were rather shocked by the story, but knew no way of breaking in on the man's unconsciousness of the evil of his deed. Besides, there was a curious atmosphere about him as he told these things that eliminated all feeling of morality; he was like some returned soldier who narrates dreadful horrors and murders to an audience that shudders and yet cannot blame. Life seems different and younger on these passionate Mexican plains; and death is an old, familiar incident in the day's monotonous melodrama. We hardly knew what to say, and rode on in thoughtful silence.

In Felipe, on his glossy, splendid horse, in his flamboyant leather costume with its silver buttons and rich decorative cordings, we seemed to see riding the incarnation of that brutal, primitive aristocracy that had weighed the Mexican worker to the dust, and that we had found still dominant wherever we had been in the Republic. It was the incarnation of all the thoughtless evil of the Latin and Indian nature, sanguinary, haughty, passionate, and lust-loving, with no mercy for the animal or man in its power. It was too proud to be hypocritical about its vices or virtues; it was the pure primitive.

We grew anxious to meet Felipe's brother Enrique. For only one sober thread of conscience had we detected in the scarlet pattern of Felipe's nature, and that was his feeling for his brother. Always in the stories Felipe dropped from time to time the brother appeared as some better angel, sad, striving and impotent before Felipe's savageries. Felipe would always say his brother was mad, but we could find in him, too, a faint spark of shame and unworthiness that made him uneasy when he spoke of the other. It was as if he knew his brother was right, but could not acknowledge it or live up to his brother's ideals, and for this reason assumed a cloak of exaggerated boyish superiority that ill-fitted him. His brother was Felipe's external conscience, his sole link to the goodness that is in Mexico.

The sun was climbing higher into the sweep of glittering sky. Heat waves shimmered like the hot breath of the sandy, scrubby wastes about us. The distant mountains were softer in the slow air. A few grouse could be heard whirring in the shade of a yucca tree off the road, and Felipe unslung his rifle and drew a bead on the speckled creatures. He did not shoot, however, for a thought crossed his mind.

"Ah! I forgot; we must not waste time!" he said, dropping his gun. "We are expected at the ranch, I think. Let us keep moving."

This was a good resolution, and it was broken not many minutes later by Felipe himself. We had started from town soon after dawn, and were due at the ranch about two in the afternoon, but

Felipe developed vagaries that ate up the hours, and that brought us to the ranch patio some time near midnight.

For though he set his horse off into a good trot that we followed, he stopped a short space thereafter, and took another drink from the bottle after we had again declined. His eye lit with enthusiasm. The momentary seriousness on his face was again wiped off, as he pointed to a dark green meadow crisscrossed by irrigation ditches, a few levels below us in the valley.

"There are bulls there!" he cried gleefully. "Now I will show you how we Mexicans can ride!"

He spurred his horse over a fence, and into the meadow where a herd of cattle was peacefully grazing. With wild cries he lassoed a huge black bull by the hind legs, and, leaping off his horse, fastened a rope around the writhing animal's middle. The bull was furious, but Felipe leaped on its back, and holding tight to the rope, and gripping his legs into the creature's side, lashed it into a frothing rage.

The bull put its head down and charged like an express train. It shook itself from side to side, and bucked and came down on all its four hoofs. It bellowed madly, but Felipe held on as if glued, and shouted and even had the bravado to take one hand from the precious rope to wave his wide hat at us. The bull tried to scrape him off against the stone fence of the corral, and then it came at last to a weary and bewildered stop, when Felipe leaped lithely from its back again. He recovered the rope and returned to us, grinning, ill-concealed vanity shining from his fishy blue eyes.

"What do you think of that?" he asked in a glow, taking another pull at the unfailing bottle. We assured him we had never seen anything like it before.

The trip was resumed, down a gentle valley, than up a circular path that ascended a hill all of grass, and on whose round summit a little square blockhouse stood, a memento of the Revolution. Felipe showed us some of the trenches the fighters had made, and pointed out some mounds marked by faded wooden crosses, the graves of the revolutionists.

"That is their reward, the fools!" he said, "and that is all they deserved to get. I often tell my brother that."

He seemed in no hurry to get home now, though the morning was advancing toward noon and the sun was stronger on our backs. It was amazing what animal spirits the man had—life overflowing and exuberant and positively aching for expression. He roared lovely sad Spanish songs of love, he beat his horse into wild gallops and trots, he drank from the bottle and told us story after story of violence and lust. He was tireless, and athirst for danger.

We went down a *barranca*, a deep mountain gorge whose paths were steep alleys of boulders on which the horses slipped and floundered. Sheer thousand-foot drops were on one hand of us, and on the other were rugged cliffs black and wet with hidden springs. Felipe would not permit his horse to pick its careful, difficult way through the stones, but whipped it on blindly, and bade us follow. Once he jumped his horse over a chasm that we went painfully around, the poor beast sliding and crashing and almost toppling over the cliff beyond. Felipe only laughed, and looked at us for admiration. He was quite foolhardy, and also vain.

At the bed of the *barranca* rushed a full, strong mountain river, deep and foaming yellow. Felipe insisted that we all strip for a swim, and we saw him dive recklessly into the rocky bottom, and fight his way out of that great, steep cup of savage boulders and stunted shrubbery. At the top we found a green, immense valley stretched beneath us, a tremendous plain of shining grass and dark clots of trees, threaded by a silver trickle of water, and with huge, billowy shadows moving over its brilliant face. It was beautiful in its broad peace, a wonderful stage set for Titans, and far off in one corner we saw a cluster of white houses from which a church tower rose, like the pistil of a flower. Felipe had stopped his horse, and was gazing thoughtfully.

"That must be the ranch there!" we cried, pointing to the distant houses. Felipe shook his head.

"No," he said, "that is the village of Tomala, about four miles from the ranch. Do you know what would be a good idea?" he added slowly, his face lighting with enthusiasm. "We ought go there instead of to the ranch for our dinner. We are hungry, and I have some important business to transact there besides."

"Are you sure of that, Felipe?" we asked, trying to divert him from we knew not what.

"*Carrajo!*" he exclaimed, "of course I am sure! The judge there has sent us a requisition for five saddled horses, to be used for two months by the military commander who is fighting the rebels. I know what they will do with those horses; they will sell them. I must go and have the order withdrawn."

"But how can you do that?" Phillips asked dubiously.

"How?" Felipe laughed gaily, tugging at his reddish moustache. "How? *Bueno,* I will get the judge drunk! Wait and see!"

So we urged the horses onward to the pueblo of Tomala. The valley grew richer and greener as we went cantering down the rough roads, there were more trees, and cultivated fields, and squat adobe houses with their little gardens and cactus fences enclosing a few pigs or a cow or two. At last the road became a street lined with these little houses side by side, the plaster walls painted in delicate shades of pink and blue. We were in Tomala; a village of about 500 peon inhabitants, the center of all the farms in the valley. Lounging men in white peon clothes and immense hats stared somberly as we clattered by, and children ran about us, and women looked up from the ditches in front of their homes where they were busy with the family washing.

Felipe pressed himself with his usual vanity, and whipped up the horses, so that we entered at a spectacular gallop into the grass-grown, sleepy plaza that is the heart of every Mexican town.

We had a dinner of beefsteak, eggs, frijoles and black coffee at a small restaurant, bare as a cell, and presided over by an unimaginably old and wrinkled crone. Then Felipe led us about his business of the Judge.

We found this dignitary sitting in the sunshine on a bench in front of his home, doggedly playing Mexican waltzes on a mandolin to which the Sheriff played accompaniments on a guitar. The Judge was a battered little old man, with matted gray hair and beard, and tiny stupid eyes that twinkled suspiciously, like a weasel's. He was clad in the white, cotton flapping clothes of an ordinary peon, his dirt-caked feet enclosed in sandals. From out the wild tangle of hair on his face a corn-husk cigarette drooped, stale and forgotten.

The Sheriff was huge and burly, with an enormous black moustache that almost reached his eyes. He too was dressed in peon clothes, with a red blanket folded over his right shoulder, and a shirt of vivid flowered pink made by his wife of some gaudy calico that had probably intrigued her soul at the village store. Around the Sheriff's waist was a heavy belt loaded with cartridges, and a 30-30 rifle stood against the wall by his side.

The officials abandoned their harmonizing as we came up, and arose to greet us.

"Felipe, my *amigo!*" the Judge called in a cracked, joyful voice, embracing our host in the Mexican style and patting his shoulder enthusiastically. "Why have I not seen you for so long?"

The proper introductions were made, and then Felipe drew the Judge aside and held a little conversation with him. We could see the serious air with which the two spoke, and the manner in which the Judge shook his head from side to side, as if in doubt. Finally Felipe took him by the arm and brought him over to us.

"Let us all go to the *cantina!*" Felipe said. "We need something to drink."

The Sheriff accepted readily, picking up his rifle and carrying it fondly under his arm. We followed with our horses, and we marched in procession about the little plaza till we came to a low, ill-smelling wooden shack with great letters painted across it in red and blue, reading, "La Lucha Por La Vida"—The Struggle for Life. That is the way Mexican merchants name their dry-goods and grocery establishments.

Inside the dark, smoky saloon there was a wooden counter, sticky with liquor and swarming with flies. Behind this were shelves with various colorful bottles standing in rows, and there was a huge barrel containing the oily, sour, thin drink called *pulque*. A few men drooped about idly, and the saturnine, fat man behind the counter greeted us with the universal bartender's smile. Felipe ordered drinks for every one, striking the bar with his fist.

"This is our holiday," he cried, "and no one must be unhappy!"

We all took *tequila*. Tongues began loosening after the third or fourth drink, and laughter arose as if by magic.

The Sheriff spoke to us solemnly, from the heart. "You have many wonderful things in the United States, you gringos," he said to us, "but there is one thing of ours you cannot have, and that is our National Hymn. It is the most beautiful in the world. Did you know," he informed us proudly, "did you know that once the United States offered ten million dollars if we would give them our hymn for their own, and that we refused? Yes, we refused, for we are poor, but men of honor and sentiment and pride. And this is a fact, it is history; my own brother heard it from a policeman he knew well in Guadalajara."

They sang the national hymn, which is really beautiful, beating on the counter with their glasses. There were other songs, and stories of women and fighting. The Judge was not holding the liquor well, for his little eyes were growing dimmer and dimmer, and he wobbled on his feet.

"The revolution set us peons free," he uttered in a hazy voice, slapping his chest. "Yes, we are free now. Do you see, I am the Judge here, and if any one should hurt person or property in this pueblo I would instantly put him in jail. No robbers, no atheists, no reactionaries are allowed here. If we find a rebel, we hang him at once. We are free!"

"You, Senor, are the best Judge in the whole state of Jalisco, aren't you?" Felipe said, putting his arm on the little man's shoulder and winking at us.

"Yes!" the Judge answered at once, glaring at him half-suspiciously. "Yes, I am! And here is the best Sheriff in the whole state of Jalisco!"

The Sheriff swelled out his chest, and lifted his gun to his lips and kissed it religiously.

"With this gun I maintain the law and order in this village!" he proclaimed, beginning to wobble a little too. "I have arrested three drunks today and not one dared to put up a fight. They know who I am."

Drink after drink, and the shadows gathering in the room and obscuring those wild, flushed faces, and outside in the sky the blue catching flame from the sun, and dying with a last shout of glory. The trees were liquid darkness, and deep dusk was filling the dusty street. Our horses champed impatiently, and we went outside, calling Felipe after us.

"Aren't you ready to go yet?" we asked politely, "and haven't you arranged that matter of the horses with the Judge?"

"Yes, I've arranged it all!" he said excitedly. "We'll only have a few more drinks and then go. Come in!"

We returned reluctantly, and continued drinking, for it is almost an insult to refuse an offer of this kind in Mexico.

The place grew wilder and noisier as the liquor mounted to all heads. Felipe began boasting, and drew a large hunting knife from its scabbard, and stuck it into the counter.

"This is my only friend, and with its aid I can do what I choose anywhere. I have killed three men with it, and am ready for more—at any time, even now!"

"But you will keep order in *this* village, Senor!" the Judge mumbled stupidly, moving up against Felipe and fronting him chest to chest.

"I will do what I choose!" Felipe sneered, waving the knife in the air. "I have a ranch of three leagues, and employ almost a hundred peons. I will do what I please!"

"No!" the Judge shouted, flushing with anger. "No! Arrest that man!"

But it was the Judge that the Sheriff took by the arm and forcibly led out into the night. "I will keep law and order here!" the Sheriff mumbled grandly, dragging the smaller man as if he were a sack of flour. "I am the Sheriff here, you must remember!"

The two came back a moment later, and Felipe bought them many more drinks. We went outside, weary and with whirling heads, and waited for Felipe there. And at last he staggered to us, after many hours of night, when the village was all gloom and dots of light, and the stars had long crowded the sky. He mounted his horse, and we started off.

The Judge and Sheriff stood waving their hands after us, and as we rode down the rocky street we could see their dark, wavering forms like clots of night in the moonshine. We reached a wide, massy tree where the street changed to fields, and Felipe turned on his horse and fired three shots toward the *cantina*. A great crash answered, a bullet sped by us somewhere, and we saw a fiery burst of flame spring where the Sheriff was standing in darkness. The friends were saluting each other.

We rode through the rich moonlight, between fields of corn that glistened like waves of the night sea. The distant mountains were formless, blue smoke against the misty sky. The air was wilder than wine. A world of mystery lay about us; the drink was in our blood, and the wind against our faces. We shouted and sang. Felipe shot his revolver off many times, and we followed with salutes to the dreaming heaven. It was romance to be living, it was ecstacy and adventure, and the sad, eternal earth, humble beneath us in the moonlight, rang again and again with the cries of man's ephemeral joy.

Felipe was in glorious mood. We too had forgotten everything in abandonment of reckless wonder. Felipe saw something stirring in the bush, and shot his revolver at it. The next moment an old, bent peon came out, and stood bowing in fright. We laughed madly, and sped on our way.

We spurred our horses over great boulders, and across a stream, and through soft purple meadows sweet to the nostrils. The moonlight drowned all the senses in silver. There were millions of colored stars in the mighty Mexican sky. Little adobe houses swam by us in the night, petals on a dark river. The mountains were ever before us.

And then, jumping a fence, and walking our horses through the corduroy roughness of a ploughed field, we saw the houses of the ranch resting quietly under the moon. Felipe fired another shot, and cried, "We're home!"

We set our horses into a furious gallop, and with flushed faces and beating hearts roared up to the biggest house of all, where the brothers lived. Felipe banged out another shot still shouting *"Viva Mejico!"*

A tall, solemn figure came out on the porch as we reined in our horses. It was Felipe's brother Enrique. He had dark, stern Indian features, and a stiff, black moustache, and he folded his arms and regarded us out of lowered eyes. His silence was ominous, and chilled our reckless joy as with a cold hand.

Even Felipe seemed sober, and somewhat sheepish under that gaze. We dismounted, and went up on the porch where Enrique stood. He fixed Felipe with his black, grave, dangerous eyes.

"You drunkard!" Enrique said, in a low, fierce voice. "You drunkard! You care for nothing but your pleasures and passions! You have been away three days now, and have probably spent all the money for the corn you sold!"

Felipe's face flamed with badly-suppressed rage. "I am the elder brother here," he muttered. "You can say nothing to me!"

"You drunkard!" the other repeated bitterly. "All that I do here you undo. You and your kind are the curse of our poor Mexico. Follies such as yours have been the ruin of our people. If you weren't my brother I would kill you!"

"I am the elder brother here!" Felipe muttered sullenly, his hand twitching at his revolver.

They stood facing each other in the vast, silent moonlight, the brothers who were the poetry and wisdom of Mexico, her good and evil, her barbarism and civilization battling each other and assuring her no peace till the younger shall have forever slain the elder.

Towards Proletarian Art

THE APOCALYPSE

IN BLOOD, in tears, in chaos and wild, thunderous clouds of fear the old economic order is dying. We are not appalled or startled by that giant apocalypse before us. We know the horror that is passing away with this long winter of the world. We know, too, the bright forms that stir at the heart of all this confusion, and that shall rise out of the debris and cover the ruins of capitalism with beauty. We are prepared for the economic revolution of the world, but what shakes us with terror and doubt is the cultural upheaval that must come. We rebel instinctively against that change. We have been bred in the old capitalist planet, and its stuff is in our very bones. Its ideals, mutilated and poor, were yet the precious stays of our lives. Its art, its science, its philosophy and metaphysics are deeper in us than logic or will. They are deeper than the reach of the knife in our social passion. We cannot consent to the suicide of our souls. We cling to the old culture, and fight for it against ourselves. But it must die. The old ideals must die. But let us not fear. Let us fling all we are into the cauldron of the Revolution. For out of our death shall arise glories, and out of the final corruption of this old civilization we have loved shall spring the new race—the Supermen.

This "mystic," Whitmanesque manifesto was to Gold the source of pride as well as embarrassment in later years. Although it is intellectually callow and un-Marxist in a lot of ways, it is also one of the major documents in radical literary theory in the United States. It was the first significant call in this country for the creation of a distinctly and militantly working-class culture. The American currency of the term "proletarian literature" can be dated from the publication of this article. It is the last work he published under the name Irwin Granich—oddly enough a month after *he had become an editor of the* Liberator *under the name "Michael Gold." It is useful to understand that this manifesto is specifically a reply to the aesthetic theories of Gold's mentor, Max Eastman, as formulated in the Preface to Eastman's collection of poetry,* Colors of Life *(1919).* Liberator, *February 1921.*

A BASIS IN THE MAELSTROM

It is necessary first to discuss our place in eternity.

I myself have felt almost mad as I staggered back under the blows of infinity. That huge, brooding pale evil all about me—that endless Nothing out of which Something seems to have evolved somehow—that nightmare in man's brain called Eternity —how it has haunted me! Its poison has almost blighted this sweet world I love.

The curse of the thought of eternity is in the brain and heart of every artist and thinker. But they do not let it drive them mad, for they discover what gives them strength and faith to go on seeking its answer. They realize in revelations that the language of eternity is not man's language, and that only through the symbolism of the world around us and manifest in us can we draw near the fierce, deadly flame.

The things of the world are all portals to eternity. We can approach eternity through the humble symbols of Life—through beasts and fields and rivers and skies, through the common goodness and passion of men. Yet what is Life, then? What is that which my body holds like a vessel filled with fire? What is that which grows, which changes, which manifests itself, which moves in clod and bird and ocean and mountain, and binds them so invisibly in some mystic league of purpose? I have contemplated all things great and small with this question on my lips. And seeking a synthesis for Life, and thus for eternity, I early found that the striving, dumb universe had strained to its fullest, expressiveness in the being of man.

Man was Life become vocal and sensitive. Man was Life become dramatic and complete. He gained and he lost; he knew values, he knew joys and sorrows, and not mere pleasures and pains. He was bad, glad, sad, mad; he was color and form; he contained everything I had not found in the white, meaningless face of pure Eternity. Eternity became interesting only in him. He had desires; he engendered climaxes. He moved me to the soul with his pathos and aspirations. He was significant to me; he made me think and love. Life's meaning was to be found only in the great or mean days between each man's birth and death, and in the mystery and terror hovering over every human head.

Seeking God we find Man, ever and ever. Seeking answers we find men and women.

IN THE DEPTHS

I can feel beforehand the rebellion and contempt with which many true and passionate artists laboring in all humility will greet claims for a defined art. It is not a mere aristocratic scorn for the world and its mass-yearnings that is at the root of the artists' sneer at "propaganda." It is a deeper, more universal feeling than that. It is the consciousness that in art Life is speaking out its heart at last, and that to censor the poor brute-murmurings would be sacrilege. Whatever they are, they are significant and precious, and to stifle the meanest of Life's moods taking form in the artist would be death. Artists are bitter lovers of Life, and in beauty or horror she is ever dear to them. I wish to speak no word against their holy passion, therefore, and I regard with reverence the scarred and tortured figures of the artist-saints of time, battling against their demons, bearing each a ponderous cross, receiving solemnly in decadence, insanity, filth and fear the special revelation Life has given them.

I respect the suffering and creations of all artists. They are deeper to me than theories artists have clothed their naked passions in. I would oppose no contrary futile dogmas. I would show only, if I can, what manner of vision Life has vouchsafed me, what word has descended on me in the midst of this dark pit of experience, what form my days and nights have taken, as they proceed in strange nebular whirling toward the achievement of new worlds of art.

I was born in a tenement. That tall, sombre mass, holding its freight of obscure human destinies, is the pattern in which my being has been cast. It was in a tenement that I first heard the sad music of humanity rise to the stars. The sky above the airshafts was all my sky; and the voices of the tenement neighbors in the airshaft were the voices of all my world. There, in suffering youth, I feverishly sought God and found Man. In the tenement Man was revealed to me, Man, who is Life speaking. I saw him, not as he has been pictured by the elder poets, groveling or sinful or romantic or falsely god-like, but one sunk in a welter of humble, realistic cares; responsible, instinctive, long-suffering and loyal; sad and beaten yet reaching out beautifully and irresistibly like a natural force for the mystic food and freedom that are Man's.

All that I know of Life I learned in the tenement. I saw love there in an old mother who wept for her sons. I saw courage there in a sick worker who went to the factory every morning. I saw beauty in little children playing in the dim hallways, and despair and hope and hate incarnated in the simple figures of those who lived there with me. The tenement is in my blood. When I think it is the tenement thinking. When I hope it is the tenement hoping, I am not an individual; I am all that the tenement group poured into me during those early years of my spiritual travail.

Why should we artists born in tenements go beyond them for our expression? Can we go beyond them? "Life burns in both camps," in the tenements and in the palaces, but can we understand that which is not our very own? We, who are sprung from the workers, can so easily forget the milk that nourished us, and the hearts that gave us growth? Need we apologize or be ashamed if we express in art that manifestation of Life which is so exclusively ours, the life of the toilers? What is art? Art is the tenement pouring out its soul through us, its most sensitive and articulate sons and daughters. What is Life? Life for us has been the tenement that bore and molded us through years of meaningful pain.

THE OLD MOODS

A boy of the tenements feels the slow, mighty movement that is art stir within him. He broods darkly on the Life around him. He wishes to understand and express it, but does not know his wish. He turns to books, instead. There he finds reflections, moods, philosophies, but they do not bring him peace. They are myriad and bewildering, they are all the voices of solitaries lost and distracted in Time.

The old moods, the old poetry, fiction, painting, philosophies, were the creations of proud and baffled solitaries. The tradition has arisen in a capitalist world that even its priests of art must be lonely beasts of prey—competitive and unsocial. Artists have deemed themselves too long the aristocrats of mankind. That is why they have all become so sad and spiritually sterile. What clear, strong faith do our intellectuals believe in now? They have lost everything in the vacuum of logic where they dwell. The thought of God once sustained their feet like rock, but they slew God. Reason was once their star, but they are sick with Reason. They have turned to the life of the moods, to the worship of beauty and sensation, but they cannot live there happily. For Beauty is a cloud, a mist, a light that comes and goes, a vague water changing rapidly. The soul of Man needs some sure and permanent thing to believe, to be devoted to and to trust. The people have that profound Truth to believe in—their instincts. But the intellectuals have become contemptuous of the people, and are therefore sick to death.

The people live, love, work, fight, pray, laugh; they accept all, they accept themselves, and the immortal urgings of Life within them. They know reality. They know bread is necessary to them; they know love and hate. What do the intellectuals know?

The elder artists have all been sick. They have had no roots in the people. The art ideals of the capitalistic world isolated each artist as in a solitary cell, there to brood and suffer silently and go mad. We artists of the people will not face Life and Eternity alone. We will face it from among the people.

We must lose ourselves again in their sanity. We must learn through solidarity with the people what Life is.

Masses are never pessimistic. Masses are never sterile. Masses are never far from the earth. Masses are never far from the heaven. Masses go on—they are the eternal truth. Masses are simple, strong and sure. They never are lost long; they have always a goal in each age.

What have the intellectuals done? They have created, out of their solitary pain, confusions, doubts and complexities. But the masses have not heard them; and Life has gone on.

The masses are still primitive and clean, and artists must turn to them for strength again. The primitive sweetness, the primitive calm, the primitive ability to create simply and without fever or ambition, the primitive satisfaction and self-sufficiency—they must be found again.

The masses know what Life is, and they live on in gusto and joy. The lot of man seems good to them despite everything; they work, they bear children, they sing and play. But intellectuals have become bored with the primitive monotony of Life—with the deep truths and instincts.

The boy in the tenement must not learn of their art. He must stay in the tenement and create a new and truer one there.

THE REVOLUTION

The Social Revolution in the world today arises out of the deep need of the masses for the old primitive group life. Too long have they suppressed that instinct most fundamental to their nature—the instinct of human solidarity. Man turns bitter as a competitive animal. In the Orient, where millions live and labor and die, peace has brooded in the air for centuries. There have never been individuals there, but family clans and ancestor worshipers, so that men have felt themselves part of a mystic group extending from the dim past into the unfolding future. Men have gathered peace from that bond, and strength to support the sorrow of Life. From the solidarity learned in the family group, they have learned the solidarity of the universe, and have created creeds that fill every device of the universe with the family love and trust.

The Social Revolution of today is not the mere political movement artists despise it as. It is Life at its fullest and noblest. It is the religion of the masses, articulate at last. It is that religion which says that Life is one, that Men are one, through all their flow of change and differentiation; that the destiny of Man is a common one, and that no individual need bear on his weak shoulders alone the crushing weight of the eternal riddle. None of us can fail, none of us can succeed.

The Revolution, in its secular manifestations of strike, boycott, mass-meeting, imprisonment, sacrifice, agitation, martyrdom, organization, is thereby worthy of the religious devotion of the artist. If he records the humblest moment of that drama in poem, story or picture or symphony, he is realizing Life more profoundly than if he had concerned himself with some transient personal mood. The ocean is greater than the tiny streams that trickle down to be lost in its godhood. The Revolution is the permanent mood in which Man strains to goodness in the face of an unusual eternity; it is greater than the minor passing moods of men.

WALT WHITMAN'S SPAWN

The heroic spritual grandfather of our generation in America is Walt Whitman. That giant with his cosmic intuitions and comprehensions, knew all that we are still stumbling after. He knew the width and breadth of Eternity, and ranged its fearful spaces with the faith of a Viking. He knew Man; how Man was the salt and significance of Eternity, and how Man's soul outweighed the splendor and terror of the stars. Walt feared nothing; nothing shook his powerful serenity; he was unafraid before the bewildering tragedy of Life; he was strong enough to watch it steadily, and even to love it without end.

Walt dwelt among the masses, and from there he drew his strength. From the obscure lives of the masses he absorbed those deep affirmations of the instinct that are his glory. Walt has been called a prophet of individualism, but that is the usual blunder of literature. Walt knew the masses too well to believe that any individual could rise in intrinsic value above them. His individuals were those great, simple farmers and mechanics and ditch-diggers who are to be found everywhere among the masses—those powerful, natural persons whose heroism needs no drug of fame or applause to enable them to continue; those humble, mighty parts of the mass, whose self-sufficiency comes from their sense of solidarity, not from any sense of solitariness.

Walt knew where America and the world were going. He made but one mistake, and it was the mistake of his generation. He dreamed the grand dream of political democracy, and thought it could express in completion all the aspirations of proletarian man. He was thinking of a proletarian culture, however, when he wrote in his *Democratic Vistas:*

> I say that democracy can never prove itself beyond cavil, until it founds and luxuriantly grows its own forms of art, poems, schools, theology, displacing all that exists, or that has been produced anywhere in the past under opposite influences.

Walt Whitman is still an esoteric poet to the American masses, and it is because that democracy on which he placed his passionate hope was not a true thing. Political democracy failed to evoke from the masses here all the grandeur and creativeness Walt knew so well were latent in them, and the full growth of which would have opened their hearts to him as their divinest spokesman.

The generation of artists that followed Walt were not yet free from his only fundamental error. Walt, in his poetry, had intuitively arrived at the proletarian art, though his theory had fallen short of the entire truth. The stream of his successors in literature had no such earthy groundwork as his, however. When they wrote of the masses it was not as Walt, the house-builder, the tramp, the worker, had, not as literary investigators, reporters, genteel and sympathetic observers peering down from a superior economic plane. Walt still lived in the rough equalitarian times of a semi-pioneer America, but his successors were caught in the full rising of the industrial expansion. They could not possibly escape its subtle class psychologies.

But now, at least, the masses of America have awakened, through the revolutionary movement, to their souls. Now, at last, are they prepared to put forth those striding, outdoor philosophers and horny-handed creators of whom he prophesied. Now are they fully aware that America is theirs. Now they can sing it. Now their brain and heart, embodied in the revolutionary element among them, are aroused, and they can relieve Walt, and follow him in the massive labors of the earth-built proletarian culture.

The method of erecting this proletarian culture must be the revolutionary method—from the deepest depths upward.

In Russia of the workers the proletarian culture has begun forming its grand outlines against the sky. We can begin to see what we have been dimly feeling so necessary through these dark years. The Russian revolutionists have been aware with Walt that the spiritual cement of a literature and art is needed to bind together a society. They have begun creating the religion of the new order. The *Prolet-Kult* is their conscious effort toward this. It is the first effort of historic Man towards such a culture.

The Russians are creating all from the depths upward. Their *Prolet-Kult* is not an artificial theory evolved in the brains of a few phrase-intoxicated intellectuals, and foisted by them on the masses. Art cannot be called into existence that way. It must grow from the soil of life, freely and without forethought. But art has always flourished secretly in the hearts of the masses, and the *Prolet-Kult* is Russia's organized attempt to remove the economic barriers and social degradation that repressed that proletarian instinct during the centuries.

In factories, mines, fields and workshops the word has been spread in Russia that the nation expects more of its workers than production. They are not machines, but men and women. They must learn to express their divinity in art and culture. They are encouraged and given the means of that expression, so long the property of the bourgeoisie.

The revolutionary workers have hammered out, in years of strife, their own ethics, their own philosophy and economics. Now, when their ancient heroism is entering the cankered and aristocratic field of art, there is an amazing revaluation of the old value manifest there. We hear strange and beautiful things from Russia. We hear that hope has come back to the pallid soul of man. We hear that in the workers' art there are no longer the obsessions and fears that haunted the brains of the solitary artists. There is tranquility and humane strength. The attitude toward love and death and eternity have altered—all the fever is out of them, all the tragedy. Nothing seems worthy of despair to the mass-soul of the Russian workers, that conquered the horrors of the Czardom. They have learned to work and hope. A great art will arise out of the new great life in Russia—and it will be an art that will sustain man, and give him equanimity, and not crucify him on his problems as did the old. The new artists feel the mass-sufficiency, and suffer no longer that morbid sense of inferiority before the universe that was the work of the solitaries. It is the resurrection.

In America we have had attempts to carry on the work of old Walt, but they have failed, and must fail, while the propagandists still lack Walt's knowledge that a mighty national art cannot arise save out of the soil of the masses. Their appeal has been to the leisured class who happen to be at present our intellectuals. Such groups as centered around the *Seven Arts* magazine and the *Little Review* tried to set in motion the sluggish current of vital American art. The *Little Review,* preaching the duty of artistic insanity, and the *Seven Arts,* exhorting all to some vague spirit of American virility, alike failed, for they based their hopes on the studios.

It is not in that hot-house air that the lusty great tree will grow. Its roots must be in the fields, factories and workshops of America—in the American life.

When there is singing and music rising in every American street, when in every American factory there is a drama group of the workers, when mechanics paint in their leisure, and farmers write sonnets, the greater art will grow and only then.

Only a creative nation understands creation. Only an artist understands art.

The method must be the revolutionary method—from the deepest depths upward.

A Little Bit of Millennium

STELTON IS in New Jersey, some fifty miles out on the Pennsylvania railroad. It is an uneventful suburban stop in country flat and green as a Dutch meadow, the evening alighting place of two score or more simple-minded American commuters. They turn to the right of the station, where the village clusters. But you, fellow-malcontent, walk left for two miles along a macadam road, and so come to the Ferrer colony, a strange exotic jewel of radicalism placed in this dull setting, a scarlet rose of revolution blooming in this cabbage patch, a Thought, an Idea, a Hope, balancing its existence in the great Jersey void. . . .

But I exaggerate. Most visitors sniff a little at the Ferrer colony. They come with preconceptions, dreams and prejudices. They have heard how five years ago Harry Kelley, Leonard Abbott, Joseph Cohen and others of the dwindling faithful in the anarchist movement of America, brought out a group of children and settled in an old farmhouse they had bought cooperatively.

Others arrived each year, bought land and built shacks, till now there is a big school and about three hundred of the comrades scratching out a hardscrabble living there. Visitors come expecting a rosy millennium. The colony started in that spirit, but the visitors find weird tar-paper shacks, fantastic in architecture as a futurist drawing, muddy roads, papers and tin cans littering the crossroads at the entrance to the colony; also intensely human scandals, rumors and jealousies thick as mosquitoes and almost as plentiful as in any other closely-knit community. It is not the millennium, the visitors exclaim, as they glumly try to make a meal off the whole wheat bread and raw salads they are offered. No, it is not, a friend of the place will say. It is merely another proletarian attempt to realize the millennium in the midst of a world of capitalism. The experiment is bound to fail, as Jesus failed in his attempt to establish Christianity in a world of stiff-necked Jews and brassy-bowelled, shrewd Romans. Such experiments always leave some mark, however, and Stelton has made its own on the page of radical history here.

I lived at the colony for a few months last summer and wish to testify for it. There are numbers of such colonies scattered throughout the country, the conditions about the same as Stelton, I suppose, the same hard-pan farming, the same slim larders and ice-bound shacks in winter and gossip and internal difficulties. I knew an old house painter in Boston who had piously worked his head off in about twelve attempts at such colonies, and had seen them all fail. I know all the theories arrayed against such colonies. They are said to be relics of the Utopian pre-Marxian Socialism. They mislead as to the purpose of the revolution, which is to enter the State and capture it, not try to change it from without. These colonies, too, take lots of precious material away from the firing line, which is in the cities, in the ranks of the class-conscious workers. There are many other good objections needless to repeat; every reader of the *Liberator* has surely shied a brick at Utopianism in his time. I have; I say again that colonies are not revolutionary in the scientific sense, that whoever sees in them the way and the path has not the diamond-hard mind of the revolutionist, that the revolution can only be fought and won by organization of the world proletariat at the centers of production.

Colonies are not scientific revolution; no, but they are a part of the art of the revolution. They are direct action by the proletarian soul. They are as spontaneous, as inevitable, as useful and as beautiful as the writing of poetry. They *are* the poetry created by the hard hands of inspired workingmen, and whoever does not understand them, does not understand something that is in the heart of the proletarian.

Those dreamy-eyed, dear people who become desperate in the mill of the capitalist cities and who escape to colonies, go there to make themselves over in the image of the proletarian Superman. They are as sick of the slime in their souls as any great sinner entering a monastery. They wish to become free workers— gentle, creative, loving, truthful men and women, toiling shoulder to shoulder in a community of friends, envying no one, commanding no one, taking no thought of the morrow or of the individual self, living according to that divinest of rules for the conduct of life, "From each according to his ability, to each according to his need."

This is communism, and in Russia they have made the first infantile steps toward it. It will come in time. But colonists cannot wait. They wish to live the good life in their own generation; the world revolution seems too far off. They thirst for perfection and righteousness with the thirst of Shelley and the passion of Danton; the cities hold them down.

How can they wait? Can a lover wait for the lips of the beloved? Can a poet wait years while a song is aching for expression within him? Can a race horse wait easily for the starter's shot, or can a Wobbly wait until Chicago sanctions a strike? Off they go, sinking time, money, labor, dreams and heartache into some scheme such as that of Stelton; impatient, impractical, narrow as youth, and as beautiful. It is the poetical folly of the proletariat; it must be allowed them, for God knows they have to be practical enough, most of the time; they walk the earth enough.

Of course colonies fail, as Stelton has failed, for how can you have communism with people who have been bred body and soul in the old capitalistic world, who, though they reject it with all the fervor of their conscious selves, have its dogmas in the very marrow of their bones?

But such failures are useful and good; they are experiments; they teach something. They are like the play of children, who with bits of wood and sea shells and old bottles, build theaters and houses, and rehearse at being men and women. These colonies are little laboratories in the real Communism. City revolutionists, intellectuals, parliamentarians and apartment-house Bolsheviki—we have forgotten what the original Communism is. Anarchists have it to their glory that they have never forgotten. They can be fools; many of them are reactionaries and obstructionists just now; as guides to the politics of today they may be reliable as so many Mad Mullahs; they are rash and arrogant and dogmatic, many of them, but they have never been wrong as to what the future must bring.

Anarchists have seen more clearly than any of the other radical parties, that the revolution is a final uprising against civilization, not capitalism alone; that it will bring forth a new man, with new desires that will transcend even that current "law" of economics that so many of us are obsessed by, the law of large scale production. They have seen that the revolution will be a bold, complete and Goth-like destruction of all the present values, the virtues as well as the vices; and that it will probably bring about the disintegration of the cities and a return to nature, simplicity, the clean daylight splendor of the free communes.

In Russia, though the military state is still necessary (as gas masks were necessary in the trenches), there are many signs that this pure and ancient anarchist-communism is at the core of the great experiment, waiting to exfoliate in its season. There are the Communist Saturdays, days of volunteer labor, which Lenin has declared to be germs of the future week of voluntary communist toil. Peasant communes are encouraged, subsidized and given preference over individual land owning. There is *Prolet-Kult,* the evocation from the masses of the art and science latent in them, the creation of the workers' culture, based on human brotherhood and not on egotistic beauty-seeking in art and idle curiosity and power-worship in science. And then there is the education of the children, the Communists of the future, with the old pedagogy rooted out like a weed, and anarchist autonomy coming into its place as the golden rule in teaching. These are all symptoms of what is in growth in Russia.

Everyone does his own work about his own little shack in Stelton. Everyone lives simply; nearly all are vegetarians. Manual labor and poverty are the rule, so that whoever is good or whoever is wise is easily recognized. A learned young Jewish philosopher, a most persuasive little pessimist, was for months the janitor at the school, lecturing occasionally on literature when he was in the mood. A German carpenter is a student of Goethe and writes poetry. A newspaper editor washed dishes at the hotel during the summer. A poet is the best farmer on the tract, and a singer built hen coops by day—and built them well. All are equal. There is private property, but everyone thinks it a sin. There are no police, however, no thieves, and no class divisions.

But I do not wish to speak of the adults at Stelton. I have already indicated that they, like myself, and you, rapid reader, and the Pope, and Jack Dempsey, and the Sultan of Sulu, and the members of Tammany Hall, and the members of local New York and of the Socialist Party, and Julius Gerber and Louis Fraina, and Alexander Berkman, and even that battered hoary paladin of 100 per cent Communism, Hippolyte Havel—all, all of us are warped and betrayed and flawed and spoiled, absolutely unfitted for the brotherly life of the communes of the future.

The most communistic person at Stelton is Harry Kelley, who began his apprenticeship under Kropotkin in London when he was a youth, and now, at his fiftieth year, bears still on his bowed shoulders community burdens most of us duck when we can. Harry has been true as the north star; has never lost faith, though on his devoted head has beaten many a storm; he is the mainspring of the group at Stelton. And yet Harry, generous as he is, has been warped, too, by capitalism, and has his moods, prejudices and moments of unbrotherly cantankerousness.

All of us are spoiled. The adults have been able to accomplish little at Stelton, beyond escaping, in their own persons, the fever and mechanistic hell of the cities. They are a group of workers who have returned to nature, and have found a little peace. Perhaps this is something. But it is the children at Stelton who make the place a spot of revolutionary importance. The cause is lost and must die with us who are grown-up; we are what we are, instruments of hatred and tears. We have adapted ourselves successfully to life under capitalism, and therefore would be failures under communism. It is the children we must look to in hope. Even though the revolution should burst tomorrow, we should have to begin training the children, as in Russia, for the life of the future. They alone, in an atmosphere free of fear, can learn to work and create and love in true equality; we have too little faith for that.

The education of the children; this is the true revolution; this is what Ferrer taught and was killed for teaching by the capitalist class in Spain. Children are first in everything in Russia, and at Stelton, where the adults have fled from the class struggle, instead of following the more heroic method of winning it, the children, too, are the center of all the communal life, and the one great good that has come from the experiment there.

The children! They are everywhere one turns in the colony, dotting the place with color so that one comes upon them with joy as upon blue flowers under the corn rows. The whole green tract is their school, and they absorb that universal education that comes to man only through all of his five senses, and that he misses if he reads only books and knows only abstractions.

They are in the barn, helping milk the cows, or currying old Fred, the horse, whom they love. They are working in the fields with Sherwood, each proud of his little garden, each planting seeds and marvelling at the mystic chemistry of Nature, that turns loam into vivid flowers and clean, sweet vegetable food. They build little houses of their own, and write plays and act them, and they dance and sing, and draw, and edit and set type for their magazine, and raise chickens, and sail rafts on the pond, and fly kites and wash dishes. They do as much useful work every day as the average man, and they learn more, and yet you would think it was all play. They do it with noise and barbaric exuberance, and it is like a constant hymn of joy sung in the worship of life.

At the beginning the children at Stelton were taught reading, writing and arithmetic by the regular academic methods— from books, in class rooms. But last summer a final test of faith was made, and all compulsory classes abandoned. The children come from proletarian families, and the proletariat still has the outsider's reverence for book culture, so that the school lost many children when this plan was dared.

I saw how it was working. A big hand press and many cases of type were set up in the basement, and Paul Scott was put in charge, a shrewd, genial, philosophical tramp printer and ex-agitator, who among a thousand other adventures was once run out of Mexico with Benjamin De Casseres for publishing a revolutionary labor paper Porfirio Diaz didn't like.

The children saw him print a few leaflets, and it would have taken all the chariots of hell after that to prevent them from learning how to print. Uncle Scott's was the most popular resort on the colony. He is not a professional teacher, but he is an easy-going, wholesome person, wise as good fathers and able workers are wise, and he just gave all of them printer's sticks, showed them the fonts, and let them find out the rest for themselves.

Day after day I came into the printing shop and saw the busy youngsters happy at their task. They printed cards with their names on them, they printed little poems they had written, they published their magazine. Uncle Scott told them stories of his travels between times; also he corrected their grammar; also he gave the youngest of them private tips as to what grown-ups meant by a and b and c, when he was asked anxiously. Thus, when the practical need arose, out of their own inner necessity, the children learned reading.

The children learn reading at Stelton, because they want to work in Uncle Scott's printing office. They learn writing and arithmetic for similar practical reasons. Every day they make raffia baskets and weave carpets and other things on a hand loom, and before they can get the material they must present a slip asking for the quantity they will need. So they learn to write; they plead, beg, fight, and commandeer one of the teachers into teaching them this little knack.

Also a group of the boys built a number of miniature shacks near the farm house, and Jimmy Dick, the arithmetic teacher, had to come down and work out fractions and other measurements for them, and teach them how to estimate the amount of wood needed, and how to fit the angles of a roof. Thus they acquired arithmetic.

These houses were interesting affairs—two being small, private dens where several cliques of poets came for that high solitude (away from girls and "kids") that is so necessary to the art. Another was a more pretentious affair, with much room, and fancy burlap wall paper, and a coat of red paint. This was intended as a guest chamber for parents, and the boys were saving their pennies to buy a cot. And the other structure was a post office, with wire netting, and a desk, and pens—everything. The children spent long afternoons here writing letters to all their friends, and those who could not write were generously taught by the others.

How it flows! What a lesson this all is to those dolts who are perpetually asking us the terrible questions: But who will do the dirty work under Communism? But how are you going to get people to keep active without competition?

The need for work, for expression, is as much a need of the human organism as is bread. Without work men decay. These children, unhampered, with no class work, with no punishments, examinations or competition, learned because it is useful to learn, worked and built things because there is something in the body and spirit of man that demands this. Capitalism has become a monstrous, evil dam that blocks the wide flowing of all of man's instincts for work and creation.

And capitalist civilization has been successfully reared on one fundamental lie: that nature is not our home. Civilization is another name for the artificial, for cities, for intellectual castes occupying themselves with their phantom studies, for sickness and jails and wealth and poverty.

I loved to watch the children at Stelton growing up in the midst of the true reality.

Let all who love art practice it; begin as the cave man began, without technique, without precedents and masters. Technique has made cowards of us all.

The children at Stelton learned to draw in such a simple direct and beautiful way that I never tired of watching them. Hugo Gellert was their teacher. He would come down in his bare feet, an old cotton shirt and corduroy trousers, and sit down at a big table on the school porch and start to draw something. Ten or twelve kids would grab paper and crayons and follow his example. They would draw anything they wanted to. Some would draw the trees standing on the lawn; others would sketch Hugo, or their pals; some would sketch Fred, the horse, from memory, or Mike, the poor old hound who had attached himself to the school; or they would just draw imaginatively, from the emotions, innocently, with the primitive sweetness and truth we all have forgotten in this tangled age.

"Hugo," they would cry, "is mine good? Is this good?"

"Yes, fine, peachy," Hugo almost invariably said, and it is strange how this easily-won praise stimulated them. Indiscriminate praise may be bad, but Hugo loves art as William Morris loved it, and when he praises a thing it is for the joy, the sincerity and the truth that went into it. Children still have all these virtues in whatever they do.

The children, last summer, took to writing poems when the printing press came and the magazine was started. Here is one of them:

AN ODE TO RUTH
By Samuel Pearl

Ruthy is a lollypop, with big round staring eyes,
And all the time she's out of doors she gazes at the skies;
She gazes at the birds that fly, and at the sky so blue,
But just the same I do believe she's a lollypop, don't you?

I drove the milk wagon for some time about the colony, while the regular milkman was working on his shack, and I always had a crowd of the kids with me. Work was a picnic, life a perpetual riot. One of my assistants was a young, pugnacious tough-nut named Herbert Spencer Goldberg, who always dodged school and hated lessons. But he was caught in the wave of poetry that swept the school when the magazine was started, and I was surprised to find three of his efforts in the last number—in free verse, as might have been expected.

The one that follows is a symbol to me of our whole society at the present moment. We fear Communism, we fear the new order where even artists and intellectuals may have to work, we fear equality and freedom. But let us not fear. Let us trust in men's instincts. Happy and great days are ahead for humanity.

THE WOODS
By Herbert Spencer Goldberg

There was a time that I used to live in front of a great wood. I used to think I would never go into the woods, but a day came that my father said, "Come into the woods and help me chop wood." I said all right, and I went. And I was so happy.

More News From Nowhere

THE PEOPLE were starving. They were lost in the desert. They were thirsty, their little ones were crying for hunger and thirst, and some died in the arms of the mothers. The wild beasts came at night and slew many of the people. The people were mad with despair.

So Moses went up the mountain to speak with God. After a day he came down to the fevered and waiting people, and spoke to them thus:

"Honor they father and mother. Fear God and His Life-Force. Read good books and be nobler. Establish a decent school system. Give over this silly wailing for food and drink, and strive for higher things. God has revealed a vision of the Promised Land to me, and I will tell you all about it. It is quite exciting. I will tell it to you in 400 closely printed pages and a preface. I have many new jokes that God whispered to me—the celestial latest. Disentangle your souls from the sordid matter that enslaves it, saith the Lord God. Of Life only is there no end; and though of its million starry mansions many are empty and many still unbuilt, and though its vast domain is as yet unbearably desert, your seed shall one day fill it and master its matter to the uttermost. And for what may be beyond, our eyesight is too short. It is enough that there is a beyond."

Thus spake Moses, and the people were strangely ungrateful and murmurous. It appeared to the more wretched and stiff-necked among them that God and His prophet had not quite met the occasion. To their materialistic eyes it seemed as if the people were about to die for want of food and drink and shelter. But Moses was not disturbed. He was glowing with secret literary pride for the beauty of some of his phrases.

There was a dark, horrible civilization in which we all lived,

---

This was ostensibly a review of G. B. Shaw's Back to Methuselah *and H. G. Wells'* The Salvaging of Civilization. *Shaw and Wells had long been fashionable on the middle-class literary left, and here, as usual, Gold looked with a more jaundiced eye than did most of his literary comrades at chic prophets of the Millennium.* Liberator, *July 1921.*

as in a prison. Then there was an earthquake called a war, in which more than ten million young men were murdered. And now there is peace—and thousands of babies are being starved to death, new armies are being raised, millions are without jobs and homes, the class war rages in every city, and old men plan new national wars. And Shaw and Wells climb to Sinai and come down with these two books, *Back to Methuselah* and *The Salvaging of Civilization.*

Here is what they hand us:

Moses Wells denounces the past in that vivid speech that has sold so many of his novels. He recognizes the black place we have wandered into; he recognizes that we need food and drink and a social way of living; he tells us this more eloquently and clearly than we could tell it to ourselves.

Then, as remedy, he suggests that we appoint a committee to collect and create a modern Bible—one somewhat on the order of Upton Sinclair's *Cry for Justice,* which Wells does not know has been in circulation for years without much visible effect on American plutocrats. This Bible is to furnish us all with that social cement, that cultural bond, that made the Middle Ages, with its elder Bible, such a charming era of brotherhood.

We are also to reform our educational system along Wellsian lines, most of which (though we are not told this), are tracings of the Communist lines already marked out in the little-known barbarous country called Russia.

Also we are to be very noble, like Mr. Wells' Samurai and Researchers Magnificent of former years, and we are able to work for a League of Nations (not the Russian brand), and for other noble ends.

The following is the attitude Moses Wells wants us to strike, we poor deluded slaves of fear and hunger and joblessness and tyranny:

> I know that in thus putting all the importance upon educational needs at the present time I shall seem to many readers to be ignoring quite excessively the profound racial, social and economic conflicts that are in progress. I do. I believe we shall never get on with human affairs until we do ignore them. I offer no suggestion whatever as to what sides people should take in such an issue as that between France and Germany, or between Sinn Fein and the British Government, or in the class war.
>
> These conflicts are mere aspects of the gross and passionate

stupidity and ignorance of our present world. It is impossible for a sane man who wishes to serve the world to identify himself with either side in any of them. [Except when Belgium is attacked by the Hun!] On one side we have greed, insensibility and incapacity, on the other envy and suffering stung to vindictive revolt; on neither side light nor generosity nor creative will. Neither side is more than a hate and an aggression.

Cease, Karl Liebknecht, from your sordid, stupid task of over-throwing the Kaiser! Cease, John Reed, from your work of bringing bread and peace and the poetry of communism to a hopeless world! Cease, Nicolai Lenin, and Maxim Gorky, from your "envious, vindictive" task of building a nation of freemen and thinkers in the center of a universe of drudges and slaves!

Let us all repent, and go into committee with H. G. Wells for the sublime object of editing a new Bible that shall be found, like the old, on the reading table of every respectable home forever.

That is Moses Wells.

Now for Moses Shaw.

Shaw grows indignant and horrified and passionately vitupera-tive as he contemplates the capitalist system. No one can do this better than Shaw. He has always been a desperate rebel and bit-ter humanitarian. He is one of Shelley's "resolutely good" men; we honor him for it. He did a great work when he began his ter-rorist attack on the nineteenth century taboos. But he is a prophet, too, and a nineteenth century intellectual, and this is the relevant thing he has to say, in effect, about the world crisis he sees so clearly:

> Darwin was wrong. I, Bernard Shaw, along with Samuel Butler, have always been a Neo-Lamarckian. I believe there is a Life-Force, and that it expresses itself in man's will. I do not believe in de-terminism, but in free will. Evolution is not a blind process, but innate will asserting itself in various experimental forms.
>
> Also, I have come to this conclusion: that it is almost hopeless to try to reform the world. Men are not intelligent enough. A man begins getting intelligent toward the end of his life, when his passions have become exhausted, and he does not want anything very hard. So the great problem for us all is to try to preserve our old men, so that they can rule us. We can do this by willing to live three hundred years, instead of the seventy allotted to us now. This can be done by willing; the human will is all powerful. Now I will prove this by my play, *Back to Methuselah*. Up with the curtain!

The play is really five plays—the first is laid in the Garden of Eden, the second is in the present era, the third takes place in the year 2170 A.D., the fourth in 3,000 A.D., the fifth comes on a summer afternoon in the year 31,920 A.D.—"As Far As Thought Can Reach," Shaw calls it.

All sorts of things happen then. Children are born, fully-matured, from huge eggs. By force of will, the Ancients, who now live forever, can grow five heads and six sets of arms. Scientists have learned how to construct human beings resembling the figures of our own dark period. Many other wonders are shown forth. It is all ingenious, remarkable, stimulating, dazzling, crowded with invention, and it all means nothing to the poor wanderers in the modern wilderness.

All through the plays run like a thick, rushing, brilliant river, those eloquent speeches of Shaw's. Everyone is a "philosopher" in this world of his, and talks large fascinating generalities.

Shaw states his complete philosophy of life in this book. He says he has never quite successfully done it before. Well, it is nothing much, after all. Bergson and William James and Nietzsche and others have taught us all we need to know about Creative Evolution. One can accept the doctrine without losing membership in the Union League Club. And the slogan of *Back To Methuselah* was projected more sanely and scientifically many years ago in a golden book by Metchnikoff called *The Nature of Man*.

Shaw is a great, good man. He was a mighty force in the last century, and he helped destroy many a Bastille. But he is not of our generation. It is simply so—we ourselves are finding ourselves appalled to realize how marked Shaw is with the stigmata of the last century. He hates the body—he thinks it is evil. In his Utopia men will finally discard the body and its appetites and live as vortices of pure thought. Shaw has not read psychoanalysis, apparently, and he does not know that there is no such thing as pure intellect. He really hates the masses of humanity, because they will not listen to him, and are slow, dumb, animal, enduring. That is nineteenth century intellectualism, too. We are finding that the masses of humanity can be aroused and can be led to greater goals than the Shavian and Fabian goals. Shaw does not see this, either.

He is one of the nineteenth century prophets. They were an irritable, unsocial and egotistic lot. They dwelt in suburban Sinais, where all manner of revelations were vouchsafed them. These they brought down to the multitudes, and they were angered, like Moses, when the masses refused to receive them. These prophets were too proud to wait for the masses, or to stay with them and lead and educate them. They refused to draw up plans based on objective possibility. It was all or nothing. It was Utopia or Hell.

The prophets were too pure to join parties. They were too proud, most of them, to recognize that most of their thought was stolen from the living platforms of these parties, from the arenas where thought was being hammered into deed. Thus Wells still talks about "my world-state," and "my plans for the new education." It would not be surprising if he secretly believed that his *New Worlds for Old* was responsible for the Russian Revolution.

The people are lost in the wilderness, and must be led forth to hope again. The world is coming to an end, and these bourgeois prophets talk to us grandiosely of the Life-Force and God and Bibles and noble aspirations. They are fiddling Neros in the midst of a conflagration; they are fussy suburbanites at sea who cannot understand that the ship is sinking; they are besotted mystics who dream that thought or culture or God or Bible can exist apart from the Life of Man—and do not know that the Life of Man is in peril at this moment.

There is something heartless and terrible about the vanity of these nineteenth century intellectuals! Longevity and Neo-Lamarckianism as a cure for the class war, Bibles and fine thinking as a panacea for unemployment and militarism!

Shaw and Wells are the irretrievable products of the age of romantic individualism and we are the products of the age of conscription, scientific revolution and mass action, and there is a dark and impassable gulf between us. They do not understand us, and we can no longer understand them.

We of the new generation are not too proud to tackle the belly problem first, we are willing to forego all the joys of constructing each his special Utopia. We are uniting in a dirty and necessary task, in a real world, where Utopias are as valuable as roses and nightingales to a man fighting a tiger.

Let us honor and forget these prophets of an elder day. They did some useful work in their time, and now they are old. Let them chatter in their vain and frivolous manner of the Life-Force and the Modern Bible. They are not too much in the way, and if they wish to abuse us, let them enjoy that privilege.

We have thought of eternity, no less clearly than Wells and Shaw. We have thought of Bibles and culture, too, and we say they are all nothing if the Life of Man is not organized and saved from sinking back into the primeval slime. That is our task, and we have the strength to face it: we are not luxuriating in the escape of Utopias and fine dreams.

Shaw and Wells scorn us: we are living in the cellar: Shaw shows us that we are irreligious, and Wells that we are hopelessly crude. Yes, yes, we admit all this, and now back to the task.

from *The American Famine*

LET US leave them, the sedentary swarm of politicians, uplifters, and place-seeking liberals, and go out into the open air again, where rain falls on starving men, and revolutions are made. Let the talkers mitigate, shorten duration, and commit all America to relief, while we seek the facts of life. Unemployment is not a thing in books, a matter of figures and graphic charts. It is the raw brutal terrible reality of starvation and cold and death. It is famine and desperation, and it must be felt as one feels the death of a friend if it is to be understood. The liberal intellectualistic attitude seems to be that one must study, ponder, collect data, write articles in the liberal journals and economists' reviews, read many books and attend many conferences. One must do nothing. To do anything is not a mark of serious thought. One must be genteel and restrained. One must not become what H. G. Wells calls the "Forgodsaker!"

Have any of these gentlemen ever really stood about in the freezing rain in thin rags, hungry, jobless, friendless, half-dead with worry? I have. Millions of men in this country are doing this today, and for them it is an emergency, not the academic problem it is for the liberals. The truth is, the college trained man who is always sure of a fair job, the minister, the lawyer, all the bourgeois thinkers, can never understand these proletarian

---

The material reprinted here is roughly the second half of the original article. The first half is a report of the recent doings of "the sedentary swarm of politicians, uplifters, and place-seeking liberals" in their response to the then current postwar economic slump. Abdul Bahai was the son and successor of Baha'u'llah, founder of the Bahai faith. Urbain Ledoux appeared during the recession of 1921 as a self-appointed leader of the unemployed. He got headlines by setting up "slave auctions" at which unemployed workers allowed themselves to be "sold" to employers for short periods of time. On September 20, the New York police broke up one of Ledoux's markets in Bryant Park, behind the 42nd Street Library, which is the scene of this part of Gold's article. Liberator, November 1921.

problems as they must be understood. What the liberal movement needs in this country is what the Russian movement needed
in the seventies, a return to the people. Let them get into labor
unions, the factories, the mines, and the farm granges. Let them
write directly to the people when they have anything to say.
Upton Sinclair seems naive and full of infantile indiscretions of
thought to the over-cultured, but he is the greatest propagandist
in America today because he has always written to the masses,
and not to the limited groups who read George Santayana and
Thorstein Veblen.

So many fine articles, so many well-spun, well balanced, well-
informed glossy articles were written on unemployment in our
liberal and radical weeklies; and then a man of simple, direct
feelings appeared on the scene and did more in two weeks than
the rest had done in ten years. Urbain Ledoux came and found
great masses of men starving. He conceived a dramatic method
of flinging their misery into the teeth of polite society, and he
acted on it. His slave market was a great inspiration, and it has
brought forth more fruit than could have been believed. No one
will ever do anything for the unemployed until they organize
themselves and force some sort of recognition from the society
that tries to forget them. Ledoux saw this. His trip to the President, with his "human documents" and his demand for a list of
the war profiteers was an event that rang from coast to coast as
no article ever could. It was an act, and acts do something.

Ledoux is a follower of Abdul Bahai; he has many sweet,
quaint, foolish metaphysical obsessions; he is an early Primitive
in economics; he does not like to worry the authorities, has a
deep respect for law and order, but nevertheless he is a man—a
full-blooded, passionate, brave and impressive social man. And
he knows the people. The American radicals can teach him economics, but he can teach them how to move the people.

"Human documents?" Yes, Ledoux is right; they are the
truest books from which one can study the facts of the class
struggle. One can controvert a theory, an article or a pamphlet,
but who can answer the dumb eyes of a starving, jobless man?
What Presidential rhetoric is there that can clothe and feed the
forsaken millions, and give them friends and warmth and a
human and happy place in life? What have statistics to say on a
cold night to the men huddling in Bryant Park, and what mes-

sage has Parsonry for the hollow bellies and aching hearts? What cheer brings Good Taste, that delicate scribe who fills the professional journals, and what east-wind nourishment are the multitudes to suck from the valiant speeches that fill the congressional halls and aldermanic chambers of the nation?

Ah! liars, hypocrites, rogues, and sluggards! word-bedazzled office men and frock-coated congressional bores! wealthy pimps of the souls of men, financiers, bankers, statesmen, economists, professors, white-collared lackeys and fools! you are digging well, silly moles, at the foundations of your stately civilization. It will fall. These slow, suffering masses who drift about your cities and whom you insult, will awake some day and will rend you. Patience and ignorance are not eternal. Do not count on them forever. Justice is a pyre that must be heaped to the heavens before it bursts into flame. But O, the great leaping, red cleansing conflagration at the end; O, the holy ashes from which the Phoenix shall rise!

I went about New York for several days with Hugo Gellert, the artist, to see the human documents of the famine in America, to see the patient, ignorant men whom the rich are killing and taming in this periodical Spartan massacre of the helots. One morning we stood before a bread line on the Bowery. The dawn had forced its way through the sullen wall of sky. There was a faint, bitter light in the city like that on drowned ships. The houses were stern and charred remnants against the sky; they were smouldering in gloom. The elevated roared by, strange dark Caliban rushing on the errands of man. All was old and bitter. Thousands of tired men and women, half asleep and bloodless, were on their way to the factories. Wagons rattled by. It was the black, black city of New York, and before a mission of Jesus Christ, who died for Love, as Keats died for Beauty, and as Liebknecht died that there might be bread and peace in the world, three hundred men were shivering in line.

They had waited for an hour or more in the darkness and cold; they were soon to be rewarded with coffee and stale crullers. Who were they? Who make up the unemployed? Workers all; three huge ruddy lumberjacks from the Maine woods, standing proudly and somberly as dying trees; dozens of sailors, in their rough clothes; battered, emaciated factory hands, dazed old derelicts with white, unshaven chins and watery eyes; strong young men, veterans of the war, hanging their heads in shame, stokers, cooks, waiters, mechanics, farmers, drivers, clerks and longshoremen, the useful citizens of the world, the creators of wealth, the hard-handed architects of society.

They did not speak; they stood there with hands thrust deep in pockets, braced against the wind; they were dumb; each understood the other's shame; it was not necessary to say anything, one to the other. I, too, felt ashamed, as I stood and watched; for I had five dollars in my pockets, besides the certainty of a month's living.

These men had nothing.

The Bowery is a little city of the damned. It is the bottom of the whirlpool that sucks forever downward the frail boat of the wage worker. Here men come when they have failed in the economic struggle, when they have made a misstep to one side or the other in the eternal tightrope balancing over the precipice of hunger that is the proletarian life. Here they come when they are weakest, and seek Lethe in drink and dirt and shiftlessness. Here they come when they are sick and friendless, and need a quiet place to die.

There are 600,000 men out of work in the imperial city of New York, 75,000 of whom are veterans of the war for democracy, freedom, life, homes, wives, children, music, laughter, recreation, health, friendship—Jobs.

The Bowery is always full of homeless wanderers, but now it is crowded with these men. The unemployed swarm on every corner, and in all the missions and lousy lodging houses, blue with pipe smoke. We went into one of the missions that are scattered so freely under the hurtling elevated structure that mounts the Bowery. These are the missions of those who are rich and who preach humility and brotherly love to those who are poor. It was a long, bare room, with a reading table at which some men sat sleeping for the few hours before they would be turned out into the night. A smuggy, cheap shrine stood in one corner, and over the reading table was hung an American flag. A hundred men in working clothes and overalls sat about—silent and sullen. They did not speak—there is nothing to say when men are hungry. They sat and waited.

No watchful priest or attendant was about, and a drunken man had come in. He staggered about, a thick-set Swede with a

raw, red face and blue, wondering babyish eyes, offering everyone a drink of rot-gut from a quart bottle. No one would take it.
No one would joke with him, or answer him.

"Aw, c'm on, less all be happy," he pleaded. "C'm on, fellas,
less be happy!"

But they were too hungry and sane to be happy in this way.
Happiness does not come out of a bottle, nor is it found in a
phrase. It will only come when men are free and creative, when
they are never hungry or afraid, when the Red Flag waves over
the whole wonderful earth, and there are no rich or poor.

Around Cooper Union, where the Bowery splits off into
Fourth Avenue, the unemployed sit on the benches under the
shadow of the statue of Peter Cooper, who invented some mar-
velous machine or other that has reduced the burden of labor.
They sit there every day and every night. They rarely speak.
They sit and wait. They read old newspapers, and watch the
busy people go by. They dream of nothing—they are hungry.
They sit and wait.

There is the Bowery Y.M.C.A., a massive red-brick structure
with hundreds of rooms and beds for those who have jobs and
can pay. The unemployed flock here, too—we saw hundreds of
them one night watching the free moving pictures that are provided for the starving. A handsome young bank president fights
on the screen a villainous Wall Street broker for the hand of the
most beautiful camel-hair-eyebrowed heroine in the world. Ah,
what a theme for the downcast hearts of starving men—what a
banquet of comfort and joy! There was a big bulletin board in
the lobby, with a bold legend chalked on it: "GOD FORGIVES
AND FORGETS—WHY NOT YOU?"

A dapper little superintendent came up to us, looking at
Hugo's portfolio with interest, as we were reading this masterpiece of the Christian brain.

"Ah, an artist!" he said with the ready professional smile, and
he offered to shake our hands, but we turned away in contempt.

Forgive and forget!

It rained the next morning as we set out on our rounds, the
city lay wrapped in a grey, weary smoke of rain. The faces of the
houses were wet, the pavements underfoot were slimy as an eel,
there was a chill wind that drove the rain. The damp must have
penetrated through the paper-thin shoes of the homeless thousands, the wind must have cut through their greasy, wrinkled

rags. Along the Bowery one saw knots of them flattened out against the walls of the damp buildings and cowering in doorways. They were still dumb—and they seemed even sadder and lonelier than yesterday; the gray wide chill solitude of the day, when there was not even the sun and the city seemed a great cortege of mourning, oppressed these sad outcasts.

About Cooper Square they had abandoned the benches and were standing in doorways and under the sheltered entrance to the Cooper Union library. They were in the reading room, scores of them, gazing like slow-witted kine through the endless page of the meadow-wide newspapers; they did not read with intelligence, as do men of brains and perception such as ourselves, they were thinking of the coming night, when they would have to go out to find a bed and a crust somehow.

Hugo and I went to the Grand Central station where the American Land Brigade had established a farm employment bureau for ex-service men. About four hundred men had applied here daily for jobs, the papers said, and about thirty and forty a day got them. The bureau took up a great marble corridor on the west side of the station, a gigantic balcony overlooking the shuffle, the chaos, the movement and splendid excitement of the main floor of the station.

Hundreds of young men were here, all with the bronze service buttons in their lapels, many with the silver button that tells of heroic wounds. These were the boys who had been martyred for Wilson's ideals. These were the boys who had been roasted in a hell hotter than the insane creation imagined by the Christian priesthood. These were the boys who had shed blood for freedom. Now they stood about in beggar's rags, hungry and jobless, with the dumb, animal look that one sees everywhere in these faces. The nation that had sainted them, that had demanded the "supreme sacrifice" of them, now turned them away like mongrel dogs.

Scores of them were lying on the bare marble floor, sleeping in all this din. Others squatted about on their haunches, miserably conversing. Above them and around them was the huge, wonderful monument of American industrialism, the superb arch of ceiling, a blue sky dotted with golden stars, the great Romanesque square columns, tall as mountains, the marble floors and walls and balustrades, luxury unbounded. It was a fitting frame to their misery. It was American shallowness, putting all its

ardor and idealism into steel and stone, and letting men decay. It
was American hypocrisy, a gorgeous body in which beat a putrid
and inhuman heart. At ten o'clock every night these veterans
were put out of the marble corridor, and they too must find the
crust of bread and the sleeping place somehow in the immense
unfriendly city.

Scores of other ex-service men make a dwelling place these
days of Bryant Park, which is a fine green square next to the
wonderful Public Library at Fifth Avenue and Forty-second
Street. Hundreds of unemployed have made this park their ren-
dezvous; the whole place can be seen crowded with hungry men
idle every day, sprawling over the benches, sleeping on the grass,
moving up and down the walks in close companionship like sheep
in a storm. They have formed some sort of organization here,
and have their own law-and-order committee and other repre-
sentatives. Charitable men and women come here and distribute
sandwiches and clothing occasionally, and Ledoux held some
meetings with them, and once or twice even the men were af-
forded the good old lesson that the State is not the friend of the
workers, and were clubbed by the police.

The cold, lustral rain that was still falling had driven all the
men out of the park on this day into doorways and other shel-
ters. Fifty of them were jammed as tightly as human beings can
be jammed without adhering into a little recruiting tent on the
grass. Five or six of them shivered under a beautiful marble
fountain, and a bunch huddled under a noble statue of William
Cullen Bryant, poet of Calm and Serenity. In the library reading
rooms we found dozens of others, prowling about disconsolately,
too distracted to read. The rain fell for about two hours more,
and when we came out at least a hundred men were again prom-
enading up and down the walks, for the grass and benches were
still wet, and it was cold.

A group of them had gathered about a little runt of a Jew, a
five-foot hobo without a collar, who had a droll, wise, shrewd
face like a gargoyle's, and the most mischievous little brown
eyes. The men loved him, he was their fun-maker and jester.
They buffeted him about, they kicked him and slapped him affectionately and he laughed and dodged their rough blows.

"Come on, Shorty, make us a speech!" they cried.

"G'wan, I ain't the Mayor!"

"Come on, ye gotta, Shorty! Give us a speech!"

They stood him on a bench, and he grinned like a satyr, and put his hand in his old dusty coat, like a statesman.

"Ahem!" he began pompously, and the crowd rocked with glee.

Other men came running up for the fun that is the great heroic gesture of mankind in misery. Someone produced a long false beard that had been gotten God-knows-where. Another stuck his derby on Shorty, and a clean, middle-aged man, who looked like a respectable clerk, took out his precious glasses from their case and lent them to Shorty.

How they roared as they saw their favorite in this wonderful makeup! They could not contain their laughter; they slapped each other on the backs, and the tears came to their eyes.

"Give us a speech, Shorty!" they shouted.

"Gen'l'men," Shorty began, lifting a dirty hand, "attenshin. I'm goin' to undress you all on a great subjec'. Lissen; I'm a Bullshevik, and I wanta ye to vote for me, see?"

"Hooray!" the crowd roared.

"I'm goin' tuh speak on unemployments. You know what that woid means, donchyer? It means bein' a millionaire without any money, see? Well, I just come back from Washington, boys, where I seen President Harding. He wuz playin' gol-luf on his front lawn when I come up to see him, and when I told him I come from the Bryant Park boys he says he's too busy; he's only got time to see the boys from Fifth Avenue. But then, when he found out that he used buy his chewin'-tobacco from a rich uncle of mine that runs a tobacco store in Marion, Ohio, he seen me, 'cause he knew I wuz honest.

"I told him about the unemployments, and he lissened. Then he says, 'Shorty, I'm sorry to see you're hangin' out with that Bryant Park bunch. They're a bad lot, and they'll spoil ye. Ye're too good for them——' "

Here the crowd hauled Shorty down with a great whoop of indignation and pummeled him amid uncontrolled laughter. Shorty dodged about like a cat; he came up on his feet every time; nothing would ever keep Shorty down for long. He was the perfect city gamin, and he was in his element here. They set him up on the bench again. He took out a few frayed cigar store coupons and held them up between his fingers.

"Some kind gen'l'men has just given me a hundred dollars for the boys out of work," he said with a big grin. "Who'll give me another hundred?"

He read several telegrams from an old yellow pad someone handed up to him.

"Bryant Park Committee—Send a hundred boys over to Blake's restaurant for supper. Tell them to walk quietly by two and threes and make no noise. We don't like noise, especially the way they eat soup. (Signed) The Holy Rollers."

There were loud cheers.

"Another telegram, gen'l'men.

"Bryant Park Committee—Send two hundred fellers over here for a job Monday morning—seven o'clock—at the workhouse. (Signed) The Board of Health."

"Yes, gen'l'men, they're doin' everything they can for us. They all got kind hearts, and some day they're goin' to give us the earth, yes, they are. And I'm goin' to be President some day, and I'll give ye all jobs, and we'll have gol-luf parties on the White House lawn, yes, we will."

It was just fooling; it was the unconscious wisdom of the proletariat, that waits for its proper time to burst through all the shells and shams; it was Gavroche predicting the tumbrils, and they understood him, these men, though he did not know all he was saying, nor did they. The grim jests of the proletariat; they have tumbled down many a throne!

Someone said to me the other night:

"But how *do* these men live?"

I don't know; they live somehow; and many of them die.

I was coming through Union Square one night. A young fellow stepped out of a doorway and asked me for a cigarette. I gave it to him, and gave him some money, too. Then I talked with him for a moment. He was a young, clean-looking chap, with a strong, lean American face, and blue, friendly eyes in which the tears shone as he unburdened himself to me.

"God, I don't know how this'll end for me. I've been out of work four months now. Haven't eaten for two days. I can ask for a cigarette, but haven't got the nerve to ask for money. The cops would pick me up, anyway, and I'd rather starve out here than behind bars. Used to be a mechanic in the Altoona railroad shops, but there isn't a thing doin' anywhere. A thousand men for every job. I get to places at six in the morning and they're already taken, and a big mob hangin' around outside. God! it's hell! I never knew I could get so low!

"How do I live? I don't know; parks, handouts, that sort of stuff. Haven't eaten for two days now, and wuz just getting to the point where I didn't care. God, look at all those autos goin' by, hundreds of them all day. It makes me sick to look at 'em sometimes; people with money, and I don't know where I'm goin' to sleep tonight. I never knew the world could be like this!"

No one seems to know. He wrapped himself again in the obscurity of the doorway, and shivered in his lonely misery. Half a million men in the city, without friends, without women, without food and shelter, without a single one of the simple, warm, human earthy things that make Life bearable! And the city does not care. The preachers preach their sermons; the poets write their delicate lyrics; the business men sit in their fine offices, solemnly conducting the world's affairs; the politicians make fine speeches; the debutantes give their dances; the actors strut about the stages; the editorial writers ladle out words of wisdom; there is laughter, life, color, wine, wealth; the whole monstrous city moves down its primrose path, like a courtesan plying her trade in the very shadow of the cross on which the Son of Man is writhing.

How clean and brave it is in Russia! How much better to starve and die there! There no one hides the hunger of millions behind the folds of a flag! There no one feasts while his brother starves! There misery is inevitable, it is the cruelty of nature, which can be borne, not the cruelty of man to man!

And here nothing will come of it all. We will know hunger and famine again. "A certain amount of unemployment will always be with us," says the President. Over there they are working, fighting, building, striving to the last nerve to abolish hunger, to create a world out of this misery that will be fair, just and beautiful, with Life for all, even the lowest.

But here all is still dark.

from *Hope for America*

ABOUT THREE weeks ago, by one of those strange combinations that are possible only in New York, I, a battered, "foiled *revolutionaire*" of the type common in this disorderly metropolis, found myself in the company of a certain young self-made millionaire. His name is well known; he is a cultured and capable individual; he would be a loved leader under any regime, and his unquenchable intelligence has led him to a deep and permanent interest in the revolutionary world. But he is sad, as are most millionaires, for their money makes them suspicious and selfish and mean, whatever their native characteristics may have been, and he was telling me that men were too vile for any improvement, that there was no hope for America, and that the ardent youth of the movement was throwing itself gallantly and foolishly under the wheel of an eternal Juggernaut.

We were walking through the bright, rushing streets, in the procession of the city's millions, and I was trying to prove the contrary to him, that there was hope for the world. He listened quietly, and then sighed.

"Ah!" he said wistfully. "But you have so much more optimism than I have!"

I could not help smiling. He had a million dollars and a million friends; the world was his wonderful, pearl-crowded, submissive oyster; while I, at the moment, a free-lance journalist, near-novelist and ex- and perhaps soon-manual laborer, was intensely occupied with the problem of raising the mighty sum of $25 for a new and absolutely necessary overcoat. The contrast was sublime. I felt like giving three cheers; this was a perfect episode in the glorious melodrama of Life. The millionaire is a pessimist; the pauper an optimist; and perhaps these are the only possible attitudes for them to take now; perhaps it is how nobil-

---

This selection represents roughly the first third of the original article, the rest of which is a detailed discussion of labor politics at the beginning of the Boom. Liberator, *December 1921.*

ity and beggardom felt on the eve of the French Revolution; the one striving upward, the other slipping down. *Ca ira!*

No, I am not an optimist, dear millionaire friend; I can be as sad and sick about the life I see as any of your gloomy comrades in his darkest hour. There is no perpetual sunrise over my world. Too many of my friends, the finest boys under the heaven, clean, freedom-loving, generous big men, who spent themselves like antique heroes, and not like modern self-constricted millionaires, are rotting in the jails of America. There is a famine in Russia, and sometimes I cannot sleep at night as I think of those hollow-eyed millions of simple human beings, the dumb men, the broken-hearted dumb mothers, the marrowless, withered children, who suffer, under the divine justice, for the sins of the capitalist statesmen. Soon the winter will come, and Death will run amuck among these victims and will crush them like insects. *Yet the whole world does not rise en masse to save them!* I think of this, and I think of all Europe that bled itself almost to death. I think of the chemists perfecting gas bombs in their laboratories for the next war; I think of the parliamentarians making speeches, and the premiers plotting alliances; I think of policemen and detectives, and big businessmen, the pillars of this unholy system; I think of ministers and other hypocrites. And I think of myself and my intimate friends (you see, I am selfish, too) and how we scramble about every day for a bare living, and are insulted, and degraded, and how we squeeze and pinch out the essentials and take no thought of the morrow, because the morrow will be like today, forever and ever, since we are the life prisoners of poverty; and my heart aches for all of us, and I assure you that this is no food for optimism, either.

No, I live in no cheerful world; nevertheless I live in a hopeful one. The world of labor is built on foundations of despair, but its columns and pinnacles are of strong granite hope. What keeps me sane is that I have studied a little in Marx, and have thrown myself a great deal into the dangerous whirlpools and rapids of the labor movement. I can be gloomy, tired, bitter, sordid, selfish, cynical and disgusted with the world, but I can never despair. I know too much for that. I know there is something greater than myself and my moods that is making for righteousness; that it is greater than all the moods of all the men in the world; that we can grow tired and old, corrupted and melancholy, but that the great thing will always be there. It will always be there while capitalism is there; it is the modern labor movement, that has been created by capitalism, and that by the laws of capitalism must go on fighting for its life, fighting on the defensive against the beast that is ever-hungry, fighting because it must conquer or die. And it will conquer, for the war spelt the failure of capitalistic production, and with its conquest of the world, labor, which is communistic, will replace capital, which is competitive, and we shall see great things; there will be all that we have dreamed of, it is certain as the sun.

Marx has never been heard of by immense multitudes of workingmen; and certain layers of the intelligentsia find a parasitic pleasure in crawling over the colossal figure and "criticizing" it with their little jaws; Marx made some mistakes, but was it not he who pointed out the tropismatic actions of humanity in the face of its economic needs, and was it not he who showed us that hope lay not in the thousand Utopian impulses toward goodness and reform of fallible men, but was in the strong-flowing, permanent mass needs of labor? It was a great lesson; and many have not yet learned it. For them Marx should be a bitter and bracing tonic during these dark days, more wholesome than the intoxicating, yet depressing, draughts of "humanitarian" poetry. Read Marx and study the labor movement closely, I would say to my sad millionaire friend, you will suddenly discover that there is room for grief, but not for despair. The Revolution is here, and capitalism is doomed, as surely as absolute monarchy was doomed when the Bastille fell. There is still a long, bloody fight ahead for the next century, perhaps, but at least revolutionists know that they are fighting on the winning side, and not on the losing.

Hereditary monarchism seemed woven into the fabric of the universe, but any thinker knew that it was doomed when the people began jeering at Louis the Magnificent. Capitalism seems firm as the mountains; in America, especially, the great machine reaches to the skies and awes us with its immensity, but it is doomed, also; it has failed in Russia and Europe, it will fail here. It is not absolute, and only the absolute does not change. It cannot bear criticism or attack. If one nation has repudiated it, all the nations will. God himself does not exist while there is one man to deny Him.

The labor movement cannot die, because it is the sole shield of the workers against capitalism. And the labor movement is fundamentally a revolutionary fact, though at any given moment all who carry it on may be reactionary in thought. Its very existence is a criticism of capitalism, a threat, a menace, a dissent and disobedience to the laws of the competitive society. Gompers is a revolutionist, for he fights the open shop. He cannot help himself, and the labor movement cannot help drifting everywhere toward its logical conclusion—which is, the world for the workers.

Things look bad here in America for the revolutionary forces. Imperialism is in the saddle; the reactionaries still maintain their deathhold on the A. F. of L.; unemployment has put a powerful labor-smashing weapon in the hands of the employers, which they are not slow in using; the Socialist Party, after committing all the errors possible to it, is breaking up; Debs and the "Wobbly" boys and the Communists are still in jail, and we have not been strong enough as yet to get them out.

But the labor movement is going on, and under the superficial veils of defeat new forces are preparing, new seeds are germinating in the harsh dark native soil.

The Password to Thought—to Culture

THE FACTORY of Shinster and Neuheim, Makers of the Hytone Brand Ladies' Cloaks and Suits, rushed along busily in its usual channels that sweet May afternoon; the machines racing and roaring; the workers gripped by their tasks; the whole dark loft filled with a furious mechanical life, hot and throbbing as the pulse of an aeroplane.

Outside the sunlight lay in bright patterns on the dusty streets and buildings, illuminating for two or three hours more the city crowds moving to and fro on their ever-mysterious errands. But the factory was filling with darkness, and the hundred silent figures at the sewing machines bent even lower to their work, as if there were some mighty matter for study before them, needing a sterner and tenser notice as the day deepened into twilight.

The pressers, at their boards at one end of the long loft, thumped with their irons, and surrounded themselves with hissing steam like a fog. The motors roared and screamed, and one of the basters, a little Italian girl, sang in a high voice a sad, beautiful love song of her native province in Italy. It ran through the confusion of the loft like a trickle of silver, but now and again its fragile beauty was drowned by the larger, prosaic voice of Mr. Neuheim, the junior partner, as he bustled about and shouted commands to one or another of his workers.

"Chaim, come here and take this bundle to Abe's machine!"

This autobiographical fiction can be fruitfully compared with the essay, "Towards Proletarian Art," published a year earlier, to discover some of the relations between Gold's early literary theory and practice. The "Sidar" spoken of in this story is the Jewish Prayer Book; it is usually spelled "Siddur." Vorwaerts (Forward) was the social-democratic Yiddish daily in New York, edited by Abraham Cahan. Liberator, February 1922.

he would shout in Yiddish, and a very old, white-bearded Jew came patiently and slowly, and took the huge bundle of cloaks on his brittle shoulders, and delivered them to the operator.

"Hurry up on this Flachsman job, boys!" Mr. Neuheim would say, rubbing his hands, as he stood behind one of the operators, and a few of them in the vicinity would frown slightly and murmur some inaudible answer from between closed lips.

Mr. Neuheim, a short, flabby man with a bald head and reddish moustache that was turning white, was the practical tailor of the firm and stayed in the factory and looked after production. His partner had been a salesman when they joined their poverty and ambition not many years ago, and there looked after the selling and business end now. Mr. Neuheim liked this arrangement, for he had sat at the bench for years, and still liked the smell of steam and the feel of cloth, the putting together of "garments." Best of all, he liked to run things, to manage, to bustle, and to have other tailors under him, dependent on his word.

He trudged about the factory all day like a minor Napoleon, and wherever he went there was a tightening of nerves, an increased activity of fingers, and a sullenness as if his every word were an insult. He was a good manager, and kept things moving. His very presence was like a lash lightly flicked at the backs of the workers. They did not like him, but they responded when they felt him near.

Mr. Neuheim trotted about more strenuously than usual on this afternoon. There was a big order to be delivered the next morning, and he was making sure that it would be on time. He sped from his basters to his pressers, from his pressers to his operators, a black, unlighted cigar in his mouth, a flush of worry on his gross, round face.

"Where are those fifty suits in the 36 size of the Flachsman lot?" he suddenly demanded of the white-bearded factory porter.

"I brought them to David an hour ago, Mr. Neuheim," Chaim said, looking at him with meek eyes.

"Good. Then they'll be sure to get off tonight," said the Boss, scowling like a busy general. "Good."

He thought a moment, and then hurried on his short legs through the piles of unfinished clothing till he came to the door that led from the factory to the shipping room. There was a glass panel in the upper part of the door, and Mr. Neuheim stopped and looked through it before entering.

What he saw made him take the cigar out of his mouth, swear, and then open the door with a violent kick that almost tore it from its hinges.

"My God!" he cried fervently, "what is this, anyways?"

His shipping clerk, David Brandt, a Jewish youth of about twenty-three, was seated on the table near the open window, staring dreamily at the grey masses of building opposite, that now were flashing with a thousand fires in the sun. He was hugging his knees, and beside him on the table lay an open green-covered book that he had evidently put aside for a moment.

David Brandt was a well-built youth, with good shoulders and chest, a body that would have been handsome had he not carried it like a sloven; tense brown eyes, and a lean face with hungry, high Slavic features. He was shabbily dressed, almost downright dirty in his carelessness of shirt and clothes, and he stood up hastily as the Boss spoke and ran his fingers nervously through a shock of wild black hair.

Mr. Neuheim strode over to him, picked up the book, and read the title.

"Ruskin's Sea-same and Lilies!" he pronounced contemptuously. "My God, boy, is this what we're payin' you good money for? What are you here for anyway, to work or to stuff yourself with fairy tales? Tell me!" he demanded.

"To work," David answered reluctantly, his eyes fixed on the floor.

"Then work, in God's name, work! This ain't a public library, ye know, or a city college for young shipping clerks to come to for a free education! What sort of a book is this, anyway?" he asked staring again at the title. "What's a sea-same, anyway?"

"It's a sort of password," David stammered, a crimson wave of blood creeping over his dark face.

"A password to what?" the Boss demanded, looking at him sternly, with the air of a judge determined upon the whole truth and nothing but the truth. "Is it something like the Free Masons?"

David floundered guiltily. "It's used only in a sort of symbolical sense here," he explained. "Sesame was used as a password by Ali Baba in the story, when he wanted to get into the robbers' cave, but here it means the password to thought—to culture."

"To thought—to culture!" Mr. Neuheim mimicked grandiosely, putting an imaginary monocle to his eye, and walking a few mincing steps up and down the room. "And I suppose, Mr. Brandt, while you was learning the password to Thought and to Culture—ahem!"—he put an incredible sneer into these two unfortunate words—"you forgot all about such little things like that Flachsman lot! Look at it, it's still laying around, and Chaim brought it in an hour ago! My God, boy, this can't go on, ye know! I been watching you for the past two months, and I'll tell you frankly, you ain't got your mind on business! I didn't know what it was before, but I see how it's this Thought"—he sneered again— "and this Culture. Cut it out, see? If ye want to read, do it outside the factory, and read something that'll bring you in dividends—good American reading."

"Yes."

"What do ye want with thought and culture, anyway?" the Boss cried, waving his cigar like an orator. "Me and Mr. Shinster was worse off than you once; we started from the bottom; and look where we got to without sea-sames or lilies! You're wasting your good time, boy."

David looked at the plump little Jew, with his glittering bald head, his flabby face, and his perfectly rounded stomach that was like some fleshly monument to years of champagne suppers, auto rides, chorus girl debauches, and all the other splendid rewards of success in the New York garment trade.

"Do you ever read Shakespeare?" Mr. Neuheim said more tolerantly, as he lit his cigar.

"Yes."

"Well, ye know in his Choolyus Caesar, this man Caesar says: Let me have men about me that are fat, and that don't think; that is, don't think outside of business, ye understand. Well, that's my advice to you, my boy, especially if ye want to hold your job and got any ambition. The last feller that held your job was made a salesman on the road after five years, and the same chances are open to you. Now let's see whether you're smart or not. I like you personally, but you gotta change your ways. Now let's see you use common sense after this—not Thought and Culture."

He laughed a broad, gurgling, self-satisfied laugh, and passed into the factory again, where the machines were warring, and the little Italian girl singing, and the pressers were sending up their strange, white fog of steam.

David spat viciously at the door that closed behind him.

II

He worked fiercely all that afternoon, in a state of trembling indignation; his hands shook, and his forehead perspired with the heat of the internal fires that consumed him. He was debating over and over again the problem of thought and culture with Mr. Neuheim, and his eyes would flash as he made some striking and noble point, and withered the fat little Boss with his scorn.

Six o'clock came at last; the factory motors were shut off, and died away with a last lingering scream. The operators and pressers and basters became men and women again. They rose stiffly from their seats, and talked and laughed, and dressed themselves and hurried away from the factory as from a prison.

The rage that sustained David died with the iron-throated wailing of the whistles that floated over the city, unyoking so many thousands of weary shoulders.

A curious haze came upon him then. He walked home weakly, as if in a debilitating dream. He hardly felt the scarlet sky above the roofs, the twilight beginning to fall upon the city like a purple doom, the air rich with spring. Mighty streams were flowing through the factory district, human working masses silent and preoccupied after the day's duties, and David slipped into these broad currents without thought, and followed them automatically.

He lived in a tenement on Forsythe Street, on the East Side, and the tides all flowed in that direction; down Broadway, through Grand Street and Prince Street and other streets running east and west and across the dark, bellowing Bowery. Then they spread again and filtered and poured out into the myriad criss-crossing streets where stand the tenements row after row, like numberless barracks built for the conscripts of labor.

It was a Friday night, the eve of the East Side's Sabbath, and Mrs. Brandt, David's little dark, round-backed mother, was blessing the candles when he entered. She had a white kerchief over her hair, and her brown eyes, deep and eager in her wrinkled face as David's own, shone with a pious joy as she read the pre-Sabbath ritual from an old "Sidar" that had come with her from Russia. She looked at David's clouded face anxiously for a moment, but did not interrupt her prayers to greet him when he came in. David did not greet her either, but limp and nerveless went directly to his room and flung himself upon the bed.

There he lay for a few minutes in the darkness. He heard the sounds of life rising from the many windows on the airshaft; the clatter of dishes and knives, the crying of babies, voices lifted in talk. He heard his mother move about; she had evidently finished her prayers, and was coming to his room. Some strange weakness suddenly assailed him; as she knocked at the door, David began weeping; quietly, reasonlessly, like a lonely child.

"David?" his mother inquired, waiting at the threshold. There was no answer, and she called his name again.

"David!"

David answered this time.

"I'm all right, mommer," he said, his voice muffled by the pillows.

"Supper'll be ready in five or ten minutes," Mrs. Brandt said. "Better come out now and wash yourself. And David. . . ."

"Yes?"

"David darling," she whispered, opening the door a little, "you should not do like you did tonight. You should always go and kiss your papa the first thing when you come home. You don't know how bad it makes him feel when you don't do that. He cries over it, and it makes him sicker. He's very sick now; the doctor said today your popper is worse than he's ever seen him. Be good, David, and go speak to him."

"Yes, mommer," David said wearily.

He washed at the sink, and ate the Friday night supper of stuffed fish, noodle soup, boiled chicken and tea. His mother chattered to him all the while, but David listened in that haze that had come on him at the end of the factory day, and answered her vaguely. When he had finished eating he continued sitting at the supper table, and was only aroused when she again suggested that he go in to see his father.

The elder Brandt was a sad, pale, wasted little Jew who had spent fourteen years in the sweatshops of America, and now, at the age of forty-five, was ready to die.

He had entered the factories a hopeful immigrant, with youthful, rosy cheeks that he had brought from Russia, and a marvelous faith in the miracle of the Promised Land that had come from there, too. The sweatshops had soon robbed him of that youthful bloom, however; then they had eaten slowly, like a beast in a cave gnawing for days at a carcass, his lungs, his stomach, his heart, all his vital organs, one by one.

The doctor came to see him twice a week, and wondered each time how he managed to live on. He lay in the bed, propped up high against the pillows, a *Vorwaerts* clutched in his weary hand.

His face, wax-yellow and transparent with disease, was the face of a humble Jewish worker, mild and suffering, but altogether dead now except for the two feverish eyes. He lay exhausted and limp, his whole attitude that of a figure noted down in the books of Death.

David's father was sucked dry, and there was only one spark of life and youth remaining in him—incredibly enough—his faith in the miracles of the Promised Land.

He put down the newspaper and looked up with a timid smile as David entered the room. David came over and kissed him, and he sat on a chair beside his father's bed.

"Well, David, boy, did you have a hard day in the shop today?" the sick man began in a weak voice, fingering his straggly beard and trying to appear cheerful.

"Yes," David answered dully.

"Are you getting on good there?" Mr. Brandt continued, in his poor, hopeful quaver.

"Yes."

"And did you ask the boss yet about that raise he promised you two months ago?"

"No," said David, vacantly, staring with lustreless eyes at the floor.

Mr. Brandt looked apprehensive, as if he had made an error in asking the question. He stroked the feather-bed quilt under which he lay imprisoned, and stole little anxious glances at David's brooding face, as if to implore it for the tiniest bit of attention and pity. Another difficult question hesitated on his lips.

"Davie, dear," he said at last, "why don't you come in to see you popper any more when you get home from work?"

"It's because I'm tired, I guess," David answered.

"No, it ain't that, Davidka. You know it ain't. You used to come in regular and tell me all the news. Do you hate your popper now, David?"

"No, why should I?"

"I don't know. God knows I've done all I could for you; I worked night and day for long years in the shop, thinking only of you, of my little son. I wanted better things for you than what you've got, I couldn't help myself; I was always only a working-man. Some men have luck; and they are able to give their children college educations and such things. But I've always been a *shlemozel;* but you must try to get more out of life than I have found."

"Yes."

"David, don't hate me so; you hardly want to speak to me. Look at me."

David turned his eyes toward his father, but he saw him only dimly, and heard in the same dim way the feeble, high voice uttering the familiar lamentations. In the flickering gaslight his father seemed like some ghostly, unreal shadow in a dream.

"David, you hate me because I'm sick and you have to support me along with your mother. I know; I know! don't think I don't see it all! But it's not my fault, is it, Davie, and I've only been sick a year, and who knows, maybe soon I will be able to take my place in the shop again, and earn my own bread, as I did for so many years before."

"Don't, popper, for God's sake, don't talk about it!" David spoke sharply.

"All right, I won't. All right. Excuse me."

They sat in silence, and then David moved uneasily, as if to go. Mr. Brandt reached over and took his hand in his own moist, trembling one, and held it there.

"Davie," he said, "Davie, dear, tell me why you didn't come tonight. I must know."

"I was tired popper, I told you."

"But why were you tired?"

"I had a fight in the shop."

"A fight? With whom?"

"With the boss—with Mr. Neuheim."

"With the boss? God in heaven, are you crazy? Are you going to lose your job again? What is wrong with you? You have never stuck to one job more than six months. Can't you do like other boys, and stick to a job and make a man of yourself?"

"Let me alone!" David cried in sudden rage, rushing from the room. "For God's sake, let me alone!"

III

With both elbows on the sill, and with his face in his hands, David sat at the airshaft window again during the next half hour.

His mind whirled with formless ideas, like the rout of autumn leaves before a wind. His head throbbed, and again a haze had fallen upon him, a stupor painful as that of a man with a great wound.

The airshaft was still clamorous with the hymn of life that filled it night and day. Babies were squalling, women were berating their children, men were talking in rapid Yiddish, there was rattling of plates and knives, and the shrieking of a clothes line pulley like a knife through it all. The aircraft was dark; and overhead, in the little patch of sky, three stars shown down. Pungent spring odors mingled with the smell of rubbish in the courtyard below.

David's mother moved about carefully as she took away the supper dishes. She knew David's moods, and went on tiptoe, and let him sit there until she had cleaned up in the kitchen. He heard vaguely the sound of her labors, and than she came and laid her rough hand, still red and damp from the dish water, on his shoulder.

"What's the matter, Davie?" she asked, tenderly. "What are you worrying about?"

"Nothing."

"Why did you fight with your popper? You know he's sick, and that you mustn't mind what he says. Why did you do it?"

"I don't know."

"You must be nice to him now; he feels it terribly because he's sick, and that you have to support him. Do you worry because you have to support us?"

"I don't know."

"It won't last forever, Davie boy. Something must happen—there must come a change. God can't be so bad as all that. Is that what worries you?"

David's eyes grew melancholy and his head sunk more deeply between his cupped hands.

"Life isn't worth living; that's what's the trouble mommer," he said. "I feel empty and black inside, and I've got nothing to live for."

"That's foolishness," his mother said warmly. "Everyone lives, and most people have even more troubles than us. If there are so many poor, we can be poor, too. What do you think God put us here for anyway? A healthy young boy like you saying he's got nothing to live for! It's a disgrace!"

"Mommer," David said, passionately, "can you tell me why you live? Why do you yourself live? Give me one good reason!"

"Me? Are you asking me this question?" David's mother exclaimed, in a voice in which there was surprise mixed with a certain delight that her usually silent boy was admitting her on an equality to such intimacies.

She wrinkled her brow. It was the first time, probably, in her work-bound, busy life that she had thought on such a theme, and she put her finger on her lip in a characteristic gesture and meditated for a minute.

"Well, Davie," she said slowly, "I will tell you why your popper and I have gone on struggling and living. It is because we loved you, and because we wanted to see you grow up healthy and strong and happy, with a family of your own around you in your old age. That's the real reason."

"But supposing I don't want to grow up," Davie cried. "Supposing you raised a failure in me. Supposing I'm sick of this world. Supposing I die before I raise a family. . . ."

"That's all foolishness. Don't talk that way."

"But supposing. . . ."

"I won't suppose anything."

"Very well," said David. "You live for me. But tell me, mommer, what do people who have no children live for? What does the whole human race live for? Do you know? Who knows anyone that knows?"

Mrs. Brandt thought again. Then she dismissed the whole subject with a wave of her hand.

"Those are just foolish questions, like a child's," she said. "They remind me of the time when you were a little boy, and cried for days because I would not buy you an automobile, or a lion we saw in Central Park, or some such thing. Why should we have to know why we live? We live because we live, Davie dear. You will have to learn that some day, and not from books, either. I don't know what's the matter with those books, anyway; they make you sick, David."

"No, it's life makes me sick—this dirty life!"

"You're a fool! You must stop reading books, and you must stop sitting here every night, like an old graybeard. You must go out more and enjoy yourself."

"I have no friends."

"Make them! What a funny, changeable boy you are! Two or

three years ago we could never keep you at home nights, you were so wild. You did nothing but go about till early morning with your friends—and fine friends they were too, poolroom loafers, gamblers, pimps, all the East Side filth. Now you read those books that settlement lady gave you; and I don't know which is worse. Go out; put on your hat and coat and go!"

"Where?"

"Anywhere! The East Side is big, and lots of things are going on! Find them!"

"But I want to read!"

"You won't! I won't let you! I should drop dead if I let you!"

David stared wrathfully at her for a moment, stung into anger by her presumptuous meddling into affairs beyond her world of illiteracy and hope. He was about to speak sharply to her, but changed his mind with a weary shrug of his shoulders. He put on his hat and coat and wandered aimlessly into the East Side night, not in obedience to his mother, but because it was easier than to sit here under the impending flow of her nightly exhortations

Thoughts of a Great Thinker

WHAT A vertiginous place this *Liberator* office is! What a harassed and important man is an Editor! I am sitting here on this wet, sunny March day, and out of my window I can see the street below, the beautiful street where life flows like blood in the body of a young tiger. The heavy motor trucks thunder by, horses jingle their harness, the people walk by so thoughtfully in their overcoats (they are all on tremendous errands) and a vegetable man, with a green and blue cargo, is shouting in a high falsetto. Opposite my window is a stately low white church with Doric columns, and it is brilliantly shining in the light of the same sun that shone on Pericles and the Parthenon. How fresh and blue is the same old sky!

(Ah! the telephone! Excuse me a moment. Yes, this is Michael Gold. No, we have not sent out checks for the December poetry. Yes, it is because we are broke, you have guessed it. No, we aren't always broke; don't believe all they tell you. What, you haven't eaten for thirty-six hours? Good-by, poor poet!)

As I was saying, I am sitting here on this lovely spring-like day, and I am about to review seven or eight books for the April *Liberator*. I am a very wise man. I know a great deal. I am an intellectual, and people read what I have to say. It was not always thus. From the tender age of twelve until the tougher period of twenty-two I practised what is known as manual labor as

---

This is a good example of the catch-all editorial article which Gold often found most congenial to write. Hugo Gellert, the artist, was Gold's lifelong friend and comrade. The Baroness Else Von Freytag-Loringhoven was a Greenwich Village eccentric (a real baroness) who contributed fey dada verse to the Liberator. *Claude McKay, the West Indian poet, was, for a year or so, co-editor of the magazine with Gold. Jim Larkin and Bob Minor, mentioned in the "spring poem" at the end of the article, were Communist leaders. H. S. Calvert was a "Wobbly" who worked with Big Bill Haywood to establish a production cooperative of American workers at Kuzbas in the Soviet Union.* Liberator, *April 1922.*

111

a means of livelihood. I was verging on twenty-three, and night porter for the Adams Express Company, I remember, when the turn for the better took place in my affairs. I got a job as cub reporter on a newspaper then. Five years have passed since I deserted manual labor, and everything has gone wonderfully for me. I am successful. I have never had to work again. I think. I am an intellectual.

(What's that, the postman? With a package for me? Eight cents due? Yes, I think I have it—here!)

The book, after I unwrap it, proves to be a massive, swollen, portentous tome, called *Civilization in the United States, an Inquiry by Thirty Americans* [Harold Stearns, *ed.*, New York, 1922]. It has 577 pages, including bibliography and index. What a startling coincidence! How fortunate! I was about to write on Civilization in the United States, and here is a book that disposes of the problem.

If only I had a few weeks in which to read this book! When I worked as porter I had so much more time to read. There was an hour and a half at midnight when things were dull at the West 47th Street depot. I ate my sandwiches then lying on the straw of an express van, and read great books, and studied French, and dreamed and thought. Now I am too busy for such things. I have to *review* books and read manuscripts and earn a living and—

(Comrade Slifsky to see me? Come in, Comrade. Sit down. Have a cigar. You want to know my views on the class struggle? I will tell them to you. I think the class struggle is hell. What do I think of the Workers' Party, free verse, Mahatma Gandhi, Art Young, Upton Sinclair, Bluebeard Landru, Jacob P. Adler, the great Jewish tragedian, and Turkish baths as a cure for colds? I agree with you on all these subjects. You have been out of work for three months? I'm damned sorry, Comrade, damned sorry. So long; come again!)

That book on civilization!

Nothing seems to have been neglected by it. Every conceivable intellectual phase of My Country has been treated by an authority—The City, Politics, Journalism, The Law, Education, Scholarship and Criticism, School and College Life, The Intellectual Life, Science, Philosophy, The Literary Life—

(Another phone ring! Curses! Hugo Gellert, who leads the Life of Art, wants to borrow five dollars from me. No, Hugo, sorry; I lead The Literary Life, as you know. Maybe I will have the five payday; come around then. Good-by!)

Music, Poetry, Art, The Theater—there is a lot more. It looks great. Max Eastman must be made to review this book next month. I think I am not competent to review such a book, anyway; I am too prejudiced. I turn over these pages carelessly, and the faint, acrid aroma of intellectual irony, cool as pine needles, breathes from them. I will wager a baked apple at Child's, with cream, that fully one-half of the writers call for a spiritual aristocracy in America, that will hold itself aloof from the sordid life of the nation, and create a great, free, cosmic Art and Culture, antiseptic and above the battle. That is all that most American intellectuals have discovered about America. I have discovered other things. There are millions of poor people in this nation, who work too hard, and are slaves to the payroll. They are the vast majority here—they are the nation. They have no time to think or lead full-orbed lives. The trouble with the poor is their poverty. And the trouble with the intellectuals is that they are Bourgeois.

(Ah, the Baroness Else Von Freytag-Loringhoven, with huge rings on her ten fingers, and her dog Sophie in her lap, is reciting her Dada poetry to Claude McKay in another room. The walls shake, the ceiling rocks, life is real and life is earnest! I see I will never get around to that review!)

BUT HERE ARE SOME THOUGHTS ON THE SATURDAY EVENING POST

Two and a half million copies of this magazine are sold weekly. Hundreds of lumberjacks live in lousy bunkhouses and stand knee-high in icy water to send the logs down for the pulp. Hundreds of workers sweat over the vats where the pulp is boiled for the paper. Hundreds of printers set up the type, and worry over the make-up, and sit at linotype machines under an electric light to make this magazine. And there are hundreds of office girls round-shouldered at typewriters, and hundreds of clerks and salesmen and bookkeepers; and hundreds of pale, nervous authors who plough their brains for this magazine.

Oh! the filthy lackey rag, so fat, shiny, gorged with advertisements, putrid with prosperity like the bulky, diamonded duenna of a bawdy house!

This magazine takes hundreds of the young creative artists of America and bribes them, in their poverty, to write stories of "Success." And these stories have become the American parallel

of that spiritual opium that is fed the poor, groping peasants of
the Catholic lands. They corrupt the writers, they corrupt the
readers, and thousands of men and women throw their lives
away to print and distribute the stories.

The magazine sells for five cents. The Editors say they are
giving the people what they want. Pimps, dope peddlers and
gold-brick merchants have the same apology for their professions.

A LABOR LEADER

I can't forget Big John Avila. He is in Leavenworth now; has
been there for four years; and he is my friend.

John Avila is a tall, sinuous young Portuguese I.W.W., with a
handsome Latin face, blue-black hair and a graceful, eager,
naive manner that makes people like him. John is like a child,
and yet he never failed in his part as a man. I knew him in Boston five years ago, when he was organizing the longshore workers and sailors. We had many great nights in Boston together, I
remember. Once we went down to Providence to take charge of
a strike of about 1,000 Portuguese Negro longshoremen, tall,
splendid-looking men, descendants of the Moors, and I remember that period best of all.

How the men loved John and how their eyes followed him as
he bustled around the hall; how they listened to his words, as if
he were the Messiah! They were in a tight hole, and did not
know how to get out; there was not one man in the thousand
who could read and write well enough to take care of the union
books; they depended on John for everything, as upon a father.

He was busy every moment of the day and night; but he was
always laughing, always joking, never despondent or hurried;
this was his life his pleasure and vocation. All the girls liked
him, and fooled with him; and the married men invited us to
their houses, and John took their children on his lap, and we
danced, and drank, and laughed and sang through that long,
anxious, bitter strike, because John was around.

He was twenty-six when I knew him, but had been a labor organizer for ten years. At sixteen he had got together a local of
weavers, in the city of Lowell, and though a boy among 500
grown men and women, he was made the secretary. He also went
through the first Lawrence strike. He married at seventeen, and

had five children when I knew him. He sent most of his pay home regularly to his wife, and never thought the responsibility hard or discouraging. Once he wrote a pamphlet in Portuguese, and translated parts of it for me. It was a beautiful, naive thing; the thoughts of the factory worker as the whistles blow in the morning, the harsh, mournful factory whistles that are like the voice of the world's despair. The worker answers the command of the whistles, and leaves the sun and sky behind, but all day at his loom he dreams of freedom, of organization, of solidarity and the struggle for the wonderful day when all men will live together like brothers. The pamphlet was written for practical ends, but it was poetry, too, the poetry of this young proletarian who had spent every day in the labor movement since his sixteenth year.

John grew very tired of things during the war, threw up his job as organizer, and went back to one of his trades, barbering, in a little mining town in New Jersey. There was no money in the I.W.W. treasury then, and he had to earn some to support his family. But he could not be quiet; he talked industrial unionism to the miners who sat in his chair, and one night a mob of respectable citizens came and kidnapped him from his room. They took him out in the woods and hung him four times, letting him down each time just before he was unconscious. They were Americans, citizens of the land of the free and the home of the brave; and he was a dangerous alien.

Two weeks later John was recovering at the home of a friend in Paterson when he was mobbed again, this time legally. He was arrested on the blanket charge against all the I.W.W. officials and was one of the big group tried in Chicago. John was given ten years. He has served nearly four now, without a chance at bail. I hear he still laughs and jokes, and makes the best of things, and even flirts with the girls through the bars on visiting day. John was always brave, and he will stand anything "for the cause," as he calls it, but I wish he were free now. I'd like to knock about the streets of New York for a week with him, I'd like to take him to dance, and shoot pool with him, and take him to theaters and Italian restaurants where there is red wine to be found, and good fellows to talk to; and I'd like to introduce him to all the pretty New York girls. How happy, after his season in hell, these simple things would make him; how John would laugh if he could walk down Sixth Avenue with three or four of us, a few dollars in our jeans, the night before us, hopeful and jolly and free as men were intended to be.

AND HERE, LADIES, IS A SPRING POEM

My love, my fragrant, blue-eyed sweetheart, child of the morning, and of the sun and the moon;

Laughter of my dark days, fragile darling, friend of my deep heart, listen! the spring is here, the sky is shining like a butterfly's blue wing; the tropics are flowing to our dreary north; it will be summer soon;

And soon, dear, I hope, the coal miners will call their nationwide strike; they will raise a black hard fist under the noses of the arrogant bosses, and shake it there, beloved.

Last night we lay under the rich, red, opiate moon, and ah! the stars were the signal fires of God, and I felt the strange delirium of Eternity in your heart-beat;

But this morning the papers are filled with news of the Genoa conference and the South African revolt,

And Gandhi has been arrested, and Jim Larkin may go free, and Emma Goodman has converted the New York *World* to anarchism,

And I must hammer out an editorial, or make a speech, for I have forgotten the great music of your body to mine, Beloved.

Shall we be young forever; shall we lie here forever in the silent, growing, young grass, while a robin sings, and the river wakes its waters to meet the Spring?

Shall we forget all that has been or will be, and dwell forever in the purple airs of Eden, forever beautiful and free?

Maybe; but next week I am planning to go to Pawtucket to cover the textile strike for the *Liberator,*

And in six months, Beloved, it is possible that I may travel to Siberia with H. S. Calvert and his 6,000 Wobbly pioneers.

Kiss me, my wild beauty; the sap of the fresh spring world is rising in my veins; I am mad as a swallow with springtime and with love,

Take my hand; tonight we will go to a meeting under the auspices of the Workers' Party,

At which Bob Minor is to speak on "The Lessons of the Paris Commune," my little darling.

O Californians! O Ladies and Gentlemen!

As A newly arrived immigrant in this beautiful nation of California, I know I am being rash and ungallant in offering a breath of criticism as I stand here on a height and regard this promised land. Yes, Californians are citizens, not of these more or less United States, but of a mountainous, motorized, movieized, irrigated commonwealth that stretches from the heathen land south known as Mexico, to the equally unredeemed state of Oregon at the north, Oregon, where no one from California dreams of going except on business. Californians are fiercely loyal to this, their country. It is dangerous for one to criticize California as it is for a poor beetle-browed slave from Serbia to criticize America, because she makes him work twelve hours a day in the steel mills of Judge Gary.

To the steel mill slave, America growls savagely in answer to his feeble wail of protest: If you don't like this country, go back to the one you came from. Californians are too polite to say this to an Easterner, but they think it as savagely. I, for one, am willing to accept this challenge at any time if some one will advance me the fare back.

I love California but if I cannot criticize what I do not like, I am willing to sacrifice the daily pleasures of life here; the morning climb up Russian Hill, the jazzy breakfasts at Leighton's Cafeteria, the Friday night jazz and wine carnivals at Begin's, the Sunday hikes in the suburbs of Sausalito, Paul Ash's "syncosymphonists" at the Granada (this is music!), my nightly view of the Carnation Mush sign at the foot of Russian Hill, the edi-

---

Gently, Brother *was a fugitive left-liberal literary magazine published in San Francisco which lasted for at least two issues in 1924. Gold's appraisal of California culture was printed in its first number (March 1924). His estimate of the Californian's jealousy and provincialism was born out when he was nearly fired by a boss who happened to read his irreverent notions of the Promised Land.*

torials in the newspapers, the dramatic columns in all of them, the delights of feeding the sad little monkeys at Idora Park, and so on.

Yes, I will give them up, and I will even lay down this wonderful climate on the altar of truth, and go away from God's country if I am not to be allowed to use my mind on the things I see and hear. For that is criticism; selection, judgment, the creation by the mind of man, out of the lawless materials of the world, of the harmonies of his own world. Why are Californians so afraid of this act of criticism? They want the new literary immigrant to accept everything; their God is a jealous God, and demands nothing but endless hymns of praise; they do not believe in evolution, in youth, in change; they have not yet heard of the Civil War, I sometimes think, but imagine history stopped with Bret Harte and the forty-niners.

Poor Bret Harte! Was he not the perfect summary and perfect father of most California art from that time to this. Here is a sensitive, finely gifted fictional artist living in one of the most stirring episodes in the history of America. It is the rush for gold into a pioneer Spanish and Indian country; the adventurers, the bad men, the hopeful and restless and disappointed crowd from every part of the world to get rich quick, to get rich at any cost. There is lynch law in these rough communities; there are prostitutes, horsethieves, professional murderers, there is gambling by day and by night, there is more whisky drunk than has ever been drunk per capita in this puritan nation.

Men who lived this rough adventurous life, with a hand ready for the gun at any moment, and the other hand as ready to take up the whisky glass and convey it to the bearded mouth—these men probably swore. They probably told smutty stories. They were probably brutal about their sex pleasures, unbridled in other passions. Good fellows in the main, and active and happy because they were living outdoors and were careless, unmarried, and healthy. But not angels. I know this sounds heretical, but I cannot believe they were red-shirted saints. Human nature is still the same everywhere, and I have seen the tribe of roughnecks in oil towns and mining camps of today. They are not like Bret Harte's characters at all.

For Bret Harte, in the midst of this crude, vigorous life, where he himself presumably took a drink occasionally and shared in the other simple dance hall sports of the founding fathers—Bret

Harte, when he sat down to write, wrote like a gentleman. With his magic pen he transmuted the rough gold of the life about him into genteel, dainty *lavallières* that would not disgrace the breast of the purest daughter of a country town banker. He was genteel. He was trying to prove that even a mining camp author is a gentleman. His characters are noble—oh, painfully and painstakingly noble! They have rough exteriors, but hearts honest as the deacon's. You can introduce them anywhere—their speech is chaste, their thoughts almost Tennysonian—you can bring them into the drawing rooms of the London literary world, into the chaste foyers of the *Atlantic Monthly,* into the rosy, romantic highschool boy's dream world that Kipling and O. Henry and Gouverneur Morris have made for fiction. Certainly, for our Bret Harte was a California gentleman, and a gentleman never tells the truth if he thinks it may offend even the feeblest of God's creatures. That is why we know nothing about the fortyniners, except indications here and there in Mark Twain. This great epic of California produced no art fruits of any soundness; and it is too bad, for Anglo-Saxon literature might have been braced, strengthened and invigorated had there been some honest and ungentlemanly artist on the scene.

This besetting sin of gentility is still the curse of Californian art. I shall not discuss here any medium of art save fiction, mentioning only in passing that most California poetry is passionless Swinburne or watery Wordsworth; most California sculpture is very bad Phidias, and very polite Michelangelo; most Californian painting is restrained Whistler, crude Corot and conscientious Sargent. Nothing wild, passionate, original, direct, or honest; no experiments, no great new dreams of form or content. All second-hand gentility; archaeology, futile scholarship, Greece, Italy, Queen Victoria, what-not, the genteel bric-a-brac deposit that has accumulated in the world and that passes for art with the middle classes everywhere.

I exaggerate of course; there are some exceptional men in all these fields who are trying to create something out of their own flesh and blood; but I shall talk only about fiction now, for when we, your little cousins of the effete East think of Californian art the names of Jack London, Frank Norris, Bret Harte and Ambrose Bierce most invariably occur to us, as they seem to occur to yourselves.

Now, before I enter on my unholy task, I wish to reassure

some of you who seem trembling with fear, and ready to rush for the door. Yes, I am about to utter blasphemies, but I am quite sure God will not notice them. I am a thoroughly experienced phophet, and have cursed other cities in my wanderings, with no evil results. Nothing will happen—do not grab your hats. I have denounced, for instance, the literary bunk one finds in New York. In New York the supreme blasphemy is to criticize the critics. They have captured the stage, and threaten to crowd off the artists therefrom. They know everything; they have their school; they argue with each other, and assume each other's tragic importance; they bustle, storm, weigh, sneer, poise, sigh, aestheticize, they make a great clamor and noise of intellectualism. They are busy telling how the thing ought to be done, but anyone who tries to do it usually disappoints them. In New York, the careful writer always carries a handful of fine cigars and kind words about him for the critices. They are like the police force of literature; innocence is no protection against them; it is better to keep in with them, for they can frame a man's life away. In a few years no authentic New York intellectual will try to write or read poetry or fiction; there will be only journals by, of, and for critics.

So that I have blasphemed in New York, and in Chicago and Boston and other places. But do not fear. Blasphemy and criticism are good; life would stop growing did we not blaspheme. If the fourteen-year-old boy became satisfied with his body and mind, he would never become a man. In California the literary plant has not had enough of this hot sun and pelting rain to make it grow; in New York there is a cloudburst of criticism, and a desert heat, and the poor things must be enormously tough and strong, or never emerge from the rocky soil. If California and New York could establish some yearly exchange of artists who write for artists who criticize! What a blessing it would be!

But let us return to our California muttons.

California is genteel. California is provincial. I submit that a literature cannot grow in such a vacuum. James Joyce has said somewhat bitterly of his Ireland: She is the mother sow who eats her young. This saying might somewhat bitterly be applied to California. This old California sow is prolific in her young; she brings forth great litters of artistic sucklings in every decade. The warmth of Golconda lies on this land; the sun shines, the deep blue waters shine, the land is brilliant with flowers and fruit blos soms, the tall redwoods support an ancient and imperial sky. Life is rich and steeped in sunlit beauty here; and, listen to my words, O Californians! O ladies and gentlemen! it is easy for the young writer to procure his Ham and Beans. Do not smile at this apparent anti-climax; artists must eat, and I assure you it is perhaps the most important problem of their lives, as it is for other men. A man may be born with a cosmology of whirling and beautiful star-mists in his brain, but the chaos will never express itself in an orderly universe unless he seizes years of leisure for the mighty task. This problem is growing more widespread every year, for all the artists are not being born into the leisure classes as formerly; the poor are becoming educated, thoughtful and sensitive, they are developing an intellectual aristocracy that may prove more rugged and more fitted for the conquest of life than were the delicate pessimists of the past. But meanwhile they must live.

It is easier to "get by" in California than in New York, the climate is balmier, rent is cheaper, some food, such as frijoles, is cheaper, and it is easier to get temporary outdoor jobs, in periods of despair. Also there are more cheery patrons of art to borrow from in emergencies, I am told. Whatever the causes, it is a fact that California's soil teems with as many embryo writers as with embryo prunes, raisins, and freestone peaches. Many of these seeds of promise fall on stony soil: some go to work; others land on newspapers; a few persist and develop, and believe me, persistence is half the battle. The old mother sow encourages her young; and that is how she devours them. It is a god-given privilege to be a young artist in California. The awe and reverence of those elders who questioned the boy Jesus in the temple surround these happy California youths. They do not need to study, work hard, discipline themselves, despair and feel; they need only produce something—anything—and all California will hail them as geniuses. Genius is the most freely used word in this opulent state, next to the more practical word for a nation of realtors: Boost. A young man writes a poem: He is called a genius. A young girl learns to dance the sailor's hornpipe without losing her balance: genius! They use it amiably and carelessly, but it is a dangerous procedure; the day will come when Californians will nudge each other and point to some young thinker and say: "He's a California genius. Yes, he can read and write!"

If the geniuses have some talent and some desire for growth, if they refuse to rest on the unripe laurels of youth and press on, they are sure to find themselves up against the Great Fog Wall of California gentility. I cannot repeat this fatal word often enough —it should be marked on the state seal of California. This is the most genteel state in the union. This is the fattest, laziest, hungriest, richest, cheeriest reactionary state in the union. Liberty has been smothered to death here in the arms of the whole-souled, money-making, hearty, happy native sons of the golden west. The middle class has established the most violent law against free speech in economics of any of the states; and it has established the most horrible law of gentility in its arts. California, the old smiling sow, has damaged all her really gifted sons who wrote fiction. Frank Norris was a great mind, but he was automatically cut off by birth from working with that mind on great materials. He tried to break through the fatal censorship; perhaps, had he lived long enough, he might have; but his real genius was wasted in producing the conventional yarns California feeds on.

Jack London was also an artist, gifted greatly; yet outside of a few true fine things, what did he do with his life but repeat the childish romantic formulas the Californian tradition had established in Bret Harte with the later aid of Robert Louis Stevenson, that perfect gentleman?

Ambrose Bierce was not genteel, but he was thwarted by provincialism. With his splendid powers of rage, indignation, and deeply-felt horror at the injustice of life, he might have built some enduring and noble monuments. California taught him, however, that a story must be something like Bret Harte; and philosophy, even when pessimistic, need not concern itself with anything deeper than the corruption of city politicians; and that, since California was more important than the wide world, satire need concern itself only with the comparatively petty history of this region.

I shall not go into the lives or works of any of these men in detail; no doubt you are already beginning to yawn. Nor shall I discuss Upton Sinclair, who is only half a Californian, and whose lifework was shaped in New York by the giant hands of the international class struggle and the international struggle of the poor to find their own spokesman in the hitherto snobbish world of fiction. And I am not trying to place the California writers; it is too amateurishly futile to arrange the men of art in a hierarchy, and then squabble and fight over their positions in it. That is work for those who compile the lists of the ten greatest books. I am only concerned here with the guiding spirit of the literature of the state; and that spirit has been as genteel as a prune-rancher's wife. There are two immense currents in life and in art; the struggle for food, and the struggle for love. What native Californian has written a great epic on either of these themes? What Californian has written truthfully on love? What Californian has given us the spiritual history of the gradual corruption of this state? I say again, there have been solitary chance books and fragments of truth flung out here and there; but what man stands for some great truth in Californian literature? What man has been true to the bitter end, to the depth of psychology or the heights and strangeness of great imaginative art? Jack London sounded a note of proletarian rebellion; it was quickly smothered by gentility, by money-making. Frank Norris wrote of the piracy of the Southern Pacific railroad; and he wrote *McTeague;* but he wrote them with one eye on the censor—the genteel prune-rancher's Iowan wife. *McTeague* is artificial; it is the novel of a slummer and tourist; it is not the life of the poor, or the underworld; it is a stunt. Jack London was nearer reality, but as you all know, California conquered him.

What of the present?

Buy a copy of any week's *Saturday Evening Post;* it is only five cents, and the mass of paper will serve many uses after your investigations. Read this journal and weep. There is the great imperial mausoleum of present-day Californian fiction.

Hired romanticists; hired liars about life; high salaried thimble-riggers, flim-flam men, and circus fakers; Rolls Royce captains of fictional industry; sob sisters; minor Irvin Cobbs; Rotary Club bards, clowns, and Balaams—O, what base uses has this Californian genius descended to! About one-half of all the fiction-cocaine of this country is produced in California, I imagine. And yet it was all inevitable. Like all parvenu roughnecks California has always strained for the genteel. In this decade gentility is no longer measured by the former standards—a knowledge of etiquette, Latin and polite literature—but by money. The middle class of America is building a country club civilization, and if you haven't any money, you don't belong. California writers would perish of envy and feel themselves failures if they could not belong, and so they are making lots of money. Let them make it. Some day, with God's help, the Bolsheviks who read the *Liberator* may take it away from them. Yes, let them make money; and meanwhile, let decent men go on writing what is true and what is great.

For the powerful genteel middle class does not want the truth in life, in art, or in love. Plutocracy, like monarchy, is built on a lie, and it needs the lies of religion, nation and cheap fiction (which has become America's religion), to sustain it. Truth is always strong, deep, revolutionary; it breaks up the bourgeois home, it makes youth restless with mere business and money-making; it gives the workers a clear vision. Art is truth or it is nothing; reaction has always been sentimental and romantic. Californians are all romantics and middle class; and their idea of art is something reaching a summit in Robert Louis Stevenson, their most eminent literary visitor.

Walt Whitman, Emerson, Thoreau could not have grown to power here; Sherwood Anderson, Eugene O'Neill, Theodore Dreiser, Carl Sandburg, and so many more would find themselves pale and insignificant here beside the genteel romantic heroes of Californian art—the Peter B. Kynes, the Cecil de Milles, and all the others of this busy set. So be it. It cannot last forever. The dead will bury its dead. If there arise any real geniuses in California, they will do three things:

First: they will turn on any bright-eyed jackass who calls them genius, and say coldly, "I am not a genius. I am an humble apprentice, learning the tools of my art and sitting patiently at the spectacle of Life."

Second: they will not read or be concerned deeply with anything Californian that is called artistic, but will immerse themselves in the art of the modern world.

Thirdly: they will not feel that they have to escape from California to the east or Paris or Europe or any other so-called art center. Life is great here, too, and worthy of the artist's deepest devotion. There are epic events here, as everywhere. They are not genteel; life is never genteel. There is the epic of the Wobblies, the migratory workers and their vast, violent, dramatic life; a story yet to be written. There is the Chinese population, the Mexicans, the old life of the Barbary Coast that the genteel writers could not touch. There are mining camps, lumber camps, fishing fleets in this state. There is even the true story of the fortyniners; it has never been told. And then there is the earthquake; who has yet made art out of that colossal event?

And, finally, there are human beings; they are the same here as everywhere; the newspapers are filled with their murders, suicides, loves, hates, plans for money-making, struggles for bread and love. No Californian has ever written about them; the field is almost virginal. Some day a genius will arise and he will write the truth about California. God help him, too; for the Vigilantes will surely hang him for his genius, or teach him it is safer to be genteel.

The Strange Funeral in Braddock

Listen to the mournful drums of a strange funeral.
Listen to the story of a strange American funeral.

In the town of Braddock, Pennsylvania,
Where steel mills live like foul dragons burning, devouring man and earth and sky,
It is spring. Now the spring has wandered in, a frightened child in the land of the steel ogres,
And Jan Clepak, the great grinning Bohemian on his way to work at six in the morning,
Sees buttons of bright grass on the hills across the river, and plum trees hung with wild, white blossoms,
And as he sweats half-naked at his puddling trough, a fiend by the lake of brimstone,
The plumb trees soften his heart,
The green grass memories return and soften his heart,
And he forgets to be hard as steel, and remembers only his wife's breasts, his baby's little laughters, and the way men sing when they are drunk and happy,
He remembers cows and sheep, and the grinning peasants, and the villages and fields of sunny Bohemia.

Listen to the mournful drums of a strange funeral.
Listen to the story of a strange American funeral.

Wake up, wake up! Jan Clepak, the furnaces are roaring like tigers,

---

This macabre prose-poem has been several times set to music. It is a good example of Gold's penchant for the grotesque in working-class life. The incident described really happened, but in Donora, Pennsylvania, not in neighboring Braddock, as Gold recalled it. Liberator, *June 1924.*

The flames are flinging themselves at the high roof, like mad yellow tigers at their cage.

Wake up! it is ten o'clock, and the next batch of mad, flowing steel is to be poured into your puddling trough,

Wake up! wake up! for a flawed lever is cracking in one of those fiendish cauldrons,

Wake up! and wake up! for now the lever has cracked, and the steel is raging and running down the floor like an escaped madman,

Wake up! O, the dream is ended, and the steel has swallowed you forever, Jan Clepak!

Listen to the mournful drums of a strange funeral.
Listen to the story of a strange American funeral.

Now three tons of hard steel hold at their heart, the bones, Flesh, nerves, the muscles, brains and heart of Jan Clepak,

They hold the memories of green grass and sheep, the plum trees, the baby-laughter, and the sunny Bohemian villages.

And the directors of the steel mill present the great coffin of steel and man-memories to the widow of Jan Clepak,

And on a great truck it is borne now to the great trench in the graveyard,

And Jan Clepak's widow and two friends ride in a carriage behind the block of steel that holds Jan Clepak,

And they weep behind the carriage blinds, and mourn the soft man who was killed by hard steel.

Listen to the mournful drums of a strange funeral.
Listen to the story of a strange American funeral.

Now three thinkers are thinking strange throughts in the graveyard.

"O, I'll get drunk and stay drunk forever, I'll never marry woman, or father laughing children,

I'll forget everything, I'll be nothing from now on,

Life is a dirty joke, like Jan's funeral!"

One of the friends is thinking in the sweet-smelling graveyard,

As a derrick lowers the three tons of steel that held Jan Clepak.

(LISTEN TO THE DRUMS OF THE STRANGE AMERI-
    CAN FUNERAL!)

"I'll wash clothes, I'll scrub floors, I'll be a fifty-cent whore, but
    my children will never work in the steel mill!"
Jan Clepak's wife is thinking as earth is shovelled over the great
    steel coffin,
In the spring sunlight, in the soft April air.

(LISTEN TO THE DRUMS OF THE STRANGE AMERI-
    CAN FUNERAL!)

"I'll make myself hard as steel, harder,
I'll come some day and make bullets out of Jan's body, and
    shoot them into a tyrant's heart!"
The other friend is thinking, the listener,
He who listened to the mournful drums of the strange funeral,
Who listened to the story of the strange American funeral,
And turned as mad as a fiendish cauldron with cracked lever.

LISTEN TO THE MOURNFUL DRUMS OF A STRANGE
    FUNERAL.
LISTEN TO THE STORY OF A STRANGE AMERICAN
    FUNERAL.

America Needs a Critic

1. SOVIET RUSSIA

Most of the younger writers and artists turn to France for that foreign cross-fertilization that has always been biologically necessary for a healthy national culture.

But intellectual France has ended in Dada. Young America can learn nothing from the 200-year old boulevardiers, except to sit at sidewalk cafés and sip aperitifs, literariously.

All that is left now in France is a café culture, and the worker's movement.

We who turn to Soviet Russia for help in self-understanding are luckier. There we find a new dynamism akin to our own American spirit. There we find titan artists who are grappling with the Machine Age. There we find a world seething with experiment, a huge fascinating art laboratory. Russia is self-conscious about the machine age, but we are not; and that is what we can learn of them.

Read a book like Huntley Carter's *The New Theatre in Soviet Russia* and if you are a playwright, you will burn to take the first boat for Moscow.

Read Trotsky's *Literature and Revolution,* and if you are a minor poet, you will be shamed out of your morbidity, your introspection, your self-pitying, God-seeking American confusion, and rise to the trumpet blast like a soldier of art.

Yes, art is not the boudoir sport of dilletantes in Soviet Russia, but a heroic spirit that moves in the streets and public squares, that marches in the Red Army, lives with the peasants,

---

In his early praise of Trotsky as a revolutionary "Leonardo da Vinci," Gold reflected the prevailing opinion of the American Left at the time. His very different later estimates of Trotsky are evident in "Trotsky's Pride" and "Renegades" which are reprinted below. The "author of Mlle. de Maupin," mentioned at the end of part six was Theophile Gautier. The subheads of both part seven and part eight were identical in the original. New Masses, October 1926.

works side by side with the factory workers, performs mighty social tasks.

Art is no longer snobbish or cowardly. It teaches peasants to
use tractors, gives lyrics to young soldiers, designs textiles for
factory women's dresses, writes burlesque for factory theaters,
does a hundred other useful tasks. Art is necessary as bread. No
one feels apologetic about Art in Russia. Carl Sandburg sells
some two thousand copies of his poems here; but Mayakovsky, a
Futurist writing the most modern and complex rhythms, sells
three million books in Soviet Russia.

Art, that was once the polite butler of the bored and esthetic,
has become the heroic and fascinating comrade of all humanity.
This is a better role for her, we think. She was meant for this
from the beginning.

2. DEATH OF ROCOCO

Before the French Revolution, the corrupt court intellectuals
had created the style of the Rococo. The decadence of the time
was expressed in those delicate and erotic curves, in all that frivolous and futile ornamentation. But the Revolution of the middle
class could not use this feudal trash, and swept it away.

David and other painters began the great vigorous tradition of
French painting, which stems not from Watteau and the Rococo,
but from the Revolution.

Diderot brought literature back to the "ancient" heroism and
simplicity. He said that art must have the purpose of glorifying
fine deeds, of branding vice, and inspiring tyrants with fear. He
also advised dramatists to "get close to real life"; he himself
wrote plays that blazed the trail ending in Ibsen and Shaw.

And in England, the French Revolution inspired the young
emerging writers to revolt. Wordsworth was a visitor to revolutionary France, and came back determined to restore the common word and the common man's emotions to the sickly court
poetry of the time.

Young Shelley was touched off by the Revolution like a glorious red rocket. Blake poured forth mystic dithyrambs of revolution, and was arrested and tried for sedition for wearing a red
liberty cap in the street, and saying in public he wished the Revolution would come to England, to purge that gross land. Burns
wrote revolutionary songs, and was proud to be a peasant, Leigh

Hunt and Hazlitt wrote revolutionary criticism, Byron flamed and sneered at the feudal order, and donned the sword for red republicanism.

The French Revolution ushered in a whole new style in English literature. The Revolution was not merely "politics," which is how our own literary men are fond of dismissing the Russian Revolution. It was a revolution in culture, too, and inevitably laid its hand on literature.

The revolution of the workers today will inevitably lay its hand on our own culture, and make it over anew. How could it be otherwise? In Soviet Russia the metamorphosis is already taking place.

3. TROTSKY

Trotsky's book on literature is an amazing performance. This man is almost as universal as Leonardo da Vinci. The Revolution shares with the Renaissance the fact that men have again become versatile. They have taken all knowledge for their province, because all knowledge is a necessary tool to the Revolution. Astronomers direct vast industries in Soviet Russia, stage directors experiment in biology, economists write plays, poets invent machinery—and Trotsky ranges as far and deep as his comrades.

Trotsky was the most single-minded of pacifists, but made himself the best general and military tactician in Europe. He is a great financial expert. He is now chief organizer of the reconstructed Russian industry. He helps direct the diplomacy. He reads and writes five or six languages, and knows the intimate affairs of every country in the world. Occupying a group of positions that would correspond to several cabinet offices in this country, combined with the presidency of the steel trust, and rubber, oil, and textile industries, this man finds time to turn out at least two important books a year, some of which serve for textbooks in economics and history, besides scores of articles on industry, international politics, the Einstein theory, finance, Freud, the American agrarian situation, Chinese history and labor movements, poetry, the atom, the stage—every phase of intelligence that the Revolution must use or understand.

His *Literature and Revolution* is an examination of Russian literature, and what happened to it after the cannons of the Revolution had battered down the blood-stained Rococo style of the Czar.

Trotsky discusses hundreds of poets, novelists and dramatists intimately. He analyzes scores of young writers whose work has not yet even been collected in books. He seems to know what the obscurest sixteen-year-old factory girl poet in Kazan has been producing recently. He quotes from the manifestoes of young insolent schools of bardlings that push to life like mushrooms in present Russia. The literary air there is charged with healthy combat, and he knows familiarly the issues raised by all the schools.

Where has he found the time for this vast and loving research? This is not a matter of mere energy—Roosevelt was energetic, and Mussolini's sole stock in trade is energy. Trotsky loathes the false theatricalism of these cheap actors on the stage of history; his style has the energy, not of a blustering he-man, but of a great, serene self-restrained general on a battlefield. No, it is not energy alone; energy alone creates an American Rotarian; but it is the spirit of the Revolution that works and ferments in Trotsky, as it once fermented in Danton, Voltaire, Shelley, Blake, Walt Whitman, and John Brown.

Art is not a plaything, it is an organic part of the Revolution, and therefore wins his concentration as intensely as the defense of Petrograd against the British invaders. It is necessary as bread.

4. THE MARXIAN METHOD

Trotsky, in every line of his book, shows that he loves literature with a deep and permanent passion. He understands its own mysterious and intuitive laws, and can become intoxicated by a magic phrase like any young defenseless poet. His is not the mechanical knowledge of the pedant. And he writes as well as Mencken, if with more science. And science is what American criticism needs most of all.

In America subjective criticism prevails almost entirely. It is worthless to the writer; it cannot help him understand himself, or his relationship to his age. At best, it is a pat on the shoulder, a prettily strung bouquet of appreciation; at worst, a kick in the rear. But Trotsky's criticism is not spun out of his inner consciousness as are the critiques of Mencken or of Waldo Frank. Trotsky comes to literature, as to other social phenomena, with the scientific tools of the Marxian methodology. He gives us, what no American critic has yet fully given us, a sense of the social changes which precede each new school of art, and which determine the individual psychology of the artist, however "free" he thinks he is.

The writer and artist of today has become a specialist. He thinks of himself merely as a craftsman, and is proud to confess that he is ignorant of history, economics, and science. This lack of universal culture has left him with the naive egotism of a child. The average artist still believes that he is child of some immaculate conception, his umbilical cord attached to Eternity though the rest of humanity is bound to Time.

Wherever the boudoir bards and the minor Oscar Wildes congregate one can hear those awful, awful clichés of the esthetic bores: Art is Eternal. Art is never *useful*. Art has nothing to do with propaganda. Art is above the battle. Art is Free, etc., etc.

But the Marxians, for at least fifty years, have been grubbing and burrowing among the economic roots of the shining rose bush of art, and have found that healthy real roots do exist there, as in all other things that live. This discovery distresses artists; as the discovery that man was descended from monkeys and not angels once distressed the pious and wishful. But we need not fear these discoveries; every such truth adds a cubit to Man's heroic mind; leads to further conquest of life and eternity; makes man a master, not a slave of life. The discovery of the law of Evolution, that we did not live in a purely accidental world, but that cause and effect penetrate each part of the universe, has not degraded us, but has advanced the human mind millenniums further on the climb upward from the monkey. Marx's discovery of the mutability and class roots of all cultures, will prove as fruitful as Darwin's discovery to culture, for it will eventually lead us to the really free, classless, human, social art of the future. To more Shakespeares and Goethes, and fewer Oscar Wildes and Carl Van Vechtens! To art still undreamed of, in its glory and vastness. To new strong styles and schools, to mass-wonders! Criticism like Trotsky's is creative criticism—the American brand is only conversation.

5. THE REVOLUTION AS TOUCHSTONE

After a year of introspection in a monk's cell, one would have known as little of oneself as at the beginning. One would have only rotted. But a year of active deeds, of experiments in art and life, would bring self-knowledge and discipline. Only action can test us.

In ordinary times writers are never tested by events. They live in a kind of parliamentary peace, and nurse, like liberals, all manner of delusions. It is when a war or revolution occurs that their social roots are most clearly exposed, even to themselves.

The Russian Revolution was the great touchstone to Russian culture. Trotsky shows how those superior schools of pure poets, the Parnassians, Symbolists and others, flocked to the White Armies or found themselves suddenly not above the battle, but on the general staff of Polish militarists in invading Russia.

Many of them became emigrés in Paris, "thought they would cheat history," and wound up in futility, like so many of our American literary emigrés.

The older writers who remained in Russia, because of their strong class roots, proved almost as futile as the emigrés in the face of the Revolution. They could not accept the present. They tried to cheat time, and remain in the past.

"The gem of this literature of discarded thoughts and feelings is the fat, well-meaning Almanac Streletz," says Trotsky, "where poems, articles and letters by Sologub, Rozanov, Belenson, Kusmin, Hollerbakh, and others, are printed and to the quantity of three hundred numbered copies. A novel of Roman life, letters about the erotic cult of the bull Apis, an article about St. Sophia, the Earthly and Heavenly; three hundred numbered copies— what hopelessness, what desolation! It were better to curse and rage! That, at least, would resemble life."

This, in the face of the greatest event in world history. But some of our American writers do the same thing in the face of an event almost as great—the rise of industrial America, which they fear and understand as little as the elder pious poets understood the new Russia.

The lyrical poets of mystic feelings have deemed themselves most especially above the social battle. But the best representative of the school in Russia, Zinaida Hippius, began writing lines like this, after the Revolution.

And swiftly you will be driven to the old stable with a club,
O people, disrespectful of holy things.

Trotsky nails her in a paragraph:

> Only yesterday she was a Petrograd lady, languid, decorated with talents, liberal, modern. Suddenly today, this lady, so full of her own subtleties, sees the black outrageous ingratitude on the part of the mob in hobnailed boots, and offended in her social holy of holies, transforms her impotent rage into a shrill womanish squeak (in iambics). Immediately she showed the real property-owning witch under her decadent mystic-erotic Christian covering.

Other writers accepted the Revolution half-heartedly. But it was the gesture of death; their work never came to flower, because they ceased being creators of life, they lived on the leftovers of a culture created by blood of the past. "I have even found a place for myself in all this; a poet observer and a bourgeois saving my life from death," one of the most gifted wrote with tender irony about himself.

Trotsky goes through all the schools; touches the falsities, the mere veneer of art that coated all of these Parnassians, Symbolists, Acmeists, and others who lived only for art, but who became transformed into hysterical enemies of the working class as soon as they came into contact with its power.

It is a masterly summary of Russian literary history for the past ten years. There have always been great writers in Russia, and each of them has some prototype in America. It is strange and amusing to meet all the familiar slogans and evasions of American literary specialists in Trotsky's pages. They are priests of the esthetic God, they are servants of a divine classless mystery, and then suddenly the worker confronts them, a giant problem against the sky, and they flock to the White Army, where their real roots had always been. This happened in England, also, during the general strike. It will happen here.

6. THE NEW AGE

But it is not only by the political upheaval that Trotsky tests these writers. The bloody events of Revolution are only as important as the blood and pain in which a child is born. After that hour of primitive violence passes, the mother begins rearing the child. It is for this child that the pain was suffered—he is the Revolution, not the pain and blood.

The real Revolution has changed the face of Russia. It has destroyed the myth of the Slavic "soul," that potent myth that Sherwood Anderson and other belated Dostoyevskians in this country still cherish. The dark inquisitorial power of the Church, that kept the peasants in dirt, savagery and holiness, has been destroyed. Machinery is being introduced, talked, hoped for, worshipped, debated like the social question it really is. An illiterate nation is beginning to read ferociously; the printing industry is almost first in size in modern industrial Russia. The Bolsheviks have been a huge party of teachers, and what they are teaching Russia is modernism, the Machine Age.

All the young writers have been influenced by the powerful Futurist school, which before the war had so heroically claimed the Machine Age for art. The Futurists were the readiest to accept the Revolution, and their writers and artists are national figures now in Soviet Russia. Every newspaper cartoon, every book cover decoration, every new building, statue, monument, factory, textile design, moving picture, poem, story and symphony, has been affected by Futurist theory and practise. This is one of the enormous surprises and revelations that come to the writer who visits Russia today.

Trotsky analyzes the Futurist school, and comes to the conclusion that while it was born in bourgeois Bohemianism, as a revolt against Philistinism, and is therefore not a true revolutionary product, it still has the proud distinction of being the bridge between the old culture and the new.

Then he goes into a profound discussion of proletarian art, advancing the thesis that the term is a misnomer. He argues that the proletariat is but a transitory class in history, and that its object is not to perpetuate itself as a class, as was the object of the bourgeoisie, but to wipe out all classes. The bourgeoisie had a long period in which to create its art, some two hundred years. But the proletarian dictatorship will only be necessary for a few decades, when it will establish the classless society, and therefore the classless human art of the future.

I do not agree with this. Even if for only fifty years the proletariat remains in subjection to capitalist society, will there not be some art growing out of this mass of intense, tragic, active human beings? Will they not sing, and need cartoons, plays, novels, like other human beings? Are they not studying, groping, reaching out hungrily for culture? It is not a matter of theory; it is a fact that a proletarian style is emerging in art. It will be as transitory as other styles; but it will have its day.

I have not done justice to Trotsky's book or its subject in this article. His approach and material are so new to American readers that one would have to write the history of the Revolution, give an account of Marxism, examine all the theories of esthetics, and analyze a hundred American writers, to demonstrate the validity of the method, or even to begin to create a common ground for discussion. America is still provincial. American writers still go to the author of Mlle. de Maupin for their theories of art. American writers still try to be Dostoyevskys in a skyscraper America. American writers still go on creating a literature of social protest, while denying the social criticism of literature. America still needs its great literary critic.

7. SEND US A CRITIC

Mencken is not that critic. He has no science—is a believer in the accidental theory of literature, as in life. He is one of the salon singers celebrating the "freedom" of the artist, but is himself the best example of the fallacy of that dogma. For his popularity with the middle class rests on the fact that he has given them a class philosophy exactly suited to their needs of the hour. He is popular, not for esthetic reasons, but because he has expressed the philosophy of our *nouveaux riches*. Upton Sinclair is popular in Russia for similar reasons; he expresses the proletariat.

Mencken has rediscovered Nero's philosophy of feasting and futility. Futilitarianism is an easy way of evading one's social ideals. An idealist is not a good money-maker, and if he is to get on the bandwagon, to share some of the immense boodle that is now circulating so freely here, he must cast overboard all his ideals. This renegadism Mencken has made seem the jolliest and most sophisticated of gestures.

Waldo Frank is not the critic. He has a dark huge Whitman-like emotion about America, but he writes for an audience of medieval saints, and not for New York. Mystics cannot run locomotives, or explain the Machine Age to us.

Van Wyck Brooks started out to be that critic. His was a large sane, social mind, attracted only by the major movements of humanity. But he is lost up the blind alley of Freud, where each in-

dividual artist is explained like a miracle, by his individual neu-
roses and complexes, and not by the social environment that
created those complexes.

Floyd Dell had all the equipment for that critic, but broke
down in purpose. Max Eastman was the finest candidate, a true
artist and scientist, but the victim of an anomaly. He was a poet
with old-fashioned tendencies, and so faced backwards. He was
at heart an aristocrat, an individualist; he could never quite consent to be a part of that collectivist organization he pleaded for.
Therefore, while he demonstrated, in some of the most beautiful
prose of our day, the Marxian roots of religion, politics, sex, and
other social phenomena, in art he stood side by side with the ac-
cidentalists.

Among the younger men: Joseph Krutch has a sound equipment but is heading up Van Wyck Brooks' alley; Edmund Wilson is a force, but is bogged in formalism, and never drives clean
to the great mark; V. F. Calverton has a wide, scholarly knowledge of the new criticism, but is undeveloped in esthetic insight
or emotion. Joseph Freeman is equipped, but writes too infre-
quently to be felt.

Randolph Bourne might have grown into the critic we need.
He knew how great mass changes create the new artists, the new
thoughts. He studied the international working-class movement.
He was undaunted in the storms of history, and accepted the fact
that capitalism must change. In his mind, the world was one—
and he examined all the political and economic facts, along with
every other fact in a period, when he discussed literature.

Never did he lose, as Van Wyck Brooks has written, "the
sense of the new socialized world groping its way upward. He
was a wanderer, the child of some nation yet unborn, smitten
with an unappeasable nostalgia for the Beloved Community on
the far side of socialism." But Bourne died of loneliness during
the war, which he fought. And no one has taken his place.

8. SEND US A CRITIC

O Life, send America a great literary critic. The generation of
writers is going to seed again. Some of them started well, but are
beginning to live fat and high, and have forgotten the ardors of
their generous youth. This generation of writers is corrupted by
all the money floating around everywhere. It is unfashionable to

believe in human progress any longer. It is unfashionable to work for a better world. It is unfashionable and unsophisticated to follow in the footsteps of Tolstoi, of Dickens, Shelley, Blake, Burns, Whitman, Trotsky. Send us a critic. Send a giant who can shame our writers back to their task of civilizing America. Send a soldier who has studied history. Send a strong poet who loves the masses, and their future. Send someone who doesn't give a damn about money. Send one who is not a pompous liberal, but a man of the street. Send no mystics—they give us Americans the willies. Send no coward. Send no pedant. Send us a man fit to stand up to skyscrapers. A man of art who can match the purposeful deeds of Henry Ford. Send us a joker in overalls. Send no saint. Send an artist. Send a scientist. Send a Bolshevik. Send a man.

Faster, America, Faster!

A MOVIE IN TEN REELS

MORNING ON THE
RANCH

THE PRIVATE train never stopped. It was like war. It smashed the peace of the dark American fields. Frogs leaped into the marsh pools as the monster passed. Birds waked and screamed. Trees bent before the storm. The blow struck the still farm-houses, and they trembled in every rafter. Fever. No more quiet. The moon reeled. The Virgin night was raped from dreams. Speed! The private train never stopped. There were two luxury cars and a locomotive.

A MYSTERIOUS
STRANGER
WANDERS IN

The private train never stopped. Its whistle and bell banged and boasted: The world is mine! They clanged: Get out of the way! The Big Boss is coming! The private train spat golden sparks into the humble face of Night. It was destined for Holly-wood. Erwin Schmidt, the German-American movie millionaire had chartered it for his youngest star and some friends. The boil-ers bellowed. The rails shrieked like dying women. Loafers at small country towns were grazed by a thunderbolt of flying steel and steam. They saw a shower of golden windows. Cities and towns roared by. Mountains raced up and down, seesawed. The

---

private train never stopped. It had the right of way from Atlantic to Pacific. It owned the American horizon. (America is a private train crashing over the slippery rails of History. Faster, faster, America!) The private train never stopped.

THE RANCHER'S DAUGHTER LOVED GUM DROPS

In a huge, wonderful armchair Mr. Schmidt leaned back and smiled. He was forty-five years old, and bald, pink, shining and perfect. He was very tolerant. He was sure. He pressed a button and the world entered with a tray, and brought him what he wished. He was a sophisticated Menckenite and connoisseur.

My dear, he said in a fatherly voice, to the raw little flapper opposite him, let me ask George to fill your glass again.

Oh, thank you, Mr. Schmidt, she stammered nervously, licking her dry lips and smiling.

My dear child, he cooed, you mustn't call me Mr. Schmidt! Mr. Schmidt indeed! So formal, aren't you? All my little girls call me Pops. Just Pops.

Yes, Pops.

That's better, Angel Face.

George, the tall Negro in white, entered with low, dramatic, oriental bowings and ceremony. He poured, with perfect art, wine into two thin glasses. He dimmed the lights in the Czarist stateroom being whirled 80 miles an hour through the ancient, humble night.

My, my, Dot, now you're a real star. Yes, at seventeen your name will be blazing in electric lights on the theaters of every city in the world. Isn't that wonderful? Yesterday a mere stenographer, tomorrow a world figure, like Gloria Swanson or Valentino, no less. Don't it thrill you, my little Cinderella?

Oh, it certainly does, Mr.—Pops.

She had baby blue eyes, soft as a mongrel's. Blond, wavy bob. Pink and white enamel face, beautiful as a flat magazine cover done by a Hearst artist. Just out of high school, and bewildered. Her little heart was beating. Her little brain was puzzled. What did Pops want?

KISS ME, MY FOOL!

In the next car, a long room decorated in gilt like the Czar's palace, a male press agent, three female movie actresses, a female scenario writer, two male movie executives, and a male British novelist were drinking and dancing to the radio. None of them needed monkey glands.

Gladys La Svelte tossed off a bumper of champagne, bit the neck of the stately British author, and wanted to pull the engine cord.

Henry a short Negro in white, uttered, with oriental bowings and humility: Please, ma'am, that cord is for emergencies only.

Let's pull it anyway. I want the train to go faster. I want speed —speed—speed.

Please, ma'am—

Speed. Faster, faster! Tell the engineer, faster, faster!

Yes, ma'am.

She didn't pull it. The radio brought the history of science to a grand climax. It transmitted *Yes Sir, She's My Baby* from Chicago. The jazz band at the Hotel Karnac was ya-hooing like mad.

It positively gets into one's blood, said the British novelist naively. What a country, what a country! Faster, faster, he chortled.

He thought of his marvellous Hollywood contract, and bit the neck of Gladys La Svelte to show his joy. He unbent. This was a riotous surprise to everyone, and they whacked him with colored toy balloons.

MEANWHILE OVER THE SLUMBERING CITY THE DAWN'S ROSES FELL SOFTLY LIKE PEARLS

The fireman was shovelling coal into the fiery furnace. He was a haggard, young American roughneck. He had been in three wrecks, and in one of them a piece of iron entered his skull.

She's going good now, ain't she? he yelled belligerently, his hard face set, as he wiped his smutty brow with a hunk of cotton waste.

Too good, said the old engineer with a sour sneer. He was disillusioned with speed; he had driven express trains for forty years. But Mr. Schmidt had promised him fifty dollars at the end of his run.

Whaddye mean, too good? Ain't I givin yuh all the steam yuh need? yelled the fireman.

The engineer couldn't hear and didn't answer. He was worrying. The fireman repeated the question belligerently. His nerves were on edge. His girl had thrown him down and had married a salesman. The fireman had been on an awful bootleg jag for three days. He was a hard, bitter drinker since that last wreck, when he was knocked on the head. But the engineer was worrying.

I must watch out. There's always a jam near Des Moines. Jim Moore got wrecked there only last month, with a clear track, too. And these specials ball up the schedule. I must watch out. Jim was wrecked. He took the hill, whistling, and there was Number 4 staring him right in the face. I must watch out.

Faster, faster, yelled the fireman. You got all the steam she can stand, ain't yuh? He was mad with rage for some reason, and slammed the coal like a furious devil into the firebox. Faster, faster, you old bastard.

The engineer was startled. Was it me you called that? he shouted, staring down with stern eyes.

Yeh you, the fireman roared, shaking his shovel at the engineer. You, you, you. His hair streamed in the gale, and the black and yellow glare of the furnace illuminated him with the fires of hell.

I LOVE YOU! MAY I, MISS SMITH? I KNOW I'M JUST A POOR COWBOY, BUT—

In the narrow pantry, George and Henry, the Negroes in white, drooped wearily like heartsick mothers at a bedside.

Ain't they awful?

Yop, plumb coo-coo.

I wish I could get some sleep.

No sleep on this trip, Big Boy.

Honest, it ain't worth even the big tips. I hate to serve them.

Last time for me, I'll tell the world.

There's that bell again. Hope the old ofay busts a blood vessel or something.

Slip a white powder in his gin.

Wish I had the nerve.

Then suddenly oriental, George purringly poured for Mr. Schmidt the finest wine money could buy, into the finest glasses money could buy.

Just turn those other lights out, too, said the magnate. They hurt my eyes.

Yes, sir. Yes, sir.

The private train never stopped.

AS IN BABYLON
OF ELD

They were Hollywooding in the next car. They were wasting life. They screamed, wrestled, frazzled, mushed, rubbed, gooed and ate huge chicken and bacon sandwiches. An executive and an actress stole off into a stateroom. The others petted, laughed, screamed, gobbled. They smeared mustard on each other. A dress was torn. The floor was cluttered with napkins, salad dressing, corks and cigarette butts. The radio yammered. The night flew by. Through the windows all the dark farmhouses, trees, rivers, flashed by like a cheap movie. The dark, old American fields roared with a mighty voice. There was a protest against this new thing. But the private train never stopped.

Haw, haw, let's serenade Dot and Pops.

No, let's tell the engineer to go faster, shrieked Gladys.

Someone stuck his head out of the window. Fast enough for me. Fast as a Keystone comedy.

Aw, come on, let's serenade Dot and Pops. He's our host aint he? Gotta show our 'preciation, ain't we?

MY WONDER GIRL!

The fireman slammed open the firebox door. He bellowed with delight when the tiger-blast struck his sweaty face. His muscles bulged. His chest gleamed. He danced like a clumsy bull. He climbed up the cab. The old engineer screamed. He hit the old engineer over the skull with his shovel. The engineer died. The fireman danced.

Faster, faster, the fireman screamed, flinging his giant arms to the gale. Faster when I tell yuh to go faster. I'm boss here now. I'm a millionaire. I'm King of the World!

The private train never stopped. It leaped ahead as if a giant had kicked it forward.

TWO SHOTS RANG
OUT!

Mr. Schmidt was slightly sweating.

I could get any girl I wanted in the world. But I want only you, my bonny daisy.

Oh, Pops, you do say such pretty things. You talk like a poet.

Little rabbit, you're first beginning to know me. People think I'm a cold, dull business man, but I have an artist's soul. That is really the secret of my success. I'll make a great artist out of you before I'm through with you. If it costs me a cool million.

Oh, Pops! You make me so happy.

Kiss me, Dottie.

I'm so young, she lisped coyly, I don't know about these things. Isn't it wrong, Pops?

MEANWHILE A LONE
RIDER—

Henry and George were badly frightened. They stuck their heads out of the pantry window. The wind smote them like an uppercut from Jack Dempsey's fist.

Gawd, she'll jump the track at this rate, sure. I never saw a train act this way.

I guess it's all right, George. I guess so. Old Gordon's driving her, and he knows what he's doing. I guess so.

It don't feel right, I tell yuh. No. Too fast, too fast!

Old Gordon's running her. Guess so. Guess so. It's all right, George. Guess so. Guess so.

A LITTLE CHILD
SHALL LEAD THEM

The gaudy mob poured in to serenade Pops. But the state-room door was locked against them. They pounded on the door with bottles and yelled Hey! Hey! They rocked on their feet. The private train was shimmying like mad. It never stopped. A few were sick. Gladys La Svelte vomited on the Czarist floor. Everyone laughed like a zoo. Britain supported America and held her head down.

Gladys grew histrionic. She wept like Jesus. He's double-crossed me, she screamed, and broke away. She kicked at the door crazily. I know what's going on in there. He's thrown me over for that little Kewpie doll, the old cradle-snatcher. But I'll show him. I'll tell the newspapers he's crazy for young girls. I'll break him. I'll sue him. He dragged me down.

The others laughed like a zoo. They rocked and shimmied with the train. Aw, forget it, Gladys. Come on and sing, Gladys. Be a sport. He's our host, ain't he? The British novelist used his monocle haughtily, and thought of his contract. Gladys was vulgar. But there was laughter of coyotes and peacocks. Everyone burst into song. Hail, hail, the gang's all here, so what the hell do—

Henry and George rushed in with immense eyes and pork-pale faces.

Too fast—too fast, they stammered—

Laughter like a zoo. They bladdered the Negroes with toy balloons.

Then—OUT!

Life exploded like a bomb.

Then—POW!

The world shot from a cannon in flame. Coney Island fireworks. Crucifix pain.

Tidal wave, earthquake, last lonely screams of little children eaten by a giant. Snap and crack. Fade out. Then quiet. A bird sang in the sudden sweet gloom. There was a smell of roasted flesh.

CAME THE DAWN

The great monster lay on its side, tons of steel writhing like a snake. Huge steam clouds hissed from the dragon's wounds. The old countryside was cool, dark and still. Yes, a bird sang.

Mr. Schmidt's pampered guts lay neglected in the ballast. The last white stars shone in the sky. Gladys was grinning with some bloody joke. She was red and nude. The British novelist was undignified; he had no arms. Negro George was long, flat and patient. The night was very dark and sweet. Little Dot hugged the grass by the track. The fireman's wild head had rolled away. There was the smell of flesh. A bird sang. The press agent's belly was like an open mouth.

Faster, faster.

A pale farmer came running from the dark. He had a sickle in his hand. A pale worker in overalls came up, with a hammer. They soberly began the rescue work. Dawn grew. The red morning star appeared.

* * *

America is a private train rushing to Hollywood.

* * *

Faster, faster, America!

Lynchers in Frockcoats

IT IS August 14th, eight days before the new devil's hour set for the murder of Sacco and Vanzetti. I am writing this in the war zone, in the psychopathic respectable city that is crucifying two immigrant workers, in Boston, Massachusetts.

All of us here fighting for the two Italians are without hope. We feel that they will burn. Respectable Boston is possessed with the lust to kill. The frockcoat mob is howling for blood—it is in the lynching mood.

If the two Italian workers do not die it will not be the fault of cultured Boston. The pressure of the workers of the world will have accomplished the miracle. But I repeat, the handful of friends working desperately here are without hope. The legal procedure in this case is nothing but a bitter joke. The blood lust alone is real.

You can't understand this case unless you are in Boston now. You must mingle with the crowds at the newspaper bulletin boards on Washington street, hear sleek clerks and ex-Harvard football players and State street stockbrokers mutter rancorously:

Gold's animus toward respectable Boston dated back to the troubled year he spent there (1914–1915) as a Harvard drop-out, journalist, bum, and "foiled revolutionaire." "Love on a Garbage Dump," reprinted below, helps explain the motives and nature of Gold's hatred for Boston gentility. During that year, he was involved in the local anarchist movement; he traveled down to Plymouth, not to celebrate the Founding Fathers, but to participate in a strike of immigrant cordage workers there. He met Vanzetti. Thus, from the very beginning of the Sacco-Vanzetti affair in 1921, Gold was deeply committed to the fight. More than any other of the New York intellectuals who joined the effort to secure justice for the condemned Italian workers, Gold was personally committed. Their tragedy was his; their enemies had been his. This desperate eleventh-hour report of the battle, which records the passion of Gold's engagement, appeared just after the two men died. George Creel was chief of the government's committee on public information during World War I. New Masses, September 1927.

"These Anarchists must die! We don't want this kind of people running America!"

They whisper, they fidget, they quiver with nervousness and fear, they jump like cats every time a pin drops. The city has lost its head. The atmosphere is like the war days, when George Creel's skilled literatry liars were scaring everyone with the news that the Kaiser's airplanes were about to bomb Chicago, New York and San Francisco.

Those who sympathize with Sacco and Vanzetti in the street crowds keep their mouths shut. They are as unpopular as a Northern friend of the Negroès would be at a Southern lynching bee.

Most of the well-dressed, well-mannered Boston bourgeoisie are frank in saying Governor Fuller should not have granted a reprieve. They openly accuse him of being too soft.

The city is under martial law. The entire State militia has been brought into Boston and is quartered on the alert in the armories. The police are on 24-hour watch, equipped with machine guns, tear-gas bombs, and armored cars. No meetings are allowed on the Sacco-Vanzetti case. If you wear a beard, or have dark foreign hair or eyes, or in any way act like a man who has not had a Harvard education or Mayflower ancestors, you are picked up on the streets for suspicion.

You must not look like a New Yorker. Two New York women, Helen Black and Ann Washington Craton, were arrested and questioned at a police station for the crime of looking like New Yorkers. You must not need a shave. Six Italians in an automobile who had come for the demonstration on August 10th were arrested and held on a bombing charge because two of them needed a shave.

Detectives dog you everywhere; yes, those stupid, criminal, blank detective faces haunt you everywhere, in restaurants, in drug stores while you are having an ice cream soda, in cigar stores, even in toilets. At night you can rise like Shelley from your dreams and stare below into the moonlit street and see a knot of evil, legal detective faces, watching you lest you go sleep-walking.

It is highly dangerous to be out in the streets after midnight. A group of us after a hard day's work at the headquarters, went searching for a restaurant at 12:30, and were followed, not by four or five of the detectives, but by a whole patrol wagon load of them.

I was one of those who picketed the State House on August 10th, the first date set for the murder of Sacco and Vanzetti. Forty of us marched up and down the concrete walk between the elm trees near the Common, gaped at by a vast curious mob of Bostonians and police and detectives, and from the capitol's ornate balconies, by the official flunkeys of Governor Fuller.

Our picket line was a good cross-section of the sentiment that has been aroused in America and the rest of the world. There were Jewish needle trade workers and Communists from New York. There were five young Finnish working girls from Worcester, Massachusetts, two of them under the age of fifteen. There was John Dos Passos, the splendid young novelist, and Dorothy Parker, a gay, sophisticated writer of light verse and satirical plays with a flavor of social conscience. There was a group of young Communist workers from Chicago and New York. There were iron workers, sailors, jewelry workers, barbers, bakers educators, agitators and waiters. There was finally a little fiery Anglo-Saxon aged 62, who made a speech in court affirming that he was opposed to anarchism, was a Harvard graduate, and wanted justice for the two doomed men, for all of which he was fined $20.

Dorothy Parker and I were arrested by the same brace of iron-handed policemen. As they hauled us off on the long walk to the police station, a crowd followed after us—a well-dressed Boston mob, of the type that lynched Lovejoy during the Abolition days.

Some of these respectables booed us, and several of them hooted and howled:

"Hang them! Hang the Anarchists!"

That is the mood of respectable Boston at this hour. A friend of mine who is a veteran newspaperman in this city says he has never seen respectable Boston in as tense a mood as now.

"If this were the South they would not wait for Governor Fuller but would storm the jail and lynch Sacco and Vanzetti," my friend said.

But Governor Fuller is in the lynching mood, though he feels constrained to decorate it with Puritan legalities. And President Lowell of Harvard is in that mood, and all those who have conspired one way or another to execute the two Italians.

They will kill Sacco and Vanzetti legally. They are determined on revenge. For decades they have seen wave after wave of lusty immigrants sweep in over their dying culture. For years these idealists who religiously read Emerson and live on textile mill dividends have had to fight rebel immigrants on strike.

New England is dying culturally and industrially. The proud old libertarian tradition of the Abolition days has degenerated into a kind of spiritual incest and shabby mediocre pride of family. The inefficiency of the blueblood factory owners has pushed the textile industry South, where there is plenty of cheap, unorganized and unrebellious native labor.

So these ghosts, these decadents, these haughty medicore impotent New Englanders have flamed up into a last orgy of revenge. They have the subconscious superstition that the death of Sacco and Vanzetti can restore their dying culture and industry. At last they have a scapegoat. At last they can express the decades of polite frosty despair.

They are as passionate against these Italian workers as white Southerners toward the Negro. They know that New England is rotten from stem to stern, and that the slightest match may prove the brand to start a general revolt in the industrial and political field. They will not be moved from their lust for a blood sacrifice —these faded aristocrats. They are too insane with fear and hatred of the new America.

All I can see now to save Sacco and Vanzetti is a world strike. Nothing less stupendous can shake the provincial Chinese wall of this region. Boston is not conducting a murder case, or even the usual American frame-up—it is in the throes of a lynching bee, led by well-spoken Harvard graduates in frockcoats.

John Reed And The Real Thing

JOHN REED was a cowboy out of the west, six feet high, steady eyes, boyish face; a brave, gay, open-handed young giant; you meet thousands of him on the road, in lumber camps, on the ranges, in fo'c'sls, in the mines.

I used to see Jack Reed swimming at Provincetown with George Cram Cook, that other Socialist and great-hearted adventurer now dead too. I went out a mile with them in a catboat, and they raced back through a choppy sea, arm over arm, shouting bawdy taunts at each other, whooping with delight. Then we all went to Jack's house and ate a big jolly supper.

He loved every kind of physical and mental life; the world flowed through him freely. He lived like an Elizabethan. Because of this, friends like Walter Lippman would say with affectionate contempt that Jack Reed was a romanticist. They said he never studied politics or economics, and rushed in where wise men feared to tread. But Walter Lippman, the Socialist, supported the war, and now supports Al Smith for President. He is wrong on everything. And Jack Reed wrote the most vivid book on the Bolshevik Revolution that has yet appeared in any language. After ten years it is as sound and fresh as at first. It was written white-hot, almost at the scene of the event. It is the greatest piece of reporting in history. It is a deathless book that sells by the million.

The Revolution is the romance of tens of millions of men and women in the world today. This is something many American intellectuals never understand about Jack Reed. If he had remained romantic about the underworld, or about meaningless adventure-wandering, or about women or poem-making, they would have continued admiring him. But Jack Reed fell in love with the Revolution, and gave it all his generous heart's blood. This the pale, rootless intellectuals could never understand. When he died they said he had wasted his life. It is they who

New Masses, *November 1927.*

lead wasted, futile lives in their meek offices, academic sanctums, and bootleg parlors.

Jack Reed lived the fullest and grandest life of any young man in our America. History is already saying this in Soviet Russia. It will say it a century from now in the textbooks of America.

At first he wrote short boyish sketches. He liked roughnecks, he gave himself to queer, far places, he loafed about cities and the underworld. His eyes were keen, his blood boiled with animal joy. The exuberant words leaped in his prose, they swam like laughing athletes, he wrote with broad humor, he exaggerated the bright suns and moons of nature, he splashed the colors on his canvas like a young god. His early stories remind me of Dickens, of Tolstoy, and of Stephen Crane—a strange mixture, but an epic one.

He burst into American writing like a young genius. Everyone followed his work eagerly, waiting for the inevitable masterpiece. At the outbreak of war Jack Reed was the best paid and most brilliant war correspondent in America. He had written some of the best short stories. Everyone waited for the masterpiece. When it came, "they" were all voting for Al Smith, and drinking bootleg with Mencken. "They" had not the great spirit which recognizes masterpieces.

Jack Reed's life was not wasted; he did write his masterpiece, *Ten Days That Shook The World*. But the "intellectuals" haven't yet recognized this.

The role of the intellectual in the revolutionary labor movement has always been a debating point. In the I.W.W. the fellow-workers would tar and feather (almost) any intellectual who appeared among them. The word "intellectual" became a synonym for the word "bastard," and in the American Communist movement there is some of this feeling.

It is part of the American hard-boiled tradition, shared by revolutionists here who believe it is unproletarian and unmanly to write a play, or study politics, or discuss the arts. Mr. Babbitt feels the same way.

This tradition is dying in the American revolutionary movement. Jack Reed was one of the "intellectuals" who helped destroy the prejudice. He identified himself so completely with the working class; he undertook every danger for the revolution; he forgot his Harvard education, his genius, his popularity, his gifted body and mind so completely that no one else remembered them any more; there was no gap between Jack Reed and the workers any longer.

He was active in forming the Communist Party in this country. He edited one of the first Communist propaganda papers. He was on trial during the war for sedition. He rose in the courtroom hitched up his pants, looked the Judge squarely in the eye, and testified boldly and frankly, like a revolutionist.

It is a difficult career being an active revolutionist. It takes all one's nerves, energy and character. It is almost as difficult to be a pioneer revolutionary writer. Jack Reed, in his short life, managed to combine both careers. But not many have this exuberance, this versatility. Robert Minor has given up his magnificent art for the revolution; is this necessary? Jack Reed did not think so, in Soviet Russia no one thinks so. But most Americans, even revolutionists, believe it unworthy for the man of action to be also a man of thought. Lenin was both.

The revolutionary intellectual is an activist thinker. This is what makes him so different from the careful men with perpetual slight colds who write for the *New Republic* and the *Nation*. Jack Reed needed for his activism a magazine like the *Masses*, and helped create it. I was working as a night porter for the Adams Express Company in New York when I began reading the *Masses*. It was the beginning of my education. It educated a whole generation of youth in America, many of whom did not survive the spiritual holocaust of the war. Those who did survive remember Jack Reed, and his courage flows in their veins. And the revolution will grow in America, and there will be a new youth and Jack Reed will teach them how to live greatly again. This depression, this cowardice, this callousness and spiritual death will not last forever among the youth of America. It cannot. Life is mean only in cycles; it sinks defeated, then it inevitably rises. There will be more Jack Reeds in America, his grandchildren perhaps. This mean decade of ours will pass on.

He had his faults. Most people have. But he was never petty in his faults. You can tell that even by his writing. It is difficult to write that way in America today. It is difficult to admit you enjoy life so hugely; that you are simple and loyal, that you are tender to the friendless and wear your heart on your sleeve. A writer must act as mean and as hardboiled as the rest of modern Americans. Maybe this is a good discipline for writers. Maybe it is the way to the strength that writers need in this age. But I am sure that the best elements of Jack Reed's spirit will be preserved in any revolutionary writers who will appear in this country. They will have the bigness to be humane. They will laugh, but they will not sneer. Jack Reed was a fierce enemy to capitalism, but in all his books you will never find a sneer at humanity. And this is difficult to refrain from, too.

Many of his bourgeois friends were always sure Jack Reed was a kind of playboy in the revolution. The revolution was just another one of his huge jolly adventures, like the one in which he dived off an Atlantic liner leaving New York, and swam back to land on an impulse. Yes, the revolution was an impulse. It would exhaust itself when the fun had gone out of it.

Walter Lippman, in his article in the *New Republic* on John Reed, smiled affectionately as he recounted how his Harvard classmate, Jack Reed, had confessed to the fact that he hadn't heard of Bergson, the latest Paris fashion among the intellectuals of the period. Walter Lippman and many others thought this showed Jack had no brains, and that his revolutionary philosophy was just a romanticist's impulse.

But Jack Reed went through the Paterson strike, and the Lawrence strike, and the Bayonne strike, and understood their significance. And he understood the economic basis of the World War, and refused to be a tool of J. P. Morgan, like Walter Lippman and many other wise men who knew so much about Bergson, and so little about the inevitable treaty at Versailles.

And he had read and thought enough to grasp the full political and economic significance of the Bolshevik Revolution for the world, when it was still a raw, bloody, chaotic, embryo, which the "intellectuals" predicted could not last a month. The book he wrote on it had an approving preface by the scientist and scholar, Lenin.

I was in Soviet Russia two years ago and visited Jack Reed's grave under the Kremlin wall. Under the rough stone, near the mausoleum of Lenin, and, in sound of church bells now forced to ring out "The Internationale," lay the splendid body of our comrade. He had not been a playboy. He had loved the Revolution when she was a haggard outlaw fighting for life against the ravening pack of capitalist nations.

He had lived with the revolution in famine, in civil war, in chaos and stern Cheka self-defense. He had seen hundreds of frozen corpses of Red Guards piled high in a railroad station. He had worked himself to the bone for this Revolution. He had wandered through typhus areas, he had been bitten by a typhus louse, and died. It was not all an impulse. It was the real thing with Jack Reed.

And what he had died for was the real thing—but what the boys whom the *New Republic* intellectuals sent out to die for was not the real thing. Walter Lippman's war to end war did *not* end war, but was the prelude to a more rapacious capitalistic imperialism and a greater imperialist war.

But Jack Reed's revolution was all about me in the Red Square of Moscow, where he lay under the rough stone. Peasants passed coming from the land given them by the revolution to lay their problems before Kalinin, their peasant premier, in Moscow. Workers passed, coming from factories where they were masters, not the slaves. Old men passed, who had learned to read and write by the millions since Jack Reed died for them. Young writers and artists passed, thousands of them growing up to express themselves as freely and grandly as Jack Reed. Women passed, walking with their heads up, the freed victims of ancient bondage. Children passed, no longer drugged by the superstitions of a medieval church. There was a new social system growing up; the Elizabethan and Greek genius that had lived in Jack Reed had flowed into a whole nation; it was spreading with red banners in every land; it was the real thing. It was the romance of the real thing.

Hemingway—White Collar Poet

ONLY MARXIANS have the slightest clue to the social basis of fashion. Fashion is as whimsical as a butterfly, neurotic as a race horse with hives, crazy as the New York weather.

What causes the cycles of fashion? The average "literary critic" can't tell you; the world is all accident to him. He is as incompetent as the average university "economist" who describes perfectly the cycles of economic expansion and depression, but knows as little of their basic laws as an Eskimo of television.

Ernest Hemingway is the newest young writer to leap into fashion among American intellectuals. He deserves recognition; he is powerful, original, would be noticed anywhere, and at any time. He has a technical control of his material as sure as a locomotive engineer's. He sees and feels certain things for himself, for 1928.

Hemingway became a best seller with his novel *The Sun Also Rises*. He had already published a volume of short stories, and a satirical novel. Neither was very popular. Hemingway was considered a member of a cult. The advance guard of American writing, most of whom live in Paris, looked upon Hemingway as one of their bannermen. He expressed their mood of irony, lazy despair, and old-world sophistication.

Suddenly this esoteric mood became popular. Thousands of simpler male and female Americans, not privileged to indulge in café irony and pity in Paris, but rising to alarm clocks in New York and Chicago, discovered and liked Hemingway. Why? His novel was an upper-class affair, concerned with the amours and drinking bouts of Americans with incomes who rot in European cafés; self-pitying exiles and talkers. Michael Arlen had already

---

This article was ostensibly a review of Ernest Hemingway's Men Without Women. *In spite of their differences, the two men remained on fairly cordial terms until the late 1930s, when the politics of world crisis divorced a good many odd bedfellows. Gold's attack on* For Whom the Bell Tolls *concludes the "Renegades" chapter of* The Hollow Men, *which is reprinted below.* New Masses, *March 1928.*

specialized in them, and fattened his bank account; why did the hard-working Babbitt Americans accept more of the same gilded sorrows in Hemingway?

It was no accident.

The middle-class youth of America is without a goal. It is shot to pieces morally and intellectually. America is the land where the businessman is the national hero. A big section of the middle-class youth, however, hates in its heart the rapacities, the meanness, the dollarmanias of business.

Part of the propaganda of the bourgeois philosopher Mencken has been to reconcile the American youth to business. In all of his writings he preaches American common sense to the young; but his common sense is that of a prosperous grocer.

American business simply cannot satisfy the mind and the heart. A thousand voices rise every day to testify against it. Mencken is losing his followers; they are discovering he is shallow. It is not his materialism one objects to; materialism offers greatness Mencken never dreamed of. Materialism is the basis of a heaven on earth, a social heaven. Mencken offers us only a fat little wholesale grocer's suburb.

The war was a profound shock to all the youth. It was an earthquake in which their world of solid Y.M.C.A. values disappeared. And they studied Versailles, and now they can sense the next war, and they have no illusions about the past or present, and they have no hopes for the imperialist future.

Mencken, Hemingway, Sherwood Anderson all the bourgeois modern American writers, whom do they write for? Not for workingmen, and not for the bankers of Wall Street. They write for, and they express the soul of, the harried white-collar class.

I know a hundred gay, haggard, witty, hard-drinking woman-chasing advertising men, press agents, dentists, doctors, engineers, technical men, lawyers, office executives. They go to work every morning, and plough their weary brains eight hours a day in the fiercest scramble for a living the world has ever known.

Men who cheerfully fought through the war become nervous wrecks under the strain of American business competition. You must never let down; you must never stop to feel or think. There is no relief except violent nights of bootlegging and Bohemian love.

Sherwood Anderson expressed the soft daydreams of this class, an epicene's dream of escape, without will, without vigor.

Hemingway offers the daydreams of a man. Liquor, sex and sport are his three chief themes, as they are in the consciousness of the American white-collar slave today.

The intelligent young American liberal who was shocked and disgusted by his helplessness in the Sacco-Vanzetti case, forgets his impotence in getting drunk and imagining himself a strong, brutal killer with Ernest Hemingway. This is literature of escape, it is a new form of the ivory tower in America.

The young American "liberal" writes advertising copy meekly all day, then at night dreams of Hemingway's irresponsible Europe, where everyone talks literature, drinks fine liqueurs, swaggers with a cane, sleeps with beautiful and witty British aristocrats, is well informed in the mysteries of bullfighting, has a mysterious income from home.

That is why Hemingway is suddenly popular. He has become the sentimental storyteller to a whole group of tired, sad, impotent young Americans, most of whom must work in offices every day—"white collar slaves."

After the first Revolution failed in Russia, in 1905, a similar situation arose. The young people lost all hope for a modern world. Artzibashev came and expressed their mood in *Sanine*. Suicide clubs and clubs for sex orgies flourished among the youth.

When the French Revolution seemed to have failed, the poets it had created, like Wordsworth, grew timid and sad.

The literary historian of America will recognize that a great wave of social revolt came to its climax in the election of Woodrow Wilson to the Presidency. It was diverted by him, as Napoleon diverted the French Revolution, to a means of vast personal power. It then collapsed in the Versailles treaty, and in the following years of this false, stinking, imperialist peace of ours.

This is the social background of the depression among the young American intellectuals; the background and reason for the new Hemingway fashion. We are living in a decade of betrayals; our time is dominated by Ramsay Macdonald, Mussolini and other Judases.

Ten years ago Hemingway could not have written in this mood; he would not have felt the mood, and no one else would have understood him, in this mood. His mood is that of the betrayed young idealist.

There is no humanity in Hemingway, as there is in Dreiser, Stephen Crane, Upton Sinclair, Carl Sandburg, all the men of the earlier decade. He is heartless as a tabloid. He describes the same material as do tabloids, and his sole boast is his aloofness, last refuge of a scoundrel. What one discerns in him as in those younger writers close to his mood, is an enormous self-pity. He romanticizes his bewilderment in a world where social problems have become the only real problems of the so-called individual. The Hemingways are always running away from something—not going to something.

Hemingway, curiously enough, is an imitator of Tolstoy. I have seen no critic who has yet pointed this out. Hemingway has the same bare, hard style of a god-like reporter; his narrative is precise and perfect as science; he is the poet of facts.

Tolstoy, the disillusioned intellectual, strove like a weary exile to return to the golden child-land of the senses; he dreamed he could be a peasant. Hemingway, weary of the Judas decade and incapable of social thought, surrenders his intellect too, and dreams that he can be an American lowbrow; a prize-fighter, a fisherman, a village drunkard.

Tolstoy had a big brain, and in his Russia for an intellectual to turn peasant meant that the Revolution had gained another recruit. This was far from a tragedy for Tolstoy and the world.

Hemingway will soon exhaust the illusion that he is a brainless prize-fighter, and since he is too bourgeois to accept the labor world, I predict he will imitate next, not Tolstoy, but those young French writers near to his mood, who have sought nirvana in the Catholic Church.

It will be a pity. Hemingway is a power; he has led American writing back to the divine simplicities of the prosaic; he has made a great technical contribution.

The revolutionary writers of the future will be grateful to him; they will imitate his style. But they will have different things to say. A new wave of social struggle is moving on the ocean of American life. Unemployment is here; hints of a financial depression; the big conservative unions are breaking up; another world war is being announced by Admirals and Generals.

Babbitt was one of the evidences of the desperation and pessimism of the middle-lass idealists during the Judas decade, Hemingway was another sign. In the decade to come we may develop Gorkys and Tolstoys to follow these Artzibashevs. The Sacco-Vanzetti case woke the conscience of the intellectuals. They brushed Mencken aside and walked on the picket lines in

Boston. Upton Sinclair is coming back in popularity in his own land. There is surely something brewing. Hemingway is not the herald of a new way of feeling, but the last voice of a decade of despair.

In Foggy California

It was in 1923–24. I had "escaped" to California to write a novel. New York is too noisy for continuous thinking. It is a machine that grinds the mind to powder. It is a battlefield. But I soon discovered that Californis was a hospital. Take your choice; the subway or the bedpan.

Here are some extracts from a diary I kept in exile:

July 4—San Francisco is a very foggy city filled with people who insist that the sun is always shining. They are obsessed with climate. I never knew the weather could be so important. Maybe it is.

July 10—Another session with George Sterling, Upton's friend. We went drinking around. He is a wonderful, generous chap, but shot to pieces, like so many California intellectuals. About one in the morning we passed an apartment house in construction. George stopped to curse it.

"The realtors and Babbitts have captured our Athens, we are Greek slaves at the court of the Roman barbarian, etc.," he shouted. Then he lit a match and tried to set fire to the house. I stopped him. It is trivial to hate apartment houses.

It has little to do with revolution. George loves these large fierce gestures, like all poets. He yanked out a big pocket knife, and said, "Mike, let's find a Babbit, and stick him for fun!"

July 30—My dentist used to be a secretary of the I. W. W. miner's union at Goldfield, Nevada. He led a big strike. Now, after ten years in California, he produces ectoplasm, and tells me he can project his body anywhere he wants to.

He is not eccentric in this. In New York, the middle-class "intellegentsia" follows Freud, Heywood Broun, the Theatre Guild, and Bernard Shaw. Here two out of three have intimate affairs with spirits, or use the ouija board.

August 5—Fremont Older, editor of the S. F. *Call,* for whom I am working, does not believe the human race has any future.

New Masses, *November 1928.*

Everyone is predetermined by glands, Mr. Older says. This man was once a hard-boiled fighter who exulted in political battles and reform. Now he has been licked, not by glands, but by California.

August 9—Save your soul! Eat raw food and rap tables. Met three today.

August 12—Went with a gang of newspapermen up to Jackson. Six months ago fifty gold miners lost their lives there in the Argonaut mine disaster. The Chamber of Commerce feels the publicity was good for their lousy little town. They want to keep it alive. So they threw this party for the reporters.

The car I went in was an old circulation speedster, driven by a jolly drunk. It burst into flames half-way up the mountains, but the driver didn't notice till his pants caught fire. We threw in some sand and pushed on.

Mark Twain's country. Poker Flat, Angel's Flat, etc. . . . The Chamber of Commerce gave us a swell banquet. Liquor in buckets. Then the Mayor got up and started a solemn publicity speech from the heart. But the newspaper gang was too drunk to listen. One Irish cub, about twenty, as snotty as they come, called the Mayor dirty names all through the solemn speech. This broke up the publicity party. All dignity went to hell. The Mayor tried to throw the kid out, but our gallant lads leaped bravely to the rescue. And all night they howled up and down the main street, smashed windows, etc. . . . What a dud for the C. of C.! They'll celebrate no more miners' funerals. They'll trust no more newspaper bums.

August 15—Met a hashslinger in a one-arm lunch, who wore a Communist button. Talked to him, and found out he is a Christian Scientist too, and believes Communism and Mary Baker Eddy are twins. This is too much.

August 19—Lectured last night in Oakland. Could not hear myself talk for the snores of my audience. Deadest audiences in the U.S. Worse than Finns.

August 25—George Sterling phoned an S.O.S. this morning. I went to his room in the Bohemian Club. This is anything but a "bohemian" club, it's an exclusive, expensive barroom and hangout for all the big bankers, politicians, society bums and Satevepost "authors" of the town. To Hell with them! George lay white as an Easter lily in a fake-antique bed. He wore plum-colored plush pajamas. He was quite sick; his voice a whisper. On the floor lay a mass of dollar bills. I looked at them.

"There's five hundred dollars there," George groaned. "Take it away Mike! I won't need money any more; I'm dying, dying!" He was suffering from a bad hangover. He once told me his father died of cancer brought on by drinking. George has a fear he will pop off in the same way. I talked him out of the obsession. But I couldn't talk him out of his philosophy of life. Even now, he argued it out lucidly. George believes the universe holds more possibilities of pain than of pleasure; that this ratio has been fixed through eternity, and that nothing can change the balances, no revolution, no human effort of any kind. I told George his philosophy was personal and emotional, not scientific. It was not statistically demonstrable, and was therefore a dogma of faith, like Catholicism. He groaned, and repeated his own arguments. He told me to please take the five hundred bucks. I am broke, but being a gentleman, took only fifty, and left. Some Babbitt had given George the roll. They do it for him on drinking parties. They like him.

September 2—George has the elements of a genius. He has written a few great poems. He was nationally famous twenty-five years ago. Now California has ruined him. He writes Elizabethan rhymed ads for the Chamber of Commerce; is a kind of poet laureate of the city. The Babbitts patronize him, and he lets them. He feels financially inferior to them; this is the secret of his pessimism. He looks like Dante, and is one of Upton Sinclair's oldest friends. He was Jack London's best pal. He gave me a purple necktie yesterday that Jack London had taken off his own neck at a party and with it had tried to strangle George.

September 10—Why does everyone here talk only of Jack London, Ambrose Bierce and Robert Louis Stevenson? Why does everyone yearn so much for the glorious saloons of the past? This state is a middle-aged bourgeois, its tone is that of a Mencken article. It has chosen a cowardly and comfortable bourgeois existence, but regrets its flaming youth.

September 23—I have found a few congenial reds to hang out with. You need to, anywhere, to feel right. Delivered my "famous" lecture on Social Tendencies in American Literature last night, at the Workers' Party hall. Afterward went to the beer hall run by the German comrades. They cater the best beer in town. It is magnificent. And then had this fine evening with five swell guys.

1. Bill Rourke; former petty officer in the U.S. Navy; then became president of waiter's union; now a Communist. Has a hearty laugh, is a born gambler, a fighting fool. "The only woman I ever loved was a Kanaka belle; she had lips like boxing gloves."

2. Joe West; born and bred in the cattle country; an ex-cowboy. Lost a leg hopping freights. Now an oxy-acetylene welder and Communist. Friends only recently induced him to part with his six-shooter. Whenever he'd get blue, he'd take his gun for a walk, fill up with German beer, and shoot up a streetcar. Fremond Older got him out of two bad scrapes.

3. Gus Schmidt; 45, pock-marked, bald-headed, jovial machinist, once helped dig a tunnel to rescue Alexander Berkman from the Pittsburgh penitentiary. Ready to dig another for any comrade in need of one.

4. Sidney McGowan; 76 years old, with a wrinkled face like an ancient Indian chief. Spent three years with Agassiz in Mexico; served in the U.S. Army; did a hundred other interesting things. Now a janitor by day; a fiery Communist at night. Drinks beer with the boys after the meetings, smokes his big cigar, cocks his black sombrero. They call this 76-year-old fighting cock "The Kid."

5. Louis Lasitis; tailor. Spinal trouble has twisted his neck, and shortened his big frame by a foot. But game as ever. A wide reader in economics and philosophy; likes to argue, and can. Active Communist. Keeps about fifty canaries all around his tailor shop, and breeds them. Has some amazing stories about his canaries.

We talked until four in the morning. It was fine to meet some witty and pugnacious people in this gloomy state. Boris Pilniak, the Russian writer, said: "I am with the Communists, because in all these years in Russia they have been the only group to feel hopefully about life." Same here.

September 26—In intervals between newspaper work, I have worked for a year on a novel. Today I tore it up, all but one chapter. It is no good. I will start another, this time dealing with the I.W.W.

September 29—Upton Sinclair is coming to Frisco. He has been putting up a splendid fight for the I.W.W. in their San Pedro strike. He has brought the strike into the newspapers. He was arrested and held incommunicado for a day. He will be given a dinner here.

October 1—The Sinclair dinner last night. Mostly tired Californian radicals. Toward the end I began seeing ectoplasm and the ghost of Minnehaha hanging from a chandelier. Upton spoke on the San Pedro strike. Told about the way the American Legion gunmen poured boiling coffee on a striker's child. Told about his own arrest.

October 3—Upton invited me to join his friends on a visit to San Quentin. We talked about Tom Mooney and Matt Schmidt, the latter mixed up in the MacNamara case. Schmidt is the kind of prisoner who dominates his guards by sheer personality. Stands erect and magnificent in his prison suit like General Pershing leading an army. Tom Mooney is a big, magnetic Irishman. Most prisoners try to hibernate, put their minds to sleep, but Tom reads everything, and has never lost touch. He asked me many questions about writers—Carl Sandburg, Theodore Dreiser, Eugene O'Neill, and so on.

After this visit Upton had a conference with the Warden, and made an eloquent plea for the I.W.W. boys, thirty of whom are in solitary. The Warden promised to do something.

We visited the death chamber, read the last greetings of condemned men scrawled in pencil all over the walls. Also saw the line of ropes hanging in another room, weighted with sandbags. They have to be seasoned a year before use. The twelve crimes aren't committed yet; but the twelve ropes are ready.

Dr. Stanley, the prison doctor proudly showed us pickle jars containing several hundred stomach ulcers he has cut out of convicts.

Then we drove south, and had lunch in a meadow. Upton Sinclair ate a whole apricot pie. "I never eat pie," he said briskly, "it is really poison, but today I shall have an orgy."

Then we visited Luther Burbank, and found him a feeble old man with a transparent face of pure kindliness and intellect. He promised Upton without any hesitation to write the Governor asking that the I.W.W. boys be pardoned. He is quite radical, in his kindly and innocent way.

REFLECTIONS ON UPTON SINCLAIR—1928

Sinclair is a surprise to all who first meet him. One expects to meet a solemn bearded Tolstoy, but finds instead a brisk American youth who is quite a star at the game of tennis. He is boyish, looks fifteen years younger than his age. He has the shiny complexion of one who makes sure of a cold shower and rubdown every day. He has bright twinkly eyes; they are paternal, naive, the eyes of a cheerful country doctor, or of a daring theological student.

He is never relaxed. I don't think he has ever deliberately done a useless thing in his life. When he decides that he needs relaxation, he carefully plans for his fun in the blithe spirit of Henry Ford planning a new carburetor. His intense single-mindedness seems to be quite American; Roger Baldwin, Robert Minor, Scott Nearing and others I know have the same trait. They play uneasily, as if doing it by a doctor's orders.

But he really is charming. He believes everything everyone tells him. He is incapable of imagining baseness in other people. He beams hopefully on the world, like a child the night before Christmas. It is not sentimentality; it is the poetry of William Blake. But he tempts you continually to fool him; you want to sell him some gold brick or other, just to teach him a lesson.

When you say something he doesn't want to hear, he goes quite deaf, and his bright eyes go blank. He draws into himself; you must stop hurting him, or boring him. Like most intense people, he is easily bored. It is a trait of the high-powered American; Roger Baldwin and Robert Minor suffer from this kind of deafness, too.

Along with his naivete goes shrewdness and strength. Upton is the perfect incarnation of the small-town American. He has all the faults and virtues of that environment; Puritanism, a simple conception of life, a democratic love for people, a passion and need for crusades, and a sturdy realism about his own business affairs. The sophisticated critics don't understand him, because they don't understand America.

But he has a touch of the fanatic. This is what makes him different from the millions of other Main Streeters. The critics think he is Puritan, and therefore a man like William Jennings Bryan. But he is a Puritan, and therefore a man like Robespierre or Thoreau, or Percy Shelley. It is this extremism which makes him hate pie for decades, then suddenly gulp a whole apricot pie in a Californian meadow. It also keeps him a lonely, stubborn Socialist writer for thirty years in a hostile land.

He is hard to explain. At times he irritates you; he seems so self-centered, so unaware of others, so completely an ego. Many

people have this impression of him. It is a false impression. He is
only as egotistic as the rest of us. But he has not learned what
every ward heeler knows; how to drape the social lies around
one's naked ego.

He answers hundreds of letters every week, from people who
want advice. He helps all kinds of people.

He really loves people, and wants to help them. But you get a
feeling as if he doesn't quite understand them. He must have
been hurt badly in his over-sensitive and difficult youth. He is
shielding himself against the real bitterness of life. Like most
poets, he doesn't want to admit to himself that there is a well of
baseness in people. Upton prefers to overlook the dirt in life.
And so he makes his heroes too perfect, and his villains too villainous.

He has a rigid Mohammedan code for himself. But he is as
loyal to his friends as a gangster; even when everything they do
shocks him. He was the friend of George Sterling for over twenty-
five years. George, the esthete and romanticist, used to say Upton
was a mystery to him, yet he loved Upton. When Upton was
kidnapped and held incommunicado in the San Pedro strike,
George was mad with excitement, and planned to take a train
down at once, to rescue Upton at the cost of his own life.

He works. His whole life has been narrowed down to a stiletto
point; he is a writing machine. Nothing else matters. He keeps
two secretaries busy; he keeps his body in a chair twelve to sixteen hours a day, and writes novels, plays, articles, manifestoes,
for the Social Revolution. I wish I were like that.

HIS WRITING

Every literary youth just out of Harvard, every mamma's boy
with pressed pants, and stacomb hair, and one of papa's checks
in the bank, has written at least one superior article in the *New
Republic,* pointing out the stylistic shortcomings of Upton Sinclair, Theodore Dreiser, Eugene O'Neill.

Those delicate orchids who thrive in the hothouse *Dial* think
they know everything about life, the revolution, America, the
arts, women, and *style.* They are real roughnecks; they have read
Tom Jones, by Fielding, and the roaring Elizabethans. They
have seen life; they have been to Paris.

Upton *has* faults. He has too successfully deodorized his mind.

I do not object to what is called his sentimentality. I prefer it to the sentimentality of Cabell, or Mencken, who weeps over beer, or Sherwood Anderson, or Ernest Hemingway. I would rather feel "sentimental" with Upton about the sufferings of Red Adams, the I.W.W., or Jimmy Higgins, than with Hemingway and the young "moderns" over the bedroom tragedies of a futile drunken aristocratic bitch in Paris.

Upton has written forty books about poverty, the class struggle, the revolution. And everyone of them is written with passion, observation, and a smooth beautiful skill that reminds one of Defoe, of Dickens, of Tolstoy, all the giants of fiction whose pens flowed with large, easy grandeur.

But in all these books there is a faint trace of the Protestant minister that I can't enjoy. It is my only quarrel with this great writer. I do not relish these easy victories of virtue. There is nobility in the revolutionary camp; there is also gloom, dirt and disorder. The worker is not a bright radiant legend like one of Walter Crane's Merrie England peasants. The worker is a man. We don't need to edit him. Let us not shirk our problems. Let us not rob the worker of his humanity in fiction. Not every worker is like Jesus; there are Hamlets, Othellos, Tom Joneses and Macbeths among them, too. And I prefer this variety of life to abstractions.

And I will confess my own obsession; I dislike pictures of cheerful and virtuous poverty such as Upton often draws. Anyone who has been really poor during a lifetime becomes a little morbid, if he has any brains. Like a stoical life prisoner, he doesn't want cheery church ladies to come and comfort him. If he can escape, he will do so; that is all that counts; the rest is bunk.

Upton wears Number 11 shoes; he has big feet made of clay, but the rest of him is quite superhuman. He is the best known American writer in the world today. American writers marvel at this, but the answer is easy. Upton, with all his faults, has one virtue; he knows there is a class struggle in America, and writes about it. Europe and Asia read him to learn about the America that counts, the workers' America, not the America of murder trials, boudoirs, and snappy stories.

Yes, bourgeois critics say Upton Sinclair is not sophisticated. One Bachelor of Arts recently made the heinous charge in the *New Republic* that Upton had never read Watson's book on behaviorism. There are many other crimes. But it all comes down to this; they don't like him because he takes the social revolution seriously.

They can understand dead revolutions, and dead revolutionary writers. They can "place" the revolutionary writings of Walt Whitman, Thoreau, Emerson, they can overlook the lack of style and "behavioristic" psychology in *Uncle Tom's Cabin.*

But Upton has written a long string of novels, some good, some bad, in each of which one finds the same faults, and the same virtue and necessity and revolutionary usefulness of *Uncle Tom's Cabin.*

He is our only pioneer writer since Whitman. He is the bard of industrial America.

"Our" sudden wealth has brought with it in America a parvenu cynicism and smartness in "our" literature. Upton, with his social passion and muckraking, is out of fashion with the American "intelligentsia." I think he feels this. He has really been neglected in America and faintly sneered at for twenty-five years. He has felt it. But he writes every day. He persists. He is one of few giants among a scramble of lapdogs. He works on. His very persistence in America is an act of faith, and a form of genius.

George Sterling told me Jack London did not really die of natural causes, but killed himself with an overdose of morphine tablets. Jack did the wise thing for him. He had been defeated by the American environment. He was a success, and had to earn $40,000 every year writing Hearst slop. This money was needed for a show ranch, a string of saddle horses, and other means of impressing weekend parties of Babbitts. Jack got to hate himself, and his false bourgeois life; then he tried to hate and forget his splendid proletarian youth. He drank like a fish and tried to drown his revolutionary emotions, his real self. Result: suicide.

There are many suicides in California, many more than in New York.*

But Upton Sinclair will never dream of such a thing; he is too busy. He is too useful. He drudges on; a Christian steamshovel scooping up great mucky chunks of American injustice and dropping them in Coolidge's front parlor.

He persists. He is a great man. He is always beginning.

---

* George Sterling committed suicide about a year ago, in San Francisco, after a night spent in conversation with H. L. Mencken.

P.S.—There are thousands in America who cannot forgive Upton Sinclair for going over to the capitalist enemy in the last war. It was the biggest mistake of his life, as he admits now; but he has staged a comeback that to me is convincing of his pure and passionate loyalty to the working-class cause. This does not mean he may not fall for the next war, due about 1940. It is certain that the Socialist parties of the world will be butchering each other again for their respective nations as bitterly as in the last war. There is as little desperate sincerity in their anti-militarism now as there was then. It is true they utter brave manifestoes; but in Germany their party votes for new battleships; in England their party bombs native villages in Iraq. They do nothing concrete about the coming war; they act only to help its coming, it would seem.

But I have never understood Upton Sinclair's politics. I will repeat, despite everything, he is our great American pioneer in revolutionary fiction, he is, to my mind, the most important writer in America.

Vanzetti in the Death House

(In his chains and prison suit, Vanzetti paces the dark cell)
One-two-three-four.
I count the steps like a miser.
One-two-three-four.
Up and down the cell, but I can find no peace.
In my heart, venom; in my brain, fire!
Doomed!
One-two-three-four!
We are doomed, Sacco and I!
We are in the death house at last!
Doomed!
One-two-three-four!
(He sits, puts his face between his hands, speaks bitterly)
After seven years of struggle, of unspeakable anguish,
To be in this dungeon without stars.
Waiting for the last farce of justice,
The three shocks in the electric chair!
(He stands and paces nervously)
I am not afraid to die.
I will walk my road to the end.
I will remain a rebel and a lover.
I will remain true to the working class.
I am in the hands of the tyrants,
Let them crucify me!
One-two-three-four.
(He sits down wearily)
For I am tired, tired, tired.
For seven years I have drunk their vinegar and gall.
All my life I have drunk their poison and poverty.

Gold called this a "worker's recitation," and he appended to it the following note: "This recitation is based on the published speeches and letters of Vanzetti. Almost every line is a verbatim extract." It first appeared in Gold's anthology, 120 Million *(New York, 1929), and is reprinted here from* New Masses, *May 1929.*

I am tired of this capitalist world. Come, Death!
>   *(He regards his chains)*
Oh, capitalist system, I know you well.
I have heard the prayers of your starving children.
I have heard the groans of your young dying soldiers.
I have seen the agony of strong men hunting for jobs.
I know your crimes, capitalism, I know your crazy houses,
Your jails, factories and hospitals filled with victims!
You are a monster, I hate you,
I am glad to die!
>   *(He drops his head between his arms bitterly)*
They prepare a new world war.
They prepare new slaveries for the masses,
They prepare new jails.
They prepare new frame-ups,
New electric chairs!
>   *(He springs up, he shouts in a red rage:)*
Fiends!
Ghouls!
Assassins of the poor!
Blood-drinkers!
We will have revenge!
Revolution!
Give me a million men,
And I will walk from this jail
And set America free!
>   *(He collapses on the bench. Then in a low voice:)*
Vanzetti, be still.
Be steady, my strong heart.
Truth has ever been your god.
Look into the eyes of Truth now, Vanzetti,
And read your fate.
You are doomed, Vanzetti.
The businessmen thirst for your blood.
The Christians thirst for your blood.
Remember Governor Fuller!
Remember Judge Thayer!
They thirst for workers' blood!
>   *(He leaps up with a bitter cry:)*
Not a scorpion, not a snake,
Not a leprous dog would they have dealt with so!
Murderers!

(He paces a moment, then lifts his fists despairingly)
But my Italy is in the death house, too,
Mussolini is her Judge Thayer,
Her murderer, O my Italy!
(He sits on the bench, looks at a photograph)
They sent me this picture of my native village,
To cheer me in the death house.
O my Italy, it is hard to die!
O my native village, I have never forgotten you,
My father's garden, and my father's vineyards,
And the guitars playing, the mountain boys singing,
The smell of fruit, and the glorious sun on my face,
O my Italy, it is hard to die!
(He kisses the picture, puts it away. He stares into space, his voice is tender)
Now I work in my father's garden again.
It is also so unspeakably beautiful in Italy.
The fig trees are in bloom, the cherry trees, plums, apricots, peaches.
The grape arbors, the potato vines, I can see them all,
And all those dear, humble vegetables of the poor,
The red and yellow peppers, the parsley and onions!
O my Italy, it is hard to die!
(He looks up. His voice is like music)
There were singing birds there:
The black merles, with golden beak,
Their sweet song even more golden,
And the orioles, and the chaffinches,
And the nightingales of Italy,
Most beautiful over all, O nightingales!
(He gazes at the ground, his voice trembles)
And there were nations of flowers, too.
In my father's garden were wild daisies and forget-me-nots.
And blue violets lived there, and the white and red clover,
And other scented, rainbow flowers,
Under the blue sky of my Italy.
(He clasps his hands and speaks with a lover's sorrow)
O Mother Nature, have I not always adored you?
Was I not ever your loving son,
So rich in mind and love I needed no money?

Needing only a roof, a few books, and some comrades,
A crust of bread and Liberty,
And wind and sun, my Mother?
>*(He stands and paces the cell. Then with tragic fierceness:)*
But I loved Humanity more, O my Mother.
The world misery tore at my heart.
In proletarian hells, in jails and factories, I beheld the crucifixion
   of the poor.
And I worked, I preached with all my heart
That the social wealth belong to all,
That Humanity be free,
And this was my crime, O Mother,
For this they locked me here,
To wait for my death,
To wait for my murderers.
>*(He shouts with hate and horror:)*
For Fuller and Thayer!
>*(He paces the cell in passionate silence. It takes him six
>turns of the cell to grow calm. Then he sits, and says in a
>strange, resolute voice:)*
Be calm, Vanzetti.
The price of perfection is a high and sorrowful one,
They will burn your body in the electric chair,
But your ideas will live.
The working class will be free.
Mother Nature whispers it to you.
>*(He speaks mysteriously, a man in a trance)*
The chains are loose, I walk freely out of my cell,
I climb the snow mountains above my native village,
I dive in the stream of living water,
I drink at the cold Alpine springs,
I climb on, and reach the highest peaks,
And see the lands, waters, sky of my Italy!
>*(He rises, he holds his hands forward)*
Farewell, Italy, my native village and beloved folk.
Farewell, crucified working class of the world.
Farewell, sun and wind and sky, and little flowers I have loved.
Farewell, America of many wheels and cruel Christians.
I accept my destiny, O Governor,
America, I accept thy electric chair!

(He then flings his arms backward in the position of one crucified, saying with slow, solemn courage:)
Yes.
Yes.
This is my career and triumph.
If it had not been for this thing,
I might have lived out my life talking at street corners to scornful men.
I might have died unmarked, unknown,
A failure.
Sacco, we are not a failure now.
Comrade, this is our career and triumph,
Never in life could we have hoped
To do such good for the working class
As we do now by dying.
Governor Fuller, take our lives,
Lives of a good shoemaker and poor fish peddler—
That last moment will belong to us—
That last agony is our triumph—
The workers will never forget—
(He flings up his arms and chants solemnly:)
LONG LIVE THE REVOLUTION!

Love on a Garbage Dump

(32ND ATTEMPT AT A SHORT STORY)

CERTAIN ENEMIES have spread the slander that I once attended
Harvard college. This is a lie. I worked on the garbage dump in
Boston, city of Harvard. But that's all.

The Boston dump is a few miles out of town, on an estuary of
the harbor. Imagine a plain 200 acres square, containing no trees

---

*This story poses as well as any the problems Gold had writing fiction
and the problems we have interpreting it: Gold often lacked a clear
sense of the distinction between fiction and autobiographical fact. The
inescapable sense that we are reading fact here is reinforced by the note
Gold appended when the story was first published: "Bourgeois friends
to whom I have related this story cannot believe it. What strikes them
as incredible is the basic fact that I ever worked on a garbage dump.
They can't understand how anyone would choose such a job. Well, I
didn't choose it; it merely happened that I was broke, hungry, without
Boston friends, and desperate for any old job. People get that way, my
fat friends, even in your fat America." But how do we interpret the
non-fact which opens the story, Gold's insistence that he never attended
Harvard? (He was enrolled as a special student in Harvard in the
autumn of 1914.) Was he ashamed of his desire for a college education,
and was he simply lying about it? Certainly he meant to be jocular
when he talked about "enemies" spreading "slander" about him. And
certainly Gold considered the story fiction. On first publication he sub-
titled it "32nd attempt at a short story," and there is little in the story
which is autobiographically exact. Gold did work on the Boston dump
for a week or two, but that was hardly "all" he did in the Boston area.
He was twenty-one or twenty-two at the time, not nineteen. The
characters in the story are more or less fancied; the women especially
are types, not real individuals. But, whatever its confusions as either
fiction or autobiography, this piece remains extremely interesting as
one of the few penetrating things Gold wrote about his troubles after
he became a radical in 1914. (Note that he was an anarchist at the time
of his Boston experience, not a Communist as the conclusion of the
story suggests; the Communist Party had not yet been founded.) New
Masses, December 1928.*

or houses, but blasted and nightmarish like a drawing by Doré, a land of slime and mud, a purgatory.

Hills of rotten fish dot this plain; there are also mountains of rusty tomato cans. The valleys are strewn with weird gardens of many-colored rags, of bottles, cracked mirrors, newspapers, and pillboxes.

Garbage gives off smoke as it decays, also melancholy smells like a zoo. The pervading smoke and odor of the dump made me feel at first as if all America had ended, and was rotting into death. Buzzards lounged in the sky, or hopped about, pecking clumsily at the nation's corpse.

I was young and violent then, and must confess this image of America's extinction filled me with Utopian dreams.

Working on the dump were 30 men, women and pale children. Unfortunate peasants of Italy and Portugal, they sat in sleet and wind on each side of a conveyor.

This moving belt was an endless cornucopia of refuse. As it creaked past them the peasants snatched like magpies at odds and ends of salvage. Bits of machinery, and wearing apparel, rubber goods, etc., were rescued from the general corruption.

Later the Salvation Army and other profiteering ghouls received this salvaged ordure, and resold it to the poorest poor.

I will not be picturesque, and describe the fantastic objects that turned up during a day on this conveyor.

Nor will I tell how the peasants whimsically decorated themselves with neckties, alarm clocks, ribbons, and enema bags, mantillas and other strange objects, so that by the evening some of them resembled futurist Christmas trees.

It was their mode of humor. As I have said, I was too young and violent then to appreciate such humor.

Seeing them at their masquerade, I was sometimes sickened, as if corpses on a battlefield were to rise and dance to patriotic jazz.

I worked in the paper-baling press.

Two Italians stood on a Niagara of old newspapers, and shovelled down newspapers to another worker and myself.

We distributed the tons of newspapers inside a great box eight feet tall. When the box was full, we packed it tight by means of an immense wooden lever from which we hung by our arms. Then we roped up the bales, and wagons hauled them to the boiling vats.

Shovelling newspapers all day, jumping on them, kicking them was not an unpleasant job for one who hated capitalism.

When my muscles ached I would sometimes rest, and pore over muddy scraps of newspaper.

As I meditated on the advice to the lovelorn section, or the *bon mots* of famous columnists, or as I studied the Broadway theater gossip, and the latest news of disarmament, my anger would rise and choke me.

Then I would be glad my job enabled me to trample on these newspapers, to spit upon them and to shovel them contemptuously into great bales meant for the boiling vat.

My working partner was a dark, gloomy man of about fifty, with queer black eyes, a saffron face, and a hawk nose. I thought he was an Italian immigrant, and could speak no English. For the first three months we exchanged no word of conversation, but grunted side by side like truck horses in harness.

One day as I cursed at the newspapers, he muttered in slow but accurate English:

"I would like to kill all them."

"Who?" I asked.

"The editors of garbage," he said, and bent again to his shovel.

So we became friends. After that my days were filled with discussions with this man on the horrors of American civilization.

He was not an Italian, but a Crow Indian, and his white man's name was James Cherry. It is unusual to find an Indian in the eastern cities, but there are a few.

Cherry's story was an odd one. He had been born on a reservation in Montana, and had attended the Carlisle Indian College maintained by the government.

This James Cherry had been gifted with a mind. But the U. S. government has never admitted that Indians have minds. At Carlisle the young students are taught only manual trades. This was Cherry's chief grievance.

James Cherry had graduated as a carpenter, with a hatred of the white government that denied him a real education. After years of brooding his hate turned to a mania. He became firmly convinced that he was a great inventor, who was on the way to inventing a death-ray machine that would kill all the white tyrants.

Cherry had an enormous craving for wholesale murder, he longed for the day when his machine would be perfect enough to wipe out by secret and terrifying means, whole regiments of congressmen, bankers, college presidents, automobile manufacturers, and authors.

I tried to point out to him that this would be of no avail, that other capitalists would rise to take their places. I quoted Marx to this madman, to prove to him our remedy lay in changing the economic system that produced such men. Only by organizing the working class for a final assault on the system could anything be accomplished, I argued.

But he was a fanatic individualist, and our debates were long, furious and without avail.

As well quote Marx to Coolidge as to this Indian whose powerful mind had coiled in upon itself, like a snake in the throes of suicide.

I am always sorry for these mental freaks one meets among the workers. There are many of them. It is the result of the ferocious ideals that are taught them in public school. They are urged to aspire to the Presidency of the United States, they are enabled to read and write, and then, with this dangerous combination of Napoleonic ambition and kindergarten learning, they are shot into factories, mills and mines, to be hopeless wage-slaves for life.

Well balanced intellectuals among the workers become revolutionists. The others become freaks and madmen.

Bill Shean, my sailor friend, who is a connoisseur of such types, once told me of an elderly dishwasher he knew. This man was obsessed with the idea that he was a great orchestral leader.

Every night he would lock himself into his hall bedroom in a cheap rooming house, and turn on a Victrola. Then, with a baton, for hours he would passionately conduct symphonies and operas. If anything displeased him, he would stop the phonograph, and in stern accents, order his orchestra to go back to a certain passage. They did so, of course. These rehearsals went on for fifteen years.

Bill Shean also told me of a shipmate, a giant stoker who went

on a long drunk in Yokohama, and staggered back in two days
with a large butterfly tattooed on his forehead. He had had it
done while drunk. He was a serious person and so humiliated by
this folly, now permanent like the brand of Cain, that he grew
morbid and read books and eventually became a Theosophist.

I was 19 years old, and a fool, and in love with two women.
One was Concha, a Portuguese girl who worked on the garbage
dump, and the other was a New England aristocrat who lived on
Beacon Hill.

I had never seen the latter, nor did I even know her name. To
reach the streetcar from the fat Armenian's rooming house
where I lived, I had to pass along a certain street on Beacon Hill.
At night, returning rankly odorous and sweaty from work, I
passed the same street.

From the window of a beautiful old colonial home on this
street, a girl played Mozart in the dusk. I would linger there and
listen with a beautiful confused aching in my "soul."

Behind the yellow shades, I could see in candlelight the girl's
silhouette as she sat at the piano.

That's all, but I was madly in love with her.

I believed then in two opposing kinds of love, the physical and
the spiritual, and that one was base, and the other noble.

Concha, I knew definitely to my shame, I wanted physically. I
had heard a Portuguese worker boast he had gone home with her
often and stopped with her. This, in my loneliness, inflamed me,
and I wanted her, too.

She spoke little English. She was 18, swarthy, tall and vital, as
handsome as a wildcat. Life burned in her full breasts, and ra-
diated from her rounded hips, legs, arms. She had too much life,
and could not contain it all. She danced, joked, sang, her eyes
sparkled, she was full of dangerous electricity. Concha had not
yet been beaten by the gray years poverty brings the worker. She
was the crazy young clown and melodious lark of our garbage
dump.

She seemed to like me. All the men flirted with her, and Juan,
the boastful young Portuguese, was considered her favored
suitor. But at lunch time, she let me take her behind the tomato can
mountain, and kiss her. This happened many days. It thrilled me
with adolescent joy and pride.

One day I asked her to let me come to her home sometimes like Juan. She smiled mysteriously, and patted her gorgeous blue black hair.

"Maybe yes," she said. "Bimeby, you see it."

Juan grew jealous of me, and I was jealous of him. Once he caught me with Concha behind the tomato cans, and scowled at us and plucked his fierce black moustache.

"Sonofagun!" he said to me. "You take my girl, huh!"

"Ah, go to hell," I said, bravely drunk with "physical love."

The whistle blew just then, and Juan walked sullenly back to work. Concha laughed as if she had enjoyed the joke.

"Juan, he crazy man!" she whispered. "No good man, you come anyway bimeby to my house, next week, maybe."

I cannot tell how marvellous this seemed to me, in my adolescent fever. Concha loved me, evidently. She preferred me to all the other men on the garbage dump. I could not sleep nights thinking about my beautiful Concha. I could scarcely wait.

It was quitting time, and I was stripping off my overalls behind the paper press, when James Cherry glaring about him to make sure no one was listening, confided to me another of his strange, dismal secrets.

"I have just invented a new machine!" he said, his black eyes burning holes in my face. "Listen, this time it's the radio-eye machine! The scientists have been hunting for it, but I have found it! I can turn it on, and penetrate into any house, see everything that is happening all over the world."

"Can you see Queen Mary taking her bath?" I asked casually, to show some interest.

"Certainly, but that is nothing, it is trivial," he whispered. "I can see the Wall Street bankers at their plots. I can see the government stealing the land from the Indians. I can see the white men who murder Negroes. I will bring them to trial! I will tell the truth to everyone!"

"That's fine, Cherry," I said, "keep it up!" I shook his hand and left him among the tons of soiled newspapers, sunk in his Olympian fantasies. In ancient times the madmen among the poor dreamed of revenging their wrongs through God; now they dream in machines.

I hurried home, and washed up. Then I ate at my beanery, and walked slowly toward the North End, sunk in fantasies as crazy as James Cherry's perhaps, but more exquisite.

That noon, behind the tomato cans, Concha had smiled quietly, and said: "Tonight maybe you come by my house." She gave me the address scrawled in a pathetic childish hand on an envelope flap. Now I was on my way there.

It was spring, I was 19 years old, and on the road to my beloved. Every nerve quivered with a foolish delight. I can never forget this all.

She lived in one of those wooden tenement shacks in the North End, near the tavern where Paul Revere mounted for his famous revolutionary ride.

She greeted me at the door with a shy little smile. The rooms were low-ceilinged, stuffy and lit by a kerosene lamp. They were exactly as they must have been in 1850—no modern improvements. An old woman and two children stared dully at me.

"My mamma, my brodder, my seest," said Concha, pointing her hand at them. The old woman looked like a Rembrandt painting in the lamplight. She was wrinkled and sad, and kept staring at me vacantly. The children had Concha's Latin beauty, but were pale and undernourished, and dressed in rags.

And so we sat and stared at each other in gloomy silence. I was embarrassed, and wondered what would happen next.

"Luis! Trinidad!" the old woman spoke sharply to the children, coming out of her stupor at last. They rose and followed her meekly into the bedroom. They shut the door.

Concha smiled then, and came over and sat on my lap.

My heart beat fast, and as I breathed the warm life-smell of her vital body, I felt a shock of joy.

She had decorated herself for my coming. She had rouged her cheeks, and hung pendants from her ears. I was sure she had found them on the garbage dump. The purple silk waist she wore I was also sure came from the dump, and the faded linen tablecloth, and the chromo pictures on the wall.

"You like-a me, boy?" Concha whispered, her burning lips at my ear.

"Yes," I said.

"Me like-a you, too," she said.

We kissed. A long time passed. I could hear the old mother and the children climbing into a creaky bed in the bedroom.

"You gimme dollar, maybe?" Concha said.

"What?"

I was startled.

"Maybe you gimme dollar," Concha repeated painfully. She saw the shocked look on my face, and it hurt her. She began talking very rapidly, earnestly, painfully.

"Me poor. Me make $8 a week. Me pappa he die. Me pappa he sick and die. Me mamma she sick. Me like-a you, no bad girl. Me send brodder, seesta, to the American school-a. Me too much poor. Sabe?"

There was an ache around my heart as I gave her the dollar.

I walked home slowly, heavy with a load of shame. Physical love had betrayed me again. I walked through Boston streets, glamorous with May, and darkness, and lights and sounds, and cursed myself, and cursed my evil doggy nature.

It had all ended in cheapness. She had done it just for the dollar, not for love, my proud wildcat beauty! My God, would I ever escape from the garbage dump of America!

Almost automatically, my feet led me to the street on aristocratic Beacon Hill. The other girl was still playing Mozart from the window. I leaned against a railing, and listened to the pure, bright flow with a breaking heart. What a contrast!

This was the world of spiritual beauty, of music, and art, and ethereal love, and I, the proletarian, could never enter it. My destiny was evident; I would die like a stinking old dog on a garbage dump.

I wanted to cry for yearning and self-pity. I was ready to give up the endless futile struggle for a living. I grew weak and cowardly, and wanted to die.

And then a policeman broke this evil spell. He loomed up out of the mysterious spring night, and poked me in the ribs with his club.

"Move on, bum," he said, "bums have got no business hanging around this part of town."

Of course I moved on, and proletarian anger boiled up in my deeps, beneficent anger, beautiful anger to save me from mushy self-pity, harsh, strong, clean anger like the gales at sea.

As I walked along the Esplanade by the Charles River, everything straightened itself out again in my head, and I came back to the strong proletarian realities.

"Mozart and candlelight and the spiritual values, to hell with you all!" I thought. "You are parasites, Concha is the one who pays for you! It's more honorable to work on a garbage dump than to be a soulful parasite on Beacon Hill.

"If Concha needed a dollar, she had a right to ask for it! It is that lazy, useless, parasite who plays Mozart who forced Concha so low!" Then unlike James Cherry, I dreamed angrily of a great movement to set the working class free. I walked home in double-quick time, in my fantasy a young Communist marching to the barricades.

Go Left, Young Writers!

LITERATURE is one of the products of a civilization like steel or textiles. It is not a child of eternity, but of time. It is always the mirror of its age. It is not any more mystic in its origin than a ham sandwich.

It is easy to understand the lacquer of cynicism, smartness and ritzy sophistication with which popular American writing is now coated. This is a product of "our" sudden prosperity, the gesture of our immense group of *nouveau riches*.

The epic melancholy of Dreiser, the romantic democracy of Carl Sandburg, the social experimentation of Frank Norris, Stephen Crane, Mark Twain, Edgar Lee Masters and other men of the earlier decades, is as dead as the Indian's Manitou.

We are living in another day. It is dominated by a hard, successful, ignorant jazzy bourgeois of about thirty-five, and his leech-like young wife.

Just as European tours, night clubs, Florida beaches and streamline cars have been invented for this class, just so literature is being produced for them. They have begun to have time, and now read books occasionally to fill in the idle moments between cocktail parties.

They need novels that will take the place of the old fashioned etiquette books to teach them how to spend their money smartly.

Ernest Hemingway is one of the caterers to this demand.

The liberals have become disheartened and demoralized under the strain of American prosperity. Are there any liberals left in America? I doubt it. The *Nation* was the last organ of the liberals in this country. It has been swinging right in the last few years. When it surrendered itself body and soul to Tammany Hall in the last campaign, I think it performed a logical suicide.

This editorial article is a summary of the progress of the New Masses *after Gold became editor in May 1928, and of the new principles by which he guided the magazine.* New Masses, *January 1929.*

Its editorials now read like the New York *World*. Its book reviews and dramatic criticisms are no different in viewpoint from those in New York *Times* or *Tribune*. In fact the same group of writers fill the columns of both liberal and conservative press, and no one can detect the difference.

There isn't any difference.

There isn't a centrist liberal party in our politics any more, or in our literature. There is an immense overwhelming, right wing which accepts the American religion of "prosperity." The conservatives accept it joyfully, the liberals "soulfully." But both accept it.

There is also a left wing, led in politics by the Communists, and in literature by the *New Masses*. Will someone inform us if there is something vital between these two extremes of right and left?

This is in some ways a depressing situation. Can there be a battle between such unequal forces? Will it not rather be a massacre of a lion carelessly crushing the rabbit that has crossed his path?

No. The great mass of America is not "prosperous" and it is not being represented in the current politics of literature. There are at least forty million people who are the real America.

They are Negroes, immigrants, poor farmers and city proletarians and they live in the same holes they did ten years ago. Upon their shoulders the whole gaudy show palace rests. When they stir it will and must fall.

It was the same in Rome, in France, in Russia; it is the same here.

Let us never be dazzled by appearances. The American orgy has been pitched on the crater of the historic social volcano.

This volcano is as certain to erupt eventually as is Mount Etna.

By default, the liberals have presented us writers and revolutionists of the left wing with a monopoly on the basic American mass. We have a wonderful virgin field to explore; titanic opportunities for creative work.

Let us be large, heroic and self-confident at our task.

The best and newest thing a young writer can now do in America, if he has the vigor and the guts, is to go leftward. If he gets tangled up in the other thing he will make some money, maybe, but he will lose everything else. Neither the *Saturday Evening Post* or the *Nation* can any longer nourish the free heroic soul. Try it and see.

When I say "go leftward," I don't mean the temperamental bohemian left, the stale old Paris posing, the professional poetizing, etc. No, the real thing; a knowledge of working-class life in America gained from first-hand contacts, and a hard precise philosophy of 1929 based on economics, not verbalisms.

The old *Masses* was a more brilliant but a more upper class affair. The *New Masses* is working in a different field. It goes after a kind of flesh and blood reality, however crude, instead of the smooth perfect thing that is found in books.

The America of the working class is practically undiscovered. It is like a lost continent. Bits of it come above the surface in our literature occasionally and everyone is amazed. But there is no need yet of going to Africa or the Orient for strange new pioneering. The young writer can find all the primitive material he needs working as a wage slave around the cities and prairies of America.

In the past eight months the *New Masses* has been slowly finding its path toward the goal of a proletarian literature in America. A new writer has been appearing; a wild youth of about twenty-two, the son of working-class parents, who himself works in the lumber camps, coal mines, and steel mills, harvest fields and mountain camps of America. He is sensitive and impatient. He writes in jets of exasperated feeling and has no time to polish his work. He is violent and sentimental by turns. He lacks self confidence but writes because he must—and because he has a real talent.

He is a Red but has few theories. It is all instinct with him. His writing is no conscious straining after proletarian art, but the natural flower of his environment. He writes that way because it is the only way for him. His "spiritual" attitudes are all mixed up with tenements, factories, lumber camps and steel mills, because that is his life. He knows it in the same way that one of Professor Baker's students know the six different ways of ending a first act.

A Jack London or a Walt Whitman will come out of this new crop of young workers who write in the *New Masses*. Let us not be too timid or too modest in our judgments. This is a fact. Keene Wallis, for instance, an ex-harvest worker and I.W.W., will take Carl Sandburg's place in five years. Why ought one to hesitate about stating such a conviction?

The *New Masses,* by some miracle, has gotten out eight issues under the present management, after the magazine had been declared bankrupt, and was about to suspend. We have received no subsidies; we have earned our way.

We can announce now that another year is certain. We feel that year will be fruitful, and may see further clarification of our groping experiment.

Once more we appeal to our readers:

Do not be passive. Write. Your life in mine, mill and farm is of deathless significance in the history of the world. Tell us about it in the same language you use in writing a letter. It may be literature—it often is. Write. Persist. Struggle.

A Letter From a Clam Digger

I HAVE been down with my old Tampico malaria. I am convalescing now; am swimming, sunbathing, walking, eating, fishing, etc., getting back to shape. One can not expect thoughts on politics of literature from a man living this way. He is a sort of happy bonehead to whom nothing matters—not even that Ramsay and Herbert are cooking up, a la Woodrow, the next pious, liberalistic and pacifistic World War.

Nothing is important here on Staten Island but the way the bluefish and whiting are nibbling, and the nightly pot of clam chowder. There is an old beachcomber here who lives all year in a shack on the beach. The shack is about as big as a cell in the Tombs. It contains a cot, a chair, an oil stove, and a box of worms, some oars, nets, and fishing poles. The walls are pasted with pictures of semi-nude chorus girls out of the rotogravures. Old Gus digs worms for bait and sells them to fishermen. He is full of bootleg and sits comfortably reminiscing about his youth as a sailor, bartender, circus man, and cook.

How in hell do you expect me to think of literature when all this is going on around me?

Most radical magazines have a political group behind them, or a wealthy angel. We have neither. But the magazine goes on and even grows. How? Ten and twelve hours a day and more, and no salary for five or six months. No one is paid a nickel for work—editors, artists, writers, etc. They are a united and enthusiastic group. It is just a miracle of hard work and sincere conviction.

The subject of this anti-review is The New American Caravan *(1929), an anthology of recent American writing, edited by Alfred Kreymbourg, Lewis Mumford, and Paul Rosenfeld. Like "Thoughts of a Great Thinker," reprinted above, this piece shows Gold at his gayest, admittedly avoiding the responsibilities at hand and talking quite at random about whatever popped into his head. The "Walt" addressed in this letter was Walt Carmen who was managing editor of the* New Masses *at the time. Gastonia, N.C., was the scene of a fiercely suppressed textile strike.* New Masses, *November 1929.*

Nothing like this is happening in fat America today. There is not another literary magazine that is being run for convictions and not for money. The *New Masses* has begun to have as much significance for its time as the old *Masses* in its best days.

I have read some of the recent letters of comment on the magazine. The readers seem to feel the paper is important. It does not matter that our circulation and advertising are not yet up to the *Saturday Evening Post*. Literariously and financially speaking, we must appear like a lot of hoboes to the Brisbanes and G. H. Lorimers of the great world. But to hell with the bassdrums.

The workers are coming up in Europe and Asia. What the workers think and do is something the bourgeoisie there have to worry about—even the bourgeois writers. The literature of the future belongs to the workers. This is nothing to argue about any longer. It is clear to the social student. The old crowd have simply nothing left to write about—nothing—except the stale old bedroom triangular farces and tragedies. They will do this for years, until it all ends in Kraft-Ebbing. Meanwhile there appear hundreds like Panait Istrati, Agnes Smedley, I. Babel, etc., in every land; young graduates of the class struggle. Simply, they tell about the working-class life. They do not adorn, stylize or pose; they put down the facts. And it is literature; it is art; it is the new and creative thing in the world.

Our labors are worthwhile. The *New Masses* happens to be one magazine in this country that is headed for some place. We need no literary manifestoes; we are. We speak for the submerged nation within the nation. We may commit a thousand crudities, puerilities and crimes against so-called good taste; but in ten years these flounderings may look like the dawn of a new kind of American writing.

I know it. And I am sure the other writing counts less in the scheme of things than my present attempts to fool the snappers and tomcods with a hook. It is just a way of passing the time.

I received *The New American Caravan* to review. I can't do it. It is worth reviewing, because it shows so clearly where another group of "avantgarde" American writers are heading.

I glanced through the pages and read some of the contributions. It is expert writing. But it gives one the weary blues. It is all as solemn and pompous as Joseph Wood Krutch. If a clam were literary it might write this way. This is not the anthology of any kind of revolt. It is just a mournful yipping in the desert. Nothing challenging, clearcut. A kind of insipid mysticizing over obscure and petty sorrows. Lots of splendid words, phrases, sentences. But no point. This is not America or life. It smells to me like the old, familiar, academic, literary introversion. Maybe I'm wrong. The book should be tried on someone else. I simply can't understand this sort of thing any more. I am getting older. I want only plain food and the plain and eternal emotions.

I am through, I guess, with the form-searchers. The movies make these painful, intricate wrenchings for a new literary technique seem small. In two or three flashes the movie can beat every one of the literary stunts of subconscious writing, simultaneity, contrast, etc., etc. To hold its own, literature will have to become simple again, realistic and socially valuable. Writers will have to find universal themes like the great historians or movie directors.

Individual tremors, lyricisms, emotions, eccentricities, will have to be merged into a large objective pattern. No, this does not mean a dead level of writing. It means a new kind of genius in writing.

New forms without a new content seem as worthless to me as walnut shells whose meat the little bugs have gnawed away.

In biology it is need that creates form, function that creates form. These "moderns" seem to have no function. I repeat, I can't get them. I suspect they are merely passing the time. I prefer fishing.

I think this letter will make you impatient. Like other comrades in the labor movement, you love literature, but dislike all kinds of shop-talk about technique. I think some of it necessary in the *New Masses,* however. Proletarian writers have no tradition to work by, as have the others. We must thrash out our problems as we go along. The *New Masses* is the one magazine in English where it can be done. This is part of its function, I think.

Now I will close this wandering letter. I feel I am on the sidelines down here. I feel guilty about loafing when so many of our people are in hell in Gastonia and other places. But a man with malaria has to loaf; he's good for nothing else. I found a few gray hairs today, Walt. My God, I thought, past thirty and still broke. Then I remembered Upton Sinclair and felt better. Though I disagree with him on almost everything, I admire him more each year. He is fifty, and has remained a Socialist writer for thirty years in capitalist America.

No one who hasn't put his sweat, gall, blood and fury into a piece of unpopular writing, while wondering at the same time how the room rent would be paid, can understand the drama of a proletarian writer's role.

But thousands of Jimmy Higginses endure as much in this prosperous country, and it will all mean something in the long run. It is certainly preferable to being a white slave for the editor of "big" magazines, or a coocoo "artist."

So long. I will send you in a mess of clams and whiting if the tide is right. Regards to the gang.

MIKE GOLD

P.S.—I read some more into the *Caravan* last night. William Rollins has a good character study of an American college freshman—a little precious, however. Joseph Vogel has a picture of a Jewish wedding that could have been a glorious farce, but got lost among the interstellar spaces of "Art." A good try. Then I read Yvor Winters' long critical article on poetry. This was too much, and I quit for the night. What pomposity! The kid writes on poetry like a sixty-five year old professor with prostate troubles. As my friend Bill Sheehan would say, he needs a dose of salts. And such are the revoltees, college professors out of regular jobs.

Trotsky's Pride

ONE POINT that struck me in Trotsky's autobiography. What Luciferian pride in every line! What thinly veiled contempt for "man, that malicious animal," as one of his phrases has it. Trotsky is another Lasalle; he is not another Marx or Lenin. He is a literary genius, he is an organizing genius, he performed great miracles during the harshest days of the Revolution. But he is also a bureaucrat and embryo Napoleon.

Every line in his brilliant book breathes the dangerous spirit of a man of destiny.

Trotsky's fall is one of the romantic tragedies of history. I, for one, can shed no tears for him; I care for something greater than Trotsky's fate; the proletarian revolution. He has chosen to endanger this revolution. Every bourgeois liberal in America and the rest of the world is now a Trotskyite, and uses his book as an argument against all the Russian Revolution. This may not be what Trotsky intended, but it is the total effect of his opposition so far.

Trotsky is too convinced that he is a great man. The world has been poisoned by such "great men." Trotsky writes of the revolution as a chess player might, or a general. He has no feeling for the pathos, the poetry and human beauty of the proletarian masses. Compare his pages on the Bolshevik uprising with John Reed's *Ten Days That Shook the World*.

Trotsky writes of telephones, manifestoes, and maneuvers. Reed tells of these, but gives us, too, the epic heroism and passion of the simple masses.

Intellectual pride; this is Trotsky's chief sin. He is always sure that he is right. But any worker could tell him why he now is

---

These observations are excerpted from Gold's editorial column, "Notes of the Month," in the New Masses *for June 1930. The balance of criticism and respect which Gold expressed here bears comparison with his adulation of Trotsky in "America Needs a Critic" (1926), and his damnation in the "renegades" chapter of* The Hollow Men *(1941) and in "The Storm Over Maltz" (1946).*

wrong. In a strike, one does not go out scabbing because one disagrees with one's comrades. The objective effect of Trotsky's labors today may be compared to this, whatever his motives.

No one wants to jeer at Trotsky. No one really can. Trotsky is now an immortal part of the great Russian Revolution. He is surely one of the permanent legends of humanity, like Savonarola or Danton. For good or evil, he will never be forgotten.

But there are no supermen. All men are fallible. Trotsky has been wrong at various times in the past. It seems to me he is grievously, dangerously wrong at the present hour.

Trotskyites like to sneer at anyone who dares to say this. The inference is everyone else is too stupid, too mediocre, too misled to attempt to criticize Trotsky. I hate this snob attitude in both Trotsky and his followers.

Every worker has the right, and has the duty, to criticize and even kick out his leaders when necessary. The worker may be wrong at different times, but it is better that a few leaders should suffer occasionally, than that the masses should be betrayed.

No one should follow any leader blindly. No, there are decidedly no supermen in the world as yet.

I have read Trotsky's manifestoes in the past few years, and the Trotskyite press. I have tried sincerely to understand, but can find nothing but a bitter and narrow partisanship—nothing basic or constructive there.

The bulk of Trotskyist thought today consists of personal abuse and hatred of the Communist leadership in every land. This is not a program of any kind.

Trotskyite tactics seem to consist of nothing but endless criticism of the mistakes and shortcomings of Communism. This, too, is not a program. There are no straight lines in history. Mistakes and experiments must be made. There is no easy road to world Communism. "Deviations" are sure to occur.

Trotskyism has degenerated into a kind of cheap cat-calling from the gallery. The working class is fighting for its life on every front and the Trotskyites stand by and sneer when it slips or retreats at necessary times.

Can any honest Trotskyite tell us that every deed, every thought of their group at present is not devoted to anything but a program of blind obstruction?

They are separated from the main stream of history. They have become a sect. It is hard to differentiate the objective value of their propaganda from that of Kerensky's. In every page of Trotsky's book, in every line of the Trotskyite press, only one dogma is hammered home to the reader: that the Russian Revolution is a failure: that there is a reaction in Soviet Russia. Emma Goldman was exactly as bigoted.

Every day brings news of some new advance toward Communism in Russia. Every day brings its demonstration that the Soviet masses are awake, alive, aflame with deathless revolutionary ardor.

No Trotskyite can deny that the Five-Year Plan is as great a social miracle as the military uprising.

But no Trotskyite will admit that *anything* is sound in Soviet Russia. What a tragic decadence in a man as great as Trotsky, what a loss to the Revolution! Personal passion has at last grown like a cataract over the eyes of one who was an eagle, and could stare into the core of the fiery sun of revolution. Blind!

Wilder: Prophet of the Genteel Christ

"Here's a group of people losing sleep over a host of notions that the rest of the world has outgrown several centuries ago: one duchess's right to enter a door before another; the word order in a dogma of the Church; the divine right of Kings, especially of Bourbons."

In these words Thornton Wilder describes the people in his first book, *The Cabala*. They are some eccentric old aristocrats in Rome, seen through the eyes of a typical American art "pansy" who is there as a student.

Marcantonio is the sixteen-year-old son of one of the group; he is burned out with sex and idleness, and sexualizes with his sister, and then commits suicide. Another character is a beautiful, mad Princess, who hates her dull Italian husband, falls in love with many Nordics and is regularly rejected by them. Others are a moldy old aristocrat woman who "believes," and a moldy old Cardinal who doesn't, and some other fine worm-eaten authentic specimens of the rare old Italian antique.

Wilder views these people with tender irony. He makes no

Gold had never read a word of Thornton Wilder before Edmund Wilson put him up to this job of reviewing half a dozen of Wilder's books in the New Republic. *In the consequent "Gold-Wilder controversy," Wilson remained one of Gold's few level-headed and cordial critics. After scandalized and vitriolic letters began deluging the magazine, Wilson published an unsigned editorial (November 26, 1930) in which he carefully appreciated the strengths and limitations of what he called Gold's "economic" interpretation of literature. Wilson asked, "Does not the outcry which Mr. Gold has provoked prove the insipidity and pointlessness of most of our criticism?" A year and a half later Wilson reviewed the affair in historical perspective in a two part article in the* New Republic *(May 4 and 11, 1932), and he reflected: "There is no question that the Gold-Wilder row marked definitely the eruption of the Marxist issues out of the literary circles of the radicals into the field of general criticism. After that, it became very plain that the economic crisis was to be accompanied by a literary one."* New Republic, *October 22, 1930.*

claim as to their usefulness to the world that feeds them; yet he hints that their palace mustiness is a most important fact in the world of today. He writes with a brooding seriousness of them as if all the gods were watching their little lavender tragedies. The style is a diluted Henry James.

Wilder's second novel was *The Bridge of San Luis Rey*. This famous and vastly popular yarn made a bold leap backward in time. Mr. Wilder, by then, had evidently completed his appraisal of our own age. The scene is laid in Lima, Peru; the time is Friday noon, July 20, 1714. In this volume Wilder perfected the style which is now probably permanent with him; the diluted and veritable Anatole France.

Among the characters of San Luis Rey are: (1) a sweet old duchess who loves her grown daughter to madness, but is not loved in return; (2) a beautiful unfortunate genius of an actress who after much sexualizing turns nun; (3) her tutor, a jolly old rogue, but a true worshipper of literature; (4) two strange brothers who love each other with a passion and delicacy that again brings the homosexual bouquet into a Wilder book, and a few other minor sufferers.

Some of the characters in this novel die in the fall of a Bridge. Our author points out the spiritual lessons imbedded in this Accident; viz: that God is Love.

The third novel is the recent *The Woman of Andros*. This marks a still further masterly retreat into time and space. The scene is one of the lesser Greek Islands, the hour somewhere in B.C.

The fable: a group of young Greeks spend their evenings in alternate sexual bouts and lofty Attic conversations with the last of the Aspasias. One young man falls in love with her sister, who is "pure." His father objects. Fortunately, the Aspasia dies. The father relents. But then the sister dies, too. Wistful futility and sweet soft sadness of Life. Hints of the coming of Christ: "and in the East the stars shone tranquilly down upon the land that was soon to be called Holy and that even then was preparing its precious burden" (Palestine).

Then Mr. Wilder has published some pretty, tinkling, little three-minute playlets. These are on the most erudite and esoteric themes one could ever imagine; all about Angels, and Mozart, and King Louis, and Fairies, and a Girl of the Renaissance, and a whimsical old Actress (1780) and her old Lover; Childe Harold to the Dark Tower Came; Prosperina and the Devil; The Flight into Egypt; a Venetian Prince and a Mermaid; Shelley, Judgment Day, Centaurs, God, The Woman in the Chlamys, Christ; Brigomeide, Leviathan, Ibsen; every waxwork in Wells's Outline, in fact, except Buffalo Bill.

And this, to date, is the garden cultivated by Mr. Thornton Wilder. It is a museum, it is not a world. In this devitalized air move the wan ghosts he has called up, each in "romantic" costume. It is an historic junkshop over which our author presides.

Here one will not find the heroic archaeology of a Walter Scott or Eugene Sue. Those men had social passions, and used the past as a weapon to affect the present and future. Scott was the poet of feudalism. The past was a glorious myth he created to influence the bourgeois anti-feudal present. Eugene Sue was the poet of the proletariat. On every page of history he traced the bitter, neglected facts of the working-class martyrdom. He wove these into an epic melodrama to strengthen the heart and hand of the revolutionary workers, to inspire them with a proud consciousness of their historic mission.

That is how the past should be used; as rich manure, as a springboard, as a battle cry, as a deepening, clarifying and sublimation of the struggles in the too-immediate present. But Mr. Wilder is the poet of the genteel bourgeoisie. They fear any such disturbing lessons out of the past. Their goal is comfort and status quo. Hence, the vapidity of these little readings in history.

Mr. Wilder, in a foreword to his book of little plays, tells himself and us the object of his esthetic striving:

> I hope through many mistakes, to discover that spirit that is not unequal to the elevation of the great religious themes, yet which does not fall into a repellent didacticism. Didacticism is an attempt at the coercion of another's free mind, even though one knows that in these matters beyond logic, beauty is the only persuasion. Here the schoolmaster enters again. He sees all that is fairest in the Christian tradition made repugnant to the new generations by reason of the diction in which it is expressed. . . . So that the revival of religion is almost a matter of rhetoric. The work is difficult, perhaps impossible (perhaps all religions die out with the exhaustion of the language), but it at least reminds us that Our Lord asked us in His work to be not only gentle as doves, but as wise as serpents.

Mr. Wilder wishes to restore, he says, through Beauty and Rhetoric, the Spirit of Religion in American Literature. One can respect any writer in America who sets himself a goal higher than the usual racketeering. But what is this religious spirit Mr. Wilder aims to restore? Is it the crude self-torture of the Holy Rollers, or the brimstone howls and fears of the Baptists, or even the mad, titanic sincerities and delusions of a Tolstoy or Dostoyevsky?

No, it is that newly fashionable literary religion that centers around Jesus Christ, the First British Gentleman. It is a pastel, pastiche, dilettante religion, without the true neurotic blood and fire, a daydream of homosexual figures in graceful gowns moving archaically among the lilies. It is Anglo-Catholicism, that last refuge of the American literary snob.

This genteel spirit of the new parlor-Christianity pervades every phrase of Mr. Wilder's rhetoric. What gentle theatrical sighs! what lovely, well composed deaths and martyrdoms! what languishings and flutterings of God's sinning doves! what little jewels of Sunday-school wisdom, distributed modestly here and there through the softly flowing narrative like delicate pearls, diamonds and rubies on the costume of a meek, wronged Princess gracefully drowning herself for love (if my image is clear).

Wilder has concocted a synthesis of all the chambermaid literature, Sunday-school tracts and boulevard piety there ever were. He has added a dash of the prep-school teacher's erudition, then embalmed all this in the speciously glamorous style of the late Anatole France. He talks much of art, of himself as Artist, of style. He is a very conscious craftsman. But his is the most irritating and pretentious style pattern I have read in years. It has the slick, smug finality of the lesser Latins; that shallow clarity and tight little good taste that remind one of nothing so much as the conversation and practice of a veteran *cocotte*.

Mr. Wilder strains to be spiritual; but who could reveal any real agonies and exaltations of spirit in this neat, tailor-made rhetoric? It is a great lie. It is Death. Its serenity is that of the corpse. Prick it, and it will bleed violet ink and *aperitif*. It is false to the great stormy music of Anglo-Saxon speech. Shakespeare is crude and disorderly beside Mr. Wilder. Neither Milton, Fielding, Burns, Blake, Byron, Chaucer nor Hardy could ever receive a passing mark in Mr. Wilder's classroom of style.

And this is the style with which to express America? Is this the speech of a pioneer continent? Will this discreet French drawing room hold all the blood, horror and hope of the world's new empire? Is this the language of the intoxicated Emerson? Or the clean, rugged Thoreau, or vast Whitman? Where are the modern streets of New York, Chicago and New Orleans in these little novels? Where are the cotton mills, the murder of Ella May and her songs? Where are the child slaves of the beet fields? Where are the stockbroker suicides, the labor racketeers or passion and death of the coal miners? Where are Babbitt, Jimmy Higgins and Anita Loos's Blonde? Is Mr. Wilder a Swede or a Greek, or is he an American? No stranger would know from these books he has written.

But is it right to demand this "nativism" of him? Yes, for Mr. Wilder has offered himself as a spiritual teacher; therefore one may say: Father, what are your lessons? How will your teaching help the "spirit" trapped in American capitalism? But Wilder takes refuge in the rootless cosmopolitanism which marks every *emigre* trying to flee the problems of his community. Internationalism is a totally different spirit. It begins at home. Mr. Wilder speaks much of the "human heart" and its eternal problems. It is with these, he would have us believe, that he concerns himself; and they are the same in any time and geography, he says. Another banal evasion. For the human heart, as he probes it in Greece, Peru, Italy and other remote places, is only the "heart" of a small futile group with whom few Americans have the faintest kinship.

For to repeat, Mr. Wilder remains the poet of a small sophisticated class that has recently arisen in America—our genteel bourgeoisie. His style is their style; it is the new fashion. Their women have taken to wearing his Greek chlamys and faintly indulge themselves in his smart Victorian pieties. Their men are at ease in his Paris and Rome.

America won the War. The world's wealth flowed into it like a red Mississippi. The newest and greatest of all leisure classes was created. Luxury hotels, golf, old furniture and Vanity Fair sophistication were some of their expressions.

Thorstein Veblen foretold all this in 1899, in an epoch-making book that every American critic ought to study like a Bible. In *The Theory of the Leisure Class* he painted the hopeless course of most American culture for the next three decades. The grim, ironic prophet has been justified. Thornton Wilder is the perfect flower of the new prosperity. He has all the virtues Veblen said this leisure class would demand; the air of good breeding, the decorum, priestliness, glossy high finish as against intrinsic qualities, conspicuous inutility, caste feeling, love of the archaic, etc. . . .

All this is needed to help the parvenu class forget its lowly origins in American industrialism. It yields them a short cut to the aristocratic emotions. It disguises the barbaric sources of their income, the billions wrung from American workers and foreign peasants and coolies. It lets them feel spiritually worthy of that income.

Babbitt made them ashamed of being crude American climbers. Mr. Wilder, "gentle as the dove and wise as the serpent," is a more constructive teacher. Taking them patiently by the hand, he leads them into castles, palaces and far-off Greek islands, where they may study the human heart when it is nourished by blue blood. This Emily Post of culture will never reproach them; or remind them of Pittsburgh or the breadlines. He is always in perfect taste; he is the personal friend of Gene Tunney.

"For there is a land of the living and a land of the dead, and the bridge is love, the only survival, the only meaning." And nobody works in a Ford plant, and nobody starves looking for work, and there is nothing but Love in God's ancient Peru, Italy, Greece, if not in God's capitalist America 1930!

Let Mr. Wilder write a book about modern America. We predict it will reveal all his fundamental silliness and superficiality, now hidden under a Greek chlamys.

Proletarian Realism

LABOR MAY lose all the battles, but it will win the class war. Labor has seemed to lose every battle, every strike and frameup for the past hundred years, and yet today there is a Soviet Russia, a nascent Soviet China, a great international labor movement. Labor is doggedly and surely winning its great war for the management of the world.

Every day this is evidenced, too, on the cultural front. It is difficult for the bourgeois intellectuals to understand or acknowledge this. One of their favorite superstitions is that culture is always the product of a few divinely-ordained individuals, operating in a social vacuum.

We know and assert that culture is a social product; as bees who feed upon sumach or buckwheat produce honey of those flavors, so will the individuals living within a specific social environment give off an inevitably flavored culture.

It could not be otherwise. Who could expect a Walt Whitman at the court of Louis the Fourteenth? Who, among the cacophonies and tensions of a modern industrial city, would ask a musician to originate bland gavottes and minuets?

But the intellectuals sneer at the idea of a proletarian literature. They will acknowledge the possibility of nationalist cultures; but they have not reached the understanding that the national idea is dying, and that the class ideologies are alone real in the world today.

I believe I was the first writer in America to herald the advent of a world proletarian literature as a concomitant to the rise of the world proletariat. This was in an article published in the *Lib-*

These comments on the theory of proletarian literature are a rationalization and codification of the views Gold published a decade earlier in the manifesto, "Towards Proletarian Art," reprinted above. They are excerpted from his editorial "Notes of the Month" (New Masses, September, 1930), where they followed a discussion of recent set-backs suffered by the American labor movement. In the original, these paragraphs bore no distinguishing title.

erator in 1921, called, "Towards Proletarian Art." Mine was a rather mystic and intuitive approach; nothing had yet been published in English on this theme; the idea was not yet in the air, as it is today; I was feeling my way.

But the little path has since become a highroad. Despite the bourgeois ultra-leftism of Trotsky in his *Literature and Revolution,* where he predicts there will not be time enough to develop a proletarian literature, this greatest and most universal of literary schools is now sweeping across the world.

One would not want a better text for a survey of the new movement than this paragraph from the conservative *Japan Magazine* on the situation in Japan.

It appears that the greatest demand for the year was for proletarian literature, due perhaps to the excitement over the arrest of so many youths and maidens for being guilty of dangerous thought. The result is that henceforth there will be a more clearly marked distinction between the writers of this school and authors in general.

In North China there is the powerful Owl Society, with a string of newspapers, magazines, bookshops and publishing houses, all devoted to the spread of proletarian literature.

Thousands of books and articles on the theories of proletarian literature have been published in Soviet Russia, in Germany, Japan, China, France, England, and other countries. There is not a language in the world today in which a vigorous bold youth is not experimenting with the materials of proletarian literature. It is a world phenomenon; and it grows, changes, criticizes itself, expands without the blessing of all the official mandarins and play-actor iconoclasts and psalm-singing Humanists of the moribund bourgeois culture. It does not need them any longer; it will soon boot them into their final resting places in the museum.

No, the bourgeois intellectuals tell us, there can be no such thing as a proletarian literature. We answer briefly: There *is.* Then they say, it is mediocre; where is your Shakespeare? And we answer: Wait ten years more. He is on his way. We gave you a Lenin; we will give you a proletarian Shakespeare, too; if that is so important.

To us the culture of the world's millions is more important; the soil must be prepared; we know our tree is sound; we are sure of the fruit: we promise you a hundred Shakespeares.

We have only one magazine in America, the *New Masses*, dedicated to proletarian literature. And there is no publishing house of standing and intelligent direction to help clarify the issues. Nearest is the International Publishers perhaps, but this house devotes itself solely to a rather academic approach to economics and makes little attempt to influence either the popular mind or our intellectuals. It is as stodgy and unenterprising, in a Communist way, as the Yale University Press, and similar organizations.

If there were a live publishing house here, such as the *Cenit* of Madrid, for instance, it could issue a series of translations of proletarian novels, poetry, criticism that might astound some of our intellectuals. There would be a clarification, too, for some of our own adherents.

For proletarian literature is a living thing. It is not based on a set of fixed dogmas, anymore than is Communism or the science of biology.

Churches are built on dogma. The Catholic Church is the classic illustration of how the rule of dogma operates. Here is a great mass political and business movement that hypnotizes its victims with a set of weird formulas of magic which must not be tested or examined but must be swallowed with faith.

In Marxism or any other science there is no dogma; there are laws which have been discovered running through the phenomena of nature. These laws must not be taken on faith. They are the result of experiment and statistics, and they are meant to be tested daily. If they fail to work, they can be discarded; they are constantly being discarded.

The law of class struggle is a Marxian discovery that has been tested, and that works, and that gives one a major clue to the movements of man in the mass.

In proletarian literature, there are several laws which seem to be demonstrable. One of them is that all culture is the reflection of a specific class society. Another is, that bourgeois culture is in process of decay, just as bourgeois society is in a swift decline.

The class that will inherit the world will be the proletariat, and every indication points inevitably to the law that this proletarian society will, like its predecessors, create its own culture.

This we can be sure of; upon this we all agree. Proletarian literature will reflect the struggle of the workers in their fight for the world. It portrays the life of the workers; not as do the vulgar

French populists and American jazzmaniacs, but with a clear revolutionary point; otherwise it is meaningless, merely a new *frisson.*

Within this new world of proletarian literature, there are many living forms. It is dogmatic folly to seize upon any single literature form and erect it into a pattern for all proletarian literature.

The Russian Futurists, tried to do this; they held the stage for a while, but are rapidly being supplanted.

My belief is that a new form is evolving, which one might name "Proletarian Realism." Here are some of its elements, as I see them:

1.

Because the Workers are skilled machinists, sailors, farmers and weavers, the proletarian writer must describe their work with technical precision. The Workers will scorn any vague fumbling poetry, much as they would scorn a sloppy workman. Hemingway and others have had the intuition to incorporate this proletarian element into their work, but have used it for the *frisson,* the way some actors try to imitate gangsters of men. These writers build a machine, it functions, but it produces nothing; it has not been planned to produce anything; it is only an adult toy.

2.

Proletarian realism deals with the *real conflicts* of men and women who work for a living. It has nothing to do with the sickly mental states of the idle Bohemians, their subtleties, their sentimentalities, their fine-spun affairs. The worst example and the best of what we do not want to do is the spectacle of Proust, master-masturbator of the bourgeois literature. We know the suffering of hungry, persecuted and heroic millions is enough of a theme for anyone, without inventing these precious silly little agonies.

3.

Proletarian realism is never pointless. It does not believe in literature for its own sake, but in literature that is useful, has a social function. Every major writer has always done this in the past; but it is necessary to fight the battle constantly, for there are more intellectuals than ever who are trying to make literature a plaything. Every poem, every novel and drama, must have a social theme, or it is merely confectionery.

4.

As few words as possible. We are not interested in the verbal acrobats—this is only another form for bourgeois idleness. The Workers live too close to reality to care about these literary show-offs, these verbalist heroes.

5.

To have the courage of the proletarian experience. This was the chief point of my "mystic" essay in 1921; let us proletarians write with the courage of our own experience. I mean, if one is a tanner and writer, let one dare to write the drama of a tannery; or of a clothing shop, or of a ditch-digger's life, or of a hobo. Let the bourgeois writers tell us about their spiritual drunkards and super-refined Parisian emigres; or about their spiritual marriages and divorces, etc., that is their world; we must write about our own mud-puddle; it will prove infinitely more important. This is being done by the proletarian realism.

6.

Swift action, clear form, the direct line, cinema in words; this seems to be one of the principles of proletarian realism. It knows exactly what it believes and where it is going; this makes for its beautiful youthful clarity.

7.

Away with drabness, the bourgeois notion that the Worker's life is sordid, the slummer's disgust and feeling of futility. There *is* horror and drabness in the Worker's life; and we will portray it; but we know this is not the last word; we know that this manure heap is the hope of the future; we know that not pessimism, but revolutionary elan will sweep this mess out of the world forever.

8.

Away with all lies about human nature. We are scientists; we know what a man thinks and feels. Everyone is a mixture of motives; we do not have to lie about our hero in order to win our case. It is this honesty alone, frank as an unspoiled child's, that makes proletarian realism superior to the older literary schools.

9.

No straining or melodrama or other effects; life itself is the supreme melodrama. Feel this intensely, and everything becomes poetry—the new poetry of materials, of the so-called "common man," the Worker molding his real world.

Why I am a Communist

In 1914 there was an unemployment crisis in America, and I was one of its victims. I was 18 years old, a factory worker and shipping clerk with five years experience, and the chief support of a fatherless family. Unemployment was no academic matter to me, but the blackest and most personal tragedy.

Well, the hungry workers were raising hell in New York. There were demonstrations, marches, and raids on fashionable Fifth Avenue churches by the unemployed. The anarchists were then still a brilliant and fearless revolutionary group in America, and they led the fight in New York.

I blundered into a big Union Square meeting, where Alexander Berkman, Emma Goldman, Leonard Abbott and other anarchists spoke. The cops, as usual, pointed the anarchist denunciations of capitalism by smashing into the meeting, cracking the skulls and ribs of everyone present. I saw a woman knocked down by a beefy cop's club. She screamed, and instinctively I ran across the square to help her. I was knocked down myself, booted, and managed to escape the hospital only by sheer luck.

I have always been grateful to that cop and his club. For one thing, he introduced me to literature and revolution. I had not read a single book in five years; nothing except the sporting page of newspapers. I hadn't thought much about anything except baseball, jobs, food, sleep and Sundays at Coney Island. I was a

This article was Gold's contribution to a collection of autobiographical sketches contributed by literary radicals to the September 1932 New Masses. Gold was twenty-one in April 1914, not eighteen as he recalled here. In later accounts of the Union Square demonstration which turned him into a committed radical, Gold recalled that it was Elizabeth Gurley Flynn (then the I.W.W. "rebel girl"; later a leader of the Communist Party) whom he heard address that rally, instead of Emma Goldman and other anarchists as he reported here. Actually, both Flynn and Goldman addressed separate rallies in Union Square in the spring of 1914, but Gold's recollection in this article is probably the accurate one. It is interesting to compare Gold's attitudes toward the Socialist Party in this article and in his "A Love Letter for France" three years later.

prize-fight fanatic and amateur boxer. Now I grew so bitter because of that cop that I went around to the anarchist Ferrer
School and discovered books—I discovered history, poetry, science, and the class struggle.

Nobody who has not gone through this proletarian experience
can ever understand the fever that seized me in the next year. I
read myself almost blind each night after work. My mind woke
up like a suppressed volcano. I can never discharge this personal
debt to the revolutionary movement—it gave me a mind.

And I think I can understand what the Soviet state means
today to millions of grateful Russian workers and peasants—it
has given them a mind.

I was an anarchist for several years. The poetry, the strong
passions and naive ideology of that movement appealed to a literary adolescent. I found a job as night porter at the Adams Express Company depot on West 47th Street. I wrestled big trunks
and half-ton cases from seven at night until seven the next morning. I sweated, but in my mind I lived in the idealistic world of
Shelley, Blake, Walt Whitman, Kropotkin. I was a revolutionist,
but it never occurred to me to do anything about it. Nothing,
really, was demanded of me.

It was the I.W.W. who made me conscious of the proletarian
basis of the revolution. I left New York, had some road experi-
ences, and was present in several Wobbly strikes. The history of
this heroic organization has still to be written. It is decadent
now, but among the finest veteran leaders of American Communism are those who went through the I.W.W. experience—
Bill Haywood, William Z. Foster, Bill Dunne, Earl Browder,
Harrison George, and others. (But of course nobody ought feel
grateful for this to the bourgeois Civil Liberties liberals who now
run the poor old Wobblies.)

The War came; the Russian Revolution; I was against the
War, I was 100 per cent with the Bolsheviks. It seemed marvellous then, beyond any words, and it still is as marvellous, that
the workers' state had come down from the clouds of Shelley's
dream and established itself on the earth.

We formed a Red Guard of about a thousand youth in New
York, which Hugo Gellert and I joined, to go to Russia and fight
for the cause. Our captain went to Washington to interview the
State Department, but they told him that if we wanted to fight we
had better enlist for France. This, of course, didn't satisfy a
bunch of young Red Guards.

And now I will end the autobiography by saying that the Russian Revolution forced me to read Lenin. I read his pamphlet, *State and Revolution,* and for the first time really seemed to understand the necessary historical steps by which the world could be changed from a filthy capitalist jungle into an earthly paradise of socialism.

Till then, the revolution had been a queer mixture in my mind that now is difficult to describe. One half of me knew the proletarian realities of bastardly foremen, lousy jobs, the misery of reading the want ads each morning, cops' clubs, etc. The other half was full of the most extraordinary mystic hash, the result of reading. Let me confess it now—I took Shelley, Blake, and Walt Whitman quite literally. They were my real guides to revolutionary action. But our great teacher Lenin, clarified everything for me.

The Communist dream is beautiful, he seemed to say in his axe-like words, the greatest man has ever formed. The revolution is this highest poetry of the human race. But to be mystic about it means admitting it is only a dream, and can never be realized. A revolutionist ought never lose sight of the wonderful goal—(Anarchism, so Lenin stated it)—but he is a traitor, a misleader and a source of dangerous confusion if for even a moment he neglects the daily class struggle, the links in the revolutionary chain.

Did one really want the socialist world? Then one must discard every bit of romantic nonsense, one must become as practical in this business as the enemy, who was never romantic, but who shot and jailed romantics and amateurs.

Yes, I learned from Leninism never to lose sight of the ultimate goal; also never to lose sight of the practical steps in attaining it. I cannot tell what a great lesson this was to me; I can only say that its effect was to make me study economics for the first time.

Today I might sum up my attitude in a few paragraphs. Communism can't be summed up that way; it is a new world larger than that found by Columbus, and thousands of poets, economists, literary critics, and above all, workers, are mapping it out and creating its history.

But this is a symposium, space is valuable, so here are a few ideas:

1. We must have a Socialist world. Capitalism is literally destroying the human race; it has broken down, it can no longer

feed the multitudes; it is a bandit, also, and must be executed before it murders another ten million young men in another war.

2. The intellectuals, the teachers, engineers, critics, art pho-
tographers, ballet masters, etc. haven't the numbers, or the economic power or the will or the *sheer necessity* of ushering in a
socialist world. Only the working class satisfies these require-
ments. To free itself it is *forced* to bring in socialism. The intellectuals have a favored servant status in capitalism; and their
chief aims will remain fascist. Like good flunkeys the majority of
them will remain incorrigibly "loyalist." They will try to patch
up the master's failing fortunes; they will invent "planning"
schemes, or elect Norman Thomas as President to stave off a
revolution (a Socialist revolution); they will flock around a
Woodrow Wilson, a Franklin Roosevelt, and then a Mussolini;
yes, they will hunt saviors for capitalism; we know too well these
liberals who are liberal in America, but now may be found in the
Fascist ranks of Europe and the Orient. Perhaps ten percent of
them really want socialism, and will join the working-class ranks
and help enormously. But this will be the cream of the intellectuals.

3. Only the working class can bring in Socialism. The one political problem of our time, therefore, is how the working class
can be organized and led to the conquest of the state and to socialism. There is no other problem.

4. Many groups have fought for this leadership. By now history has given all of them a chance at power, and it is possible to
state exactly what each will do to bring in socialism.

5. The anarchists may be dismissed as a small and moribund
sect. Their chief form of action today is not against capitalism,
but against the Russian Revolution. The I.W.W. and syndicalist
movement can be described in the same terms. The Socialist and
Communist parties are the chief international rivals for leadership of the working class. And both have controlled great nations.

6. The Socialists may best be analyzed, perhaps, by their actions in Germany, where they made a revolution. The Socialist
leaders there have swung into the ranks of reaction. They murdered Liebknecht and Luxemburg at the beginning of their regime, and they ended by advising the working class to vote for
Von Hindenburg. They established no socialism. They tolerated
fascism, even made compacts with it, until it grew strong enough

to destroy them. Their political strategy had as goal not the defense of workers' rights and the establishment of socialism, but the patching up of capitalism. The same story could be told of Ramsay MacDonald's England, or Chiang Kai-Shek's China, or of Japan, where two-thirds of the Socialist party moved over into a new Fascist party to back their native imperialists in the rape of Manchuria. Is all this true, or isn't it? How can anyone defend such a party? How can anyone say any longer that this international Socialist party can be trusted to bring in socialism? Even in America they run true to form, as in the case of their leader, Morris Hillquit. He acted as lawyer for certain Czarist millionaires who tried to seize Soviet funds on the grounds that their oil wells had been nationalized (socialism). Yes, Hillquit, the Socialist leader, pleaded in a long brief that socialism is illegal. And Norman Thomas, the Socialist president, in a long speech said that socialism meant confiscation, and that he was against confiscation. In Milwaukee a Socialist mayor gives $1.31 worth of food to each starving unemployed family per week, and beats them up when they demonstrate for more. Is this a fact, or isn't it? And is it socialism?

7. The Socialists are the great alibi merchants of the modern world. Their constant plea, when in power, has always been that the time was not yet ripe for socialism. But the time was not ripe either, in Russia, when the Communists took power. The difficulties were the most enormous and heartbreaking that ever faced a group of leaders. But in the midst of war, revolution, famine, an armed intervention by seventeen capitalist nations, the Communists struck the first blow for socialism. They have gone on; nobody lies any longer that Russia is swinging back to capitalism. While capitalism strangles in the fatal web of its own contradictions, the Soviet state grows stronger and wins new victories for socialism. The majestic thunder of the Five-Year Plan has shaken the world. We can trust this party to bring in socialism, therefore; it has already begun the historic task.

8. It is an international party, with units in each country. It has developed tactics, a discipline, a literature; and to it daily are attracted the most fearless and intelligent elements of the working class. It makes mistakes. It suffers defeats. But it marches on. Its discipline may seem harsh at times, but when the world war comes the Communist International will not split up into national units fighting each other under the capitalist flags,

as did the Socialist International. It will not betray us; for it purges itself constantly of every taint of capitalist influence. We can trust this party; but we *cannot* trust the Hillquits, Ramsay MacDonalds and Scheidemanns of the Socialist movement.

9. Is there another instrument, another political party in the world today, as well-tempered, as fearless, as studious and flexible, in as deadly earnest about the birth of socialism as this Communist Party? If there is not, then whoever injures or criticizes this party without helping it, whoever forms rival parties or sects, is of necessity a traitor to the coming of socialism.

10. I have wanted for fifteen years one supreme thing. I have wanted it more than love, health, fame or security. It is world socialism that I want—for I know this alone can banish the miseries of the world I now live in. It will free the factory slaves, the farm drudges, it will set women free, and restore the Negro race to its human rights. I know that the world will be beautiful soon in the sunlight of proletarian brotherhood; meanwhile, the struggle. And I want socialism so much that I accept this fierce, crude struggle as my fate in time; I accept its disciplines and necessities; I become as practical and realistic as possible for me; I want victory.

Whoever really desires the victory of socialism is forced today into only one party—the Communist. Whatever strengthens the Communist Party brings socialism nearer. The liberal and opportunist roads seem smoother and fairer, but they lead nowhere. The Communist road is rough, dangerous and often confusing, but it happens to be the only road that leads into the new world.

A Report from the Dakotas

Folks on the prairie is getting desperate
Because the wheat is burned, Comrades, a fifth year
And grasshoppers fly in big brown clouds
The young wheat, the truck gardens all gnawed away
So folks is despondent in the Dakotas—
Young ones go a-lookin and come back
"Farmers, it is just as cruel in Idaho—"
And folks wish they'd never homesteaded this land
Where, if the bankers don't get you, the grasshoppers must
    —Our light on the sod huts, the tarpaper shacks
    Our Saga making in the dry Dakotas
    I, Oscar Swanson, have seen it clear
    Lenin's word shining in a world of death
    And we build the United Farmers—
Comrades, the Red Poppy grows on the forsaken prairie
Last February the Red Cross broke our hearts
It was 40 below in the iron month of hunger and ice
The charity store locked up the food and underwear
I tell you it hurt to see the blue-lipped children
And it warmed us, and we took what was ours—
    The Indians marched in bright blankets and war feathers
    That night lit a bonfire and leaped us a war dance
    Swedes, Danes, Norse, we remembered the Sagas
    We sang of the heroes, the Sioux drummed, and the Yanks
    Shouted the John Brown song of the marching on
    Skoal! skoal! O wonderful light of Lenin!
    Come again! again! bring hope to the lost Dakotas!

One of the ways Gold invented to meet his daily assignment as a columnist was to furbish up in the form of prose-poetry letters which rank-and-file party workers sent in to the Daily Worker *describing their activities. This report is one example of Gold's series of "Workers' Correspondence." The text here incorporates a few minor changes which Gold pencilled in on a clipping of the original column after it appeared.* Daily Worker, *September 2, 1933.*

Night in a Hooverville

THE NATION that year was covered with these miserable colonies of the men without jobs. Here it was in New York, too; the familiar landscape again, a garbage dump and shacks by a river.

It smelled, like the others, of urine and melancholy. A great white moon blazed on the tin-roofed shacks. The sour earth was choked with tomato cans, rotten rags and newspapers and old bedsprings. A prowling tom-cat sniffed at the fantastic skeleton of a dressmaker's model. The moon glittered on a black abandoned boiler. On the river, hung with red and green lamps in the velvet dark, a passing tugboat puffed and moaned.

The tall kid from Iowa had been bumped around in boxcars for three days and nights. When he arrived in New York he was too tired to care where he slept; a cinderpile under the stars was good enough.

So he had found the shantytown, and now was hunting in the moonlit garbage for his bed. He found a woman's society magazine, slimy with the muck. He brushed it clear and stuck it for a chest protector under his khaki shirt. Then he discovered a tin can once used for motor oil; it would make a fine pillow. Then he made the real find; an old soggy mattress, heavy with months of heavenly tears.

Some local Mark Twain had nailed up a signpost reading "Headache Boulevard." In a nearby mound of gravel and coke clinkers the boy lay down, pulling the mattress over him for warmth.

The night was frosty, flashing with hard bright clarity like a crystal. Up there, in the blue and silver firmament, loomed the

---

When it first appeared in a Daily Worker *column (October 17, 1933), this piece was titled "'Arfa Maroo'; from Shantytown Sketches." The title here is the one Gold adopted when this cryptic grotesquerie was reprinted in his 1935 anthology,* Change the World. *The "shantytown sketches" were to have been a novel about life among the desperately unemployed in the impromptu squatter communities they established in the early Depression.*

strange skyscrapers of New York. It was Walt's first visit to this city, this dangerous magnet of all the youth of America. He meant to explore New York tomorrow. Now he wanted to sleep.

But a drunk party was going on in one of the shacks. Men were howling and singing. A gang of demons, they shrieked like murder, and it was really impossible to sleep.

Walt found himself remembering. That night, for instance, at the Salvation Army flophouse, where on the walls a poster announced in big red and white letters: "God Answers Your Prayer." And Al Kruger the clown had asked the prissy little clerk if God would also answer one's prayer for a chocolate malted milk. Then socko! the two boys found themselves slugged and kicked out on the street for this wisecrack.

That was Louisville, Kentucky. Next night in the jungles the old hoboes got drunk on corn and ganged up on the kids there. Davenport, Iowa, how long ago that seemed. Poor Dad, what was he doing now? But to hell with Davenport! And Toledo, Ohio! "Us boys do hunt for work, Your Honor. We ain't just bums." But the judge vagged them just the same.

Walt had once started to learn the saxophone. The exercises tootled through his head. And then the devils got to howling again; it was in the end shack. But the moon was strong as opium; it hypnotized him like a crystal ball. The flowing river gleamed with the white magic, and the Iowa kid was asleep.

But in McMurra's shack they went on howling. They had finished three pints of "smoke," the alcohol sold in Bowery paint stores in cans labeled "Poison."

McMurra, once a solid Gael and self-respecting family man, was quite insane now with the drink. Under a wild, black mat of hair his eyes glittered red like evil jewels. He was "mayor" of this shanty town and the other men were his henchmen. They always quarreled at their orgies.

Ed Budke pushed his long hollow face like a snake at McMurra and sneered through yellow teeth: "Every day in the trenches we used to bump off rats like you! Officers and all!" And Short Line Casey, who'd worked on section gangs, jumped and flapped his arms exactly like a holy roller. His bald head was inflamed as though with prickly heat, he couldn't focus his eyes. Monotonously he shrieked: "What did yuh do wit' dat four dollars last Chuesday? Dat four dollars?"

Incredibly enough, Tammany politics were played in this shanty town. Like all such gangs, this one never failed to quarrel over the miserable loot. Foul and hot, the room was suffocating as a sewer. It stank of burning kerosene, rusty iron and old putrid clothing and underwear. McMurra, like many others, bartered in junk. An anchor lay in a corner. Bundles of tinfoil and pulp magazines rotted under the bed.

This was about the foulest shack in the colony. The floor was thick with a carpet of cigarette butts, sputum and potato peelings. The ceiling had been varnished a cockroach brown by months of cooking grease and tobacco. Al Smith's smiling face was pasted on a wall, the room's only decoration other than cobwebs.

McMurra glared about him in the lamplight. His brow wrinked like a puzzled gorilla's. His neck muscles seemed ready to crack. With lifted fists like Hickory clubs he advanced on the shrieking little Casey to destroy him.

But old lean Pat O'Hara moodily smacked a chair over the Mayor's skull. Then followed an orgy of battle, the mingled scream of butchered fowl and the roaring of trapped bulls. Then all the henchmen formed a united front and threw their Mayor out of his own shack.

It woke the kid from Iowa. He yawned sleepily as he heard them. He saw McMurra flung out in a twisted somersault, landing heavily on his face.

It looked like murder. The man lay still, then lifted himself painfully. Sobbing and groaning, he crawled like a wounded animal to the river bank. There, his face a bleeding steak, he rested on hands and knees, his open muzzle gasping for air.

Fascinated, the kid watched him. The melancholy gorilla-man studied the river and its marvelous silver sparkle. It oppressed him with a mysterious heartbreak. He was being tortured. Throwing back his shaggy wild mane, the gorilla howled to the moon.

"Arfa maroo!" he wailed. There was no reason in it that Walt could find. The words meant nothing but the anguish seemed real. "Arfa! Arfa maroo!"

Against his own better judgment, Walt moved slowly to help the wounded man. The kid had learned never to interfere. You got into trouble that way. But maybe the man was dying; his tragic cry was certainly a call for help. Primitive and strange, it could not be resisted.

McMurra saw him coming, and slowly, too, he arose and waited. And then Walt caught the gleam in the madman's eye, and in a spasm of regret, knew his mistake.

He started to run, but it was too late. Dripping blood and foam, like a baited bull, McMurra charged the boy. He slugged and kicked, his thick arms rose and fell. The kid fought back, but was no match for the solid madman. He screamed, but nobody heard him; none came to help.

This was the city of the men without jobs. This was the home of the defeated. In the melancholy shacks men drugged themselves with checkers and booze. Others snored. A textile worker looked at a breadknife and thought of suicide. A carpenter lay in a lousy burlap bed and read stories of optimism in a magazine. Subway diggers dreamed of Italy. A Finn ground his broad sailor's knife.

Arfa maroo! The kid was finally battered into unconsciousness. He sprawled like a corpse in the garbage. Arfa! howled the whiskey-ape to the moon. There was no reason in it all. Workers mouldered like junk in the putrid shacks. Hunger, horror and holy ghost! Maroo, maroo! Arfa maroo!

In a Home Relief Station

THE LINE is long and extends from the staircase at the end of the school courtyard to the door at the entrance. There must be at least two hundred people in the line at a time. And more come in. Every minute new ones come in. They pour through the door at the entrance where there are four big cops and a special dick with a badge on his coat lapel. Inside there are two more big cops. They seem to pick the biggest cops in the precinct for the job. You never can tell what may happen here. There are two lines like that. Two hundred workers at least in each line. Backed up against the tiled wall. Single file. Four hundred people. Waiting. Waiting for hours. Waiting until everything aches with waiting. Feet and back and shoulders. Waiting and standing up for hours. No benches. Or just one. The bench that holds four at a time in front of the interviewer's table. That's where you hand in your application slip. That's where they check up on you. Four at a time. It takes hours. And you stand and wait. Wait. Until everything aches. Feet and back and shoulders.

That's why you can never tell what may happen. That's why every ten minutes the police car comes driving around to the Home Relief Bureau. That's why there are so many cops. In case all these poor and jobless and hungry people got tired of waiting? In case they got tired and desperate standing up against the wall for hours, while the thin long line creeps forward a bare inch, an imperceptible shove at a time? In case they used those hands, toughened and hard as iron with countless years of labor, now hanging at their sides, to take over the management of this relief station? What then? They would destroy this line. There wouldn't be any standing for hours then. They'd give themselves

---

This article was untitled when it first appeared as a Daily Worker *column; the title here is that adopted in* Change the World *(1935) in which the piece was reprinted. The last sentence was negligently truncated in the* Daily Worker *column and the whole sentence deleted in* Change the World. *The last word of that sentence is here supplied by the editor on the basis of an educated guess.*

the relief they need because each knows the need of the other. That's why you never can tell what may happen. That's why there are so many cops and every ten minutes the police car comes driving around.

It happened once before here. They lost their temper once. They got tired of standing and answering stupid questions. They were hungry and they wanted relief. It began with a woman, a big brawny Swedish woman. For hours she had been standing in line. If you've never been on a line in the Home Relief Bureau you don't know what it is. You don't know the feeling you get standing there, hour after hour, like an animal, like a dog waiting to be fed. Nobody talks. Nobody says anything. You just stand. Somebody asks a question. What do they ask you? How much relief do you get? Somebody tells you how tough he's been having it. How long he's been out of work. How they're going to be put out if something isn't done soon.

The city has set up these Home Relief Bureaus. They had to set them up. Everybody knows that. They had to set them up. But they made it as difficult as possible to get relief. It is given grudgingly, and wound around with yards and yards of red tape. And they herd you like dogs there. Beggars ain't choosers. Workers ain't human. They don't deserve better. Courtesy? Why, you ought to be glad they don't let you die in the streets. You ought to be glad they don't let you freeze to death in the winter. You ought to go down on your knees and thank the big shot that his heart is big and his liver is red and his pocket is full. Thank him for the check that can't support one person decently, no less a family of four. Thank him for the rent that pays for two rooms in which five people are crowded. This is relief.

This is what the big brawny Swedish woman got tired of. Suddenly, she walked out of line, just walked right out, and plunked herself down in the chair of the interviewer. In the interviewer's chair! The staff of the Home Relief Bureau must have had a fit. Imagine, having the nerve to sit down in a chair! But she sat there, the big woman, folding her hands deliberately across her broad breast and waited. For a moment the big fat cop, the ugly one, just stood and stared at her. Then he asked her to get back in line. She refused. She said she was sick and tired of standing up there. She had children to attend to. She had a home to take care of. Hadn't she worked and slaved long enough? Did she have to come crawling on her hands and knees to get a piece of bread from the city? Was it her fault her husband was out of work? She wanted to be taken care of. She refused to stand any longer in that line that moved forward an inch at a time, while the staff went gossiping to each other. If they were shorthanded why didn't they hire more people? They took the people's money through taxes, why didn't they use it to help the people instead of grafting it?

The cop said: "You gotta get up or get out." But he forgot something. He forgot that four hundred people standing on line there felt just as the big brawny Swedish woman felt. He forgot that her words were the words of all, her thoughts were the thoughts of all. He thought he was dealing with one woman, but he was facing four hundred people who had suffered as she had and felt as she did.

She refused to leave the chair. The cop moved over to grab her arm. And then it happened. It looked as though he had grabbed the arm of four hundred people, so quickly did those two long lines move. It looked as though there was only one voice shouting, "Let me alone!" so quickly did the four hundred workers move.

And before it was over, they had not one police car sirening through the streets, but half a dozen. It looked as though they had called out all the cops in the city. But nobody was arrested, except a member of the Unemployment Council in the district whom the cops had been trying to grab for some time. He wasn't even there. But many times he had been in the line, talking, explaining the need for organizing. The cops picked him up but it was like arresting a thunderstorm. It was something that was in the minds of those four hundred people and in the minds of millions of other workers scattered throughout the land. It was the thoughts which poured out of the mouth of the big brawny woman who walked out of the line and plunked down in the interviewer's chair.

This is only a slight instance. A brief little episode in the class struggle. But it flares up in the great battles of the workers in great strikes. It will flare up in the great struggles coming. This time it was only about a chair. An interviewer's chair. The papers called it a "riot." Someday it will be not for a chair in a Home Relief Bureau but for a government. And there will be not four hundred, but millions. And they won't call it a "riot." They will call it a revolution.

The Gun is Loaded, Dreiser!

A CHILD finds a loaded gun and thinks it a fine toy. He points it at his brother playfully and pulls the trigger. The gun goes off and kills the brother. The child does not comprehend what he has done; bewildered, he stares at the silent little corpse of his brother, and runs off to some less puzzling game.

How can we punish a child for such a crime? We do not punish him; he is not responsible. But a grown man we must consider responsible for all his actions.

Recently, Theodore Dreiser stumbled in some manner upon the Jewish problem. Almost playfully, without any real study of this blood-stained question, he arranged a symposium with his fellow-editors on that rather trivial journal, the *American Spectator*. It was a symposium, according to their own account, "with the accompaniment of wine." Eugene O'Neill, James Branch Cabell, Ernest Boyd, and that example of all the vulgar froth in the Jewish bourgeois mind, George Jean Nathan, were among those who drank the wine and indulged themselves in the planned, self-conscious wit.

The tone was one of sophisticated banter. All seemed to agree with Dreiser, even the very clever Jew present, that the Jews as a

---

The "symposium" in which Theodor Dreiser first stated his "anti-Semitic" opinions appeared in the American Spectator *for September 1933; the issue was reopened in 1935 when the old anarchist, Hutchins Hapgood, published in the* Nation *(April 17, 1935) an exchange of letters between himself and Dreiser in which he attacked Dreiser's attitude toward the Jewish people and Dreiser stood pat. With Hitler strong in power now, the issue was a monumental one, especially since Dreiser had long been close to the Left. The prevailing attitude on the literary Left seems to have been to conciliate Dreiser in hopes that the famous man would come to his senses. Gold, however, could not hold his peace. Not only had he been raised on tales of the pogroms, but also he had many years earlier conducted Dreiser on a tour through the poverty of the Jewish East Side of Manhattan, including a sabbath supper in his mother's home on Chrystie Street. Gold knew that Dreiser should have known better.* New Masses, May 17, 1935.

race were too clever for the Gentiles to live with. The Jews must be put on an intellectual quota of some sort. If they refused to practice intellectual birth control, the Gentiles would be justified in asking these clever and dangerous guests to depart to some country of their own.

The Hitlerish symposium was noticed for what it was in a few journals, including the *Daily Worker*. The liberal Hutchins Hapgood wrote an indignant letter of protest to the *American Spectator*. That gallant and airy paper edited by grown men, one of them even noted for his beard, assumed the child's prerogative of irresponsibility, and simply refused to print it. But Mr. Dreiser replied privately to Mr. Hapgood. The latter wrote a second note, and Dreiser made another reply.

Recently, in the *Nation,* a year after the event, the letters have been printed with the permission of Theodore Dreiser. They have aroused a small storm of shocked indignation. Theodore Dreiser had come to be regarded in our country as our outstanding symbol of the literary artist who brings his genius to the aid of the oppressed. Like Romain Rolland in France, or Maxim Gorky in Russia, here was a writer who had become, in the fine words of Zola, the conscience of his land. Twenty years ago Dreiser was already writing essays of protest and rebellion in the socialist and anarchist press. His fiction has always been deeply laden with the compassion and brooding tenderness of a man who feels in his own spirit the wounds of the humiliated mass. Dreiser went to the aid of the Kentucky miners. He aided other groups of persecuted workers. He wrote a book of straightforward condemnation of capitalism. He defended the Soviet Union, and even called himself by the proud name of Communist.

Was this the man who was now repeating so airily many of the familiar slogans of the *Judenfressers* Hitler and Streicher? It was unthinkable; if true, it was an American tragedy, infinitely worse than that which befell Clyde Griffiths.

To Mr. Dreiser all this hullabaloo about his letters seemed almost humorous. After all, he had expressed only his private opinion, and was he not entitled to that? He was not an anti-Semite, but a friend of the Jews. In advising them to form their own country he was helping them. But he was still a "Communist," and what did this Jewish question have to do with communism?

The simplest and most basic discovery made by Marx is that there are no indivisible races or nations, but that all the races and nations are split sharply by the war of two classes, the war of owners against workers.

This war can be detected as easily among the Jews as among the British, the Germans or the Japanese. It rages most strongly on Mr. Dreiser's very doorstep in New York, and it is a marvel that he has never noticed it.

New York is the center of the clothing industry of America. The industry is controlled by Jewish capitalists, and almost a quarter of a million Jewish workers are exploited by them in their factories and shops.

> They [the Jews] do not, in spite of all discussion of the matter, enter upon farming; they are rarely mechanics; they are not the day laborers of the world—pick and shovel; they are by preference lawyers, bankers, merchants, money-lenders and brokers, and middlemen [says Mr. Dreiser]. If you listen to Jews discuss Jews, you will find that they are very money-minded, very pagan, very sharp in practice, and usually, insofar as the rest is concerned, they have the single objective of plenty of money.

Yes, this is true of the bourgeois Jews. They are sharp in practice and money-minded, like the rest of their class, Jewish and Gentile. Mr. Dreiser says he has been fleeced by these Jewish associates of his, cheated by these crooked publishers and lawyers.

But does he think these Jewish exploiters are more tender in their mercies to their fellow-Jews who happen to be of the working class? Hasn't Mr. Dreiser ever seen any of the fierce and bloody strikes in the clothing industry of New York? They have been raging for more than thirty years. Jewish bosses hire gangsters to slug and kill their Jewish workers. They even hire Irish and Italian gangsters, they can never get enough Irish policemen to break the skulls of their "brothers."

Neither were the American nationalists, Anglo-Saxon and proud of their pioneer stock, who own the coal mines in Kentucky, any more backward in killing and starving their blood-brothers, the Kentucky miners. This you did see, Mr. Dreiser. It is capitalism. Would you say of the Kentucky miners that since they are also Anglo-Saxon like the mine owners, "they have the same single objective of plenty of money"? But you say it of these Jewish workers all over the world, who are as much the victims of the capitalist Jews as you think yourself to be.

I must confess that whenever I hear anyone glibly repeating this old vulgar lie of anti-Semitism, "All the Jews are rich, all the Jews are money-minded," it makes me want to howl like a dog with rage and fight.

Shame on those who insult the poor! More shame to you, Mr. Dreiser, born in poverty, and knowing its bitter humiliations! Don't you know, can't you understand that the Jews are a race of paupers? You ramble around with your George Jean Nathans and your slick Jewish lawyers and bankers, and think this is the Jewish race.

Ten years ago or more I took you around on a tour of the East Side. You were gathering material for your sensitive and compassionate play about Jews, *The Hand of the Potter*. What did you see on the East Side, Mr. Dreiser? Do you remember the block of tenements I pointed out to you, famous among social workers as having the highest rate of tuberculosis per square foot of any area in the world? Do you remember the ragged children without playgrounds who darted among the streetcars and autos? Do you remember the dark, stinking hallways, the hot congested ant-life, the penny grocery stores?

This was only one Jewish ghetto. All over the world the mass of Jews live in such hell-holes of poverty, and have been living in them for centuries. The ghetto has been the historic home of the Jewish race, and the ghetto is not picturesque, I can assure you; it is bedbugs, hunger, filth, tears, sickness, poverty!

Yiddish literature and music are pervaded like the Negro spirituals with all the hopeless melancholy of ghetto poverty. This is our tradition. How do you account for the fact that so many young Jews may be found in the radical movements of all the lands? It is because they have known the horror of poverty, and have determined to revolt and die, if need be, rather than suffer such a fate. And the first spiritual operation a young Jew must perform on himself, if he is to become a fighter, is to weed out the ghetto melancholy, defeatism and despair that centuries of poverty have instilled in his blood.

The majority of Jews, like the mass of every other race, are workers and paupers. You do not believe in statistics, but as a "Communist" you should have learned this basic truth from

Marx and Lenin, and it would have saved you from this cruel taunt.

As for the rich Jews, the exploiting Jews who are your friends, Jewish poverty has never disturbed them. Many of them live off it. Many of them, bankers and industrialists, are even complacent under anti-Semitism. As long as capitalism endures, they will endure. Many of them helped Hitler in Germany with funds and advice, and still are at ease in their Nazi capitalist Zion.

There is a residue of truth, however, in Theodore Dreiser's complaint (it is Hitler's also) that too large a proportion of Jews are shopkeepers, professionals, and middlemen, *luftmenschen,* as they are named in Yiddish, and compete with the Gentile parasites. There is a historic reason for this in the centuries of Europe when Jews could not own or farm land, or engage in any form of skilled labor (this is coming again in Germany).

Historic reasons, however, do not heal a political danger. What is needed is a change. Even among the bourgeois Jewish nationalists the brand of the *luftmensch* has become hateful. The Zionists know they cannot attempt to build Palestine with lawyers and storekeepers. There is a great agitation among them for a Jewish peasantry and working class; though in a capitalist Palestine, it would mean the same old exploitation.

In the Soviet Union the Jewish masses have in a single generation weeded out their middlemen into workers and farmers.

In the Soviet Union it is being done by the Jews themselves. The Soviet government does not put a quota on the Jews in the professions. It does not tell them only a certain percentage can go to the universities, or write books, or practise medicine or law.

There is no nationalist chauvinism in the Soviet Union, though there are many national cultures. Here is another Marxian-Leninist truth that Theodore Dreiser has never understood.

He says, "I am a Communist." And he also says, "I am for nationalism, as opposed to internationalism," and thinks, probably, he means the culture-nationalism practised in the Soviet Union. This leads him to the reactionary argument that the Jews ought to have a nation of their own, and ought to be glad to leave America and Europe *en masse* to found this new nation.

The Zionists would agree with him, of course, just as the Ku Klux Klan at one time had a compact with Marcus Garvey, who wanted to lead all the American Negroes back to Africa. Both Zionist and African nationalists agree with their persecutors that two races cannot live side by side in a country. This theory is completely anti-Communist, for in the Soviet Union over a hundred races now live peacefully and equally side by side.

Mr. Dreiser wants the Jew to become assimilated in America, or leave it and found a nation of his own.

> The Jew insists that when he invades Italy or France or America or what you will, he becomes a native of that country. That is not true. He has been in Germany now for all of a thousand years, if not longer and he is still a Jew. He has been in America all of two hundred years, and he has not faded into a pure American by any means, and he will not.

This sudden preoccupation with "pure" Americanism is shocking, coming from Theodore Dreiser, son of German immigrants. It is the same spirit that one finds today behind the mass deportation of foreign-born workers. Half the working population of this country is foreign-born, and part of the technique of capitalist exploitation is to terrorize these workers with the threat of one-hundred-per-cent Americanism.

Dreiser denies he is with the Nazis, and we believe him, but any theory of nationalism which forces cultural assimilation of its citizens is a big step toward fascism. Can't he see where such a theory leads him?

In the Soviet Union there is no such cultural imperialism. The Jews who have nationalist feelings have been given a great territory of land, large as France, for their own autonomous republic. Other Jews are scattered throughout the Soviet Union, in factories and collective farms. Those who wish to carry on the old Jewish culture are helped to do so. Those who wish to be assimilated find no prejudices in the way. The choice is free; but Mr. Dreiser points his chauvinist gun at the head of this racial minority, the Jews, and says, "Either assimilate or get the hell out."

I am one of those who see only good in assimilation. I want to see the time come when all the races have intermingled, and there is an end to this disgusting and barbarous race hatred. I want to see a single, strong, beautiful and united human race, and I am more than willing to surrender all that I know is good in the Jewish tradition in return for a greater good.

But does Mr. Dreiser think he can force assimilation on any people? All the imperialists have tried it with their racial minorities and it has ever been violently and successfully resisted. So long as the Jews are oppressed, they will be forced to cling to each other. Under freedom, they have always assimilated. One of the reasons many orthodox Jewish rabbis hate the Soviet Union is because, under the flag of Soviet freedom, the Jews are assimilated so rapidly there.

Theodore Dreiser, you will not assimilate the Jews to your "pure" Americanism by force. And you cannot persuade four million people to leave the country where so many of them were born; it is too impractical. There are some ten million other Jews in the world, and if each country followed your plan, where is there a virgin land that could take care of fourteen or fifteen millions?

They won't assimilate, they won't leave, and so what is the next step, Mr. Dreiser? Hitler has given one answer.

As for the working-class Jew, the radical Jew, he has already been assimilated to a better America than the one you offer him, Dreiser: the America of the future, the America without capitalism and race hatred, socialist America! In the working-class movement there is no race problem; that is a problem made by capitalism.

The child didn't know the gun was loaded. Some slick Jewish lawyers and publishers fleeced Theodore Dreiser; he brooded on the crime; stumbled on the remarkable idea that the Jew ought to be happy to leave Gentile America, and then he announced this idea.

Frederick Engels once called anti-Semitism the socialism of fools. Theodore Dreiser is not an anti-Semite, but he has invented a kind of socialism directed only against capitalist Jews which smells and sounds dangerously like anti-Semitism.

Here is where, in a time like ours, murder begins. It is a historic fact that every reactionary movement for the past century has begun with anti-Semitism. We are hearing it in America today in the speeches of Father Coughlin and other potential fascists. Capitalism, in danger, finds a scapegoat. It begins with a mock attack on Jewish capitalists, and then gets down to its real business, which is destroying the labor unions, crushing every vestige of liberal thought, burning books, culture and freedom in a grand medieval bonfire.

It is not the slick Jewish lawyers and bankers who have been put in danger by your carelessly spoken words, Mr. Dreiser. They can always take care of themselves. It is the Jewish workers who will suffer, and then the working class of America, those Kentucky miners you met. We have seen all this before, in Czarist Russia, in Hungary, in Rumania, in Germany. Theodore Dreiser has damaged his own great name and the cause of the oppressed by his carelessly spoken words. It is my belief he can now undo this damage only by years of devoted battle against anti-Semitism and fascism. The times are too dangerous for any lesser proof, or for childishness.

A Love Letter for France

IT'S SAD, wet, cold, the gray Atlantic and the gray skies are drab as eternity or a hungry man's sleep in a flophouse and the people in the third class are seasick and all my thoughts are of Paris.

I think of the easy-going, friendly city, Paris of the innumerable fine bookshops, Paris of the chestnut trees, colleges, gardens and crazy taxicabs, Paris with its lovely girls and fat, vain clerks and shopkeepers with the elaborate whiskers and the Legion of Honor. I think of the spirit of revolution and art that haunts every street and I think of the workers of Paris—these gay, ardent, talented people who have such an instinct for fine living.

Our "exiles" have slandered Paris. I never wanted to go there because of their tourist café gossip. They were escapists and Paris was their opium.

But now I am glad that for even a month I was permitted to see this Paris, so different from their adolescent dreams.

France has had three revolutions and the workers have never lost their self-respect. Waiters will familiarly discuss politics with you, or literature, or your family problems. This is the most democratic land I have ever been in, outside of the Soviet Union.

Everywhere, in subways, streets and parks, one meets soldiers —France has the largest standing army in Europe. It is a conscript army of young peasant boys with fresh naive faces, just up from the provinces. They are the least militaristic soldiers I have known—no swagger or toughness, just boys in uniform, sons of the people.

It is hard to put the thing in words, but the attitude of the people to these soldier boys is different from that of Americans or Germans to their own army. It is more like the Soviet Union

Gold was one of the delegates sent by the newly formed League of American Writers to the International Congress of Writers in Defense of Culture held in Paris, June 1935. His reports of the business of the Congress appeared in the New Masses *(July 30 and August 6, 1935). This retrospective account of his extracurricular activities and impressions of France followed in the issue for August 13.*

—the people act as if these boys belonged to them and show no self-consciousness in their presence.

And every day, in the papers, one reads of strikes and protests in the barracks—the boys, too, refuse to be considered mechanical robots in a military scheme, but insist on their human rights as workers and peasants. Every day reports come of another regiment of young conscripts that as it marches home after the year of service, raises the Red Flag and sings the "Internationale" in the streets.

The fascists will not easily turn this army against the people.

Everywhere one sees cripples—men without legs, arms, noses, faces, the mutilated of the last war. There are so many of them that special seats are reserved for them in the subways and buses. Most of the Army of Mutilés are Socialists and Communists. It is their miserable pensions that Laval and the bankers are attacking, "to economize" and to save the bankers' gold.

It is the wages of the state functionaries, too, that are being attacked. These state employes are organized in trade unions and are in the United Front. I attended a meeting of delegates from all the customs houses of France, deliberating under pictures of Lenin and Stalin. This radicalization of the rank and file of the state apparatus infuriates the banker-fascists. They are always wailing about the "Moscow" enemy within the state machine. Fools, hogs, they themselves have done it with their shameless taxation of the workers' life, their wage cuts and their currency juggling!

Life is more expensive in France than in New York. And the wages for those who work are so much pitifully less that one wonders how the people manage to keep alive.

Unemployment is increasing rapidly. France was the last country to be hit by the crisis, but now this grows in momentum like a rockslide. You find signs of it in Paris—every morning, on my way to the Writers' Congress, I saw a couple out of Steinlen, a ragged old woman and her man, resting in the same doorway, her poor old weary head on his lap, "waiting for nothing." You see them around, lying under the bridges, the groups of pale, hungry men sleeping on newspapers.

The price of horse meat has doubled and wine is dearer. There are state taxes on everything, even on the rent. The Seine flows through Paris; and along its banks there are hundreds of fishermen. Maybe this looks picturesque to tourists, but I know why these workingmen are not at work, but are fishing in day-light—it is not for pleasure. When you travel through our own South you will see Negro men and women fishing at every stream —and also, not for fun. It is because they are out of work and are fishing desperately for their next meal.

The fascists propose to solve this all a la Hearst, by deporting the foreign workers, for whom life has already been rendered so difficult.

They propose to solve it by increasing the army budget (the Armament Trust subsidizes the fascists). They propose to solve it by abolishing the republic and regimenting the French people so that they will learn to enjoy starvation, because it is patriotic (but the Metal Trust, which subsidizes the fascists, has never paid bigger dividends).

But the polite, the gay, the passionate French people still dance to accordions in the little *bal musettes* and drink their wine and kiss their girls. In the open air markets where the workers buy their cheap meat and vegetables they also are care-ful to buy little bouquets of field flowers, blue lupins and white lilies for the breakfast table. Nothing will crush their spirit. The subway guards openly read *l'Humanité,* the Communist daily, or *Le Populaire,* the Socialist paper.

Everywhere the great tide rolls up of the United Front, soon strong enough, perhaps, too for a government. The French peo-ple are not ready for revolution. But they are passionately aroused against the fascists, the bankers and wage-cutters. Thirty per cent of France now votes Socialist or Communist. If the ex-ploiters press the people too far, there *will* be a revolution.

A little fact: the achievements of the Soviet Union are daily described and praised in the republican and socialist press of France; you would think you were reading our own Communist *Daily Worker.* Leon Blum, the outstanding Socialist leader, for years opposed the United Front; but I chuckled when I read a recent article in which he spoke warmly of our "good friends, the Communists."

The Abe Cahans and Jim Oneals, those poisonous enemies of the Soviet Union and the United Front against fascism, ought perhaps to be deported to France and there forced to study the program of their own party.

In France, anyone who tries to break up the United Front is considered an enemy of the working class and an ally of the fascists. I wonder whether one ought not to feel this way in America, too.

I spent one day walking around the Jewish quarter of Paris with Isaac Babel, the artist who fought under Budenny and who wrote *Red Cavalry*.

As everyone must now know, writers are not at all like their books. Some are much better and some are amazingly rottener. Babel is neither better nor worse but different. He is stocky and baldheaded, with a kind, broad, homely face and he doesn't seem like a poet or ex-cavalryman but like the principal of a village school.

If you will read his work, you will find that his is an intensely romantic nature, which sometimes distorts reality because he is vainly trying, like Arthur Rimbaud, to pierce behind all its veils. But the frenzied poet, Isaac Babel, for the past six years has been the manager of a big horse-breeding collective farm in the North Caucasus. He had come to Paris for the Writers' Congress, because he is a famous Soviet writer, but he was also visiting French stud farms to study their methods.

(Sholokhov, the author of *Quiet Flows the Don,* recently took a trip abroad, too, and spent his vacation not among the literary men of Europe but in studying the model dairy farms of Denmark—he is passionately interested in cows. The Soviets are developing a new sort of writer in a world that has grown tired of tales about the dark souls of writers.)

Yes, Babel is a practical and humorous human being. He made one of the most original speeches at the Congress. He sat simply at a table and chatted in French with an audience of several thousand, telling them anecdotes about the Soviet peasants and the naive way in which they went about the historic task of acquiring culture; witty, tender, proud anecdotes that made one see intimately the new Soviet life.

Babel loves France and Paris. I was glad to hear him say this, for I myself had feared to say it, thinking it was American naiveté on my part and also because I remembered the "exiles" and their escapism.

"You cannot be a writer until you know French," said Babel earnestly. "No writer can acquire a feeling for literary form unless he has read the French masters in their own tongue. Of this I am sure."

(There must be something in this dogmatic theory; after visiting the gardens of Versailles and the Luxembourg, I was impelled, for the first time in my life, to attempt the writing of a sonnet!)

Babel and I sat in a Jewish restaurant on a Friday night in Paris and I told him about the East Side and he told me about Odessa.

He was surprised and glad to hear about the militant Jewish workers of New York. "In the Soviet Union one forgets one is a Jew. The whole race question has already become dim, like ancient history. But here in Paris it comes back to me." Babel is soon to publish a new book, an experiment in a new form, but the novel that he has been writing for six years he isn't satisfied with; this horsebreeder has one of the most painful artistic consciences in the Soviet land.

André Malraux is lean, intense and young, the restless aviator type. I saw him first in the office of the Congress, where he was swamped like a commissar in a mass of organization detail. He was one of the active organizers of the Writers' Congress, spending weeks at the "dirty work," like Aragon and Jean-Richard Bloch and the others. These French writers throw themselves into what they do with passion and directness. How is one to explain it? America is supposed to be the land of energy, but so many of our authors seem afraid of *doing* anything. It is as if working with other human beings were somehow dangerous. But Malraux did not seem afraid of losing his "individuality."

And he was not afraid of banging on the table and shouting at the top of his voice like a human being when the Trotzkyites made their mean little disruption foray and tried to turn a United Front congress against fascism into a demonstration against the Soviet Union. Malraux was chairman at that session.

Aldous Huxley, lanky, pale, boyish, shy, was more like some of our own intellectuals. Is it because Anglo-Saxons still believe with the philistines of commerce that there is something unmanly and unworthy about being a writer? Only the stock that produced a Shakespeare has brought this attitude into the world. It is a real mystery.

After the Congress ended, Malraux left for Algiers, to address a huge anti-fascist meeting. The fascists threatened to break up the demonstration and to attack Malraux. In the Socialist *Popu-*

laire, I read the lyric report of its correspondent, who said, "Our brave young Socialists and Communists formed a defense corps and were sufficient protection for Comrade Malraux, this author who charmed us all with his ardor, his intellect, his youth and his devotion to our great cause." That's what French authors are like these days; would that a few more British and American authors might learn from them.

Or from Martin Andersen-Nexö.

It is years since I first read the working-class epic, *Pelle the Conqueror.* I have never had the lust to meet famous authors; the best of them is in their books. But I had always wanted to meet the great Andersen-Nexö, whose book had such a deep influence on my youth.

He is a solid and powerful man, like some ruddy sea captain or master-workman. He is simple, like a worker; he likes babies and wine and food and fresh air and working with his hands and jokes and simple men and women; he despises stuffed shirts, be they authors or politicians, and he has that organic hatred of the parasites, the emotion that finally crystallizes into communism.

The King of Denmark once invited him for a visit to the palace. Andersen-Nexö informed the King he had no objections to meeting him but since the King knew his address, he could call on him first, on Martin Andersen-Nexö, good shoemaker, trade unionist and proletarian author, as good as any king. The king dropped the whole matter.

Andersen-Nexö told us many stories, gay and sad, about his life. He is a happy man, because he has lived for the working class and every day this class comes nearer to its goal. It happened to be his sixty-fifth birthday and several of us made a little party of the event. We toasted him in champagne and told him (Ralph Fox, James Hanley and Pearl Binder of England, two Australian authors and myself were there) what his books had meant to us in the English-speaking lands.

"But meeting you younger revolutionary writers means more to me," said the old fighter. "I am happy when I see our youth and know that the great work will never die." It sounds, perhaps, like politeness as I write it, but it is a feeling all good revolutionists have as they grow on in years. It is what keeps them happy.

"The first portion of Pelle, the childhood, is largely invention. I wanted a story of lyric pathos and tenderness to win my read-

ers. You see, at that time there had been nothing like a proletarian novel in Europe. They would have flung my book away
had I plunged at once into the story of a trade union organizer
and his spiritual life. The critics would have been bored with
such a vulgar theme. They could accept only lurid, sordid, sensa-
tional tales of the workers' degradation. But I wanted to write
about a class-conscious worker who was a conqueror of life, not
a victim. So I had to use strategy and I began my novel with pathos and weakness." (The trilogy was written in 1905–7.)

"But the latter portions are not invention—they are my own
story. Like Pelle, I was apprenticed to a shoemaker and worked
at this trade for many years. Then I helped form our trade unions and was one of the leaders in our great general strike. Yes, I
have lived as a worker for many years; only out of the depths of
revolutionary experience will come our proletarian art.

"As to form; it has never troubled me. I believe that one must
write from the heart; the form will follow naturally. One must, of
course, knead and knead the material; slow, as the proverb has it
—slowly one must grow a tree or write a book or make love. But
above all, follow the deepest instincts of your youthful heart.
Give my heartfelt greetings to the youth of your countries."

Paul Vaillant-Couturier, a rugged Gascon with a barrel chest,
innocent blue eyes and the free and fearless manners of a
pioneer, is the author of some six novels, a book of poetry and as
many political essays. He is a horseman, a crack shot, an aviator and a boxer. He fought all through the war in the tank corps.
He is one of the editors of *l'Humanité,* the Communist daily, and
one of the party leaders on the central committee and also the
Mayor of Ville Juif, a workers' suburb of Paris.

About a year ago, Comrade Paul was given a six-month term
in prison by a fascist judge for something he had written. He was
naturally bored with his vacation and persuaded the prison authorities to permit him to have some paint and canvas. Paul had
been too busy to experiment in this art, which, like all good
Frenchmen, he adored. So in prison he painted and painted and
accumulated canvases. When he came out, his friends persuaded
him to hold an exhibition. It made quite a stir; even the bourgeois critic praised the prison artist.

But now Paul is up to his neck in party work again. He is one
of the most popular Communists in France. His painting adven-

ture has not handicapped him politically. I wonder what would happen to Clarence Hathaway if he began to write sonnets or to Earl Browder if he should join the Composers' Collective and write proletarian songs. Bob Minor felt it necessary to suppress his great art in order to do political work. Nobody would have felt that way in France, I believe.

Comrade Vaillant-Couturier is also a remarkable cook. Babel and I visited his suburb with him one Friday morning. We first visited the clinic, where for less than fifty cents workers get a thorough medical examination, with X-rays and the finest apparatus. (Unemployed free.) Then Mayor Paul sat in his office and the workers poured in with their troubles—unemployed workers, mostly, who'd been cut off relief and the like. Then Mayor Paul went shopping in the butcher shops and groceries, and smiling chauffeurs, street cleaners and housewives came up to shake hands, saying "Comrade!"

At home, the Mayor turned into a master cook; I tasted nothing better in France, home of the world's greatest cooks, than his sauces, delicate as the herbs of the springtime.

As we were sitting at lunch, the bell rang. A very fat and stylish man of the middle class came puffing in. He mopped his brow and talked to Comrade Paul earnestly. He was the owner of a laundry. During the war he had served with Comrade Paul in the tanks and was one of his best friends. For years, however, they hadn't seen each other; but during the past year, this man, a Radical Republican, grew deeply aroused against the fascist menace. This had brought him around to seeing Comrade Paul now and again.

Well, the day before, a friend of his who owned a café had had a group of fascists eating in his place and had listened in on their talk. They were gleefully planning, it seems, to make an armed raid soon on the home of Comrade Paul.

"You must be on your guard, Paul," said the fat, respectable businessman, earnestly. "Whenever there is a sign of trouble, you must phone me at once. I will bring my friends with our guns and we will finish these people."

Paul thanked him and said he would be sure to phone. When the friend had left, he smiled and said, "Do you see how some of our businessmen feel these days?"

The Sunday before that was one of the great days at the Communist suburb, Ville Juif. A new main boulevard that runs to

Fontainebleu was to be opened. The Communist suburb had decided to name it after Maxim Gorky. Everywhere on the walls were red posters calling on the people to assemble in homage to the great proletarian writer, Maxim Gorky.

Ten thousand men, women and children were gathered on the hot asphalt of a burning summer day. The fireman's band played the "Internationale." André Gide unveiled the name-plaque and Michael Koltzov spoke briefly.

Red flags, gray old leonine workers in red sashes and velvet pants, smoking their pipes; the lively, happy Pioneer kids in their red scarfs and khaki shorts; gymnasts, mothers in shawls pushing baby carriages, the lean, fighting youth, in berets and overalls; workers with big moustaches and beards, wearing caps, shopkeepers and clerks, the people of France.

Vaillant-Couturier introduced André Gide as "our great comrade who has risen to the defense of world culture and the working class." And the crowd of proletarians shouted, *"Vive la culture!"* André Gide dedicated the Maxim Gorky Boulevard. He was deeply moved. He said later it was the first time in his sixty years that he had spoken to workers at a demonstration in the streets.

Then we marched for several miles behind the firemen's band to the athletic stadium. Songs, cries, slogans; and from the sidewalks, other workers cheered from their front doors and little gardens.

I will never forget a fiery old man in the procession who was the delegate of the Paris Commune. He shouted and sang at the top of his powerful lungs, this rugged septuagenarian, and by the hand he led a little boy of three.

The old Communards have an organization in Paris and he was here to represent them, dressed in a red sport shirt, like Garibaldi's, a big red sash and an armband that said, *"Vive la Commune, 1871."* He sweated with excitement, his eyes flashed, his long white hair waved in the breeze. He taught the little boy, who was carrying a red pennant, to raise his little fist in the Red Front salute and to sing the "Internationale."

I talked to the old Communard. His name was Louis Gomet and he was a Socialist. "Ah, it is a great day! I am rejoiced to see this day of the young. If my wife were only here! She is not in her first youth, you understand, but still charming. Yes, charming! Do you know, I spent three days in prison last month for fighting a fascist in a café. He had insulted my Communard shirt. Here is the warrant they served me. I am proud of it. Here, little one, let's sing the 'Carmagnole.' I will show you the way we sang it on the barricades."

We visit the Karl Marx Children's School, one of the finest in the world. Designed by André Durcat and a collective of Red architects, erected by the Red carpenters, stone masons and plumbers of Ville Juif, in the year 1932. The first modern children's school in France. Architects and other visitors have come to see it from all over the world. It is well worth seeing; an enhancing monument to a new and freer life, built in the midst of the old.

I have always had a slight prejudice against modernist architecture. Much of its seems faddist, a straining to be different at any cost. Inhuman and cerebral exercises by bourgeois artists who are removed from the people, it gives one no joy. But this school is both modernist and human and a joy to the heart and the mind.

It was built, not to please the architects, but the children. But the architects were Communists and loved and understood the children, so they too found a joy in the task. Great glass walls everywhere; so that the sunlight pours in on the children all day; it is like being outdoors, even in the wintertime. Beautiful yellow and blue tiling, murals everywhere, to delight the children; beautiful laboratories for little scientists, great porches to play games in on rainy days; marvelous maps and a dining room and model kitchen; classrooms that are interesting as little theaters; a children's palace, clean, happy and bright with color, sunlight and a new spirit.

All the Socialist and Communist suburbs are now building such schools for the workers' children. But in wealthy New York, under capitalism, many children still spend their days in dismal old firetrap buildings, where the toilets stink and the air smells like prison and the teachers are driven like factory slaves.

A little banquet had been arranged for the visiting authors in the dining room of the school. Here, surrounded by the workers, we drank toasts in champagne to Karl Marx, to the Soviet Union, to the Communist Mayor Paul Vaillant-Couturier and to the Socialist and Communist workers of Ville Juif.

Then back to the stadium; where through the loudspeakers,

each of us made a brief address of salutation—Alexei Tolstoy, Michael Koltzov, Louis Aragon, André Gide, Isaac Babel, Erich Weinert and others. And as each speaker ended, a worker of Ville Juif stepped forward with a great bouquet of roses, lilies, gladioli and fern, all from the local gardens, and presented it to the visting author and kissed him on both cheeks.

Good-bye, Paris; *au revoir,* beautiful city that for centuries has held the world's imagination. I am going back to my own raw, young city and land that I love painfully, the way a man loves a woman who is bad for him. France, your devoted sons love you in a different manner. Did I not hear Leon Moussinac, the gifted and passionate Communist novelist and critic, argue with great fervor that a revolution was necessary soon, if the glorious wines of France were to be saved, if the traditions of the great vineyards were not to be destroyed by the capitalist depression?

Au revoir, Paris. Your generals and bankers love blood and gold but your ditch-diggers and machinists love flowers and song and love. Your clerks dream of painting and poetry and your scientists and artists are ready to fight on the barricades for humanity against fascism.

Au revoir. I can understand why Americans, like the rest of the world, have ever been fascinated by your charm. Some of them have found only the tourist perversion and filth in you but your real self has been revealed to the artist and the revolutionist. *Au revoir.* I shall never forget your streets where the great story of humanity is revealed on every corner, where one meets memorials to a Danton, a Pasteur, a Claude Bernard, where side by side with an ancient monastery one finds a statue to a young student who was tortured by the Inquisition or to the first printer of libertarian books, his arms tied behind his back as he proudly awaits the executioner.

The great tradition of democracy and science that began here in the Renaissance hovers with wings of terror and beauty over every one of your alleys. Paris, it is an old story to you but to me it was still thrilling to travel by subway to stations bearing such names as Danton, Jean Jaurès, Saint Simon, Place de la Bastille and to walk on streets named after Balzac, Baudelaire, Laplace and Lenin.

Au revoir, dear Paris. Now I know that the bourgeois dilettante lied about you. You are not a city of cheap vice and easy emotions. You are deep, serious and passionate unto the death over the great human things. You have always been so. It is no accident that you were the birthplace of the Commune, which served as model for Marx and Lenin and the proletarian democracy of the Soviets.

Your working people, as I studied them in mass meetings, in cafés, in streets, have a collective soul beautiful as anything I have seen. Hungry, cheated and oppressed, they have never been degraded. They have a deathless instinct for culture and beauty and through blood and anguish, you must beat the fascists, for they would destroy all this, they will take this soul of your people and make of it a dull, senseless cog in a brutal military machine.

The free soul of French culture and the French people is too good for such a fate. But the Soviets will release all this mass genius, this wonderful spirit. Your people have traveled far, they are ready to be a super-race, when the wisdom of your past is incorporated in the daily life, when culture will be free to all, when democracy releases every talent, when workers and intellectuals build a new socialist France.

Les Soviets partout! Soviets everywhere! Until then, *au revoir,* Paris, and accept the gratitude and hopes of another infatuated American!

The Second American Renaissance

A SHABBY genteel scorn for the people and an equally shabby contempt for life were the predominant strains of the literary Twenties. Joseph Wood Krutch, the *Nation's* critic, expressed some of the prevailing sentiment in several dreary books, out of which one can pluck as an underlying thesis this line: "We have come, willy-nilly, to see the soul of man as commonplace and its emotions as mean." T. S. Eliot, a young man writing poetry concerned with the emotions of tired and burned out old men, named the period "the wasteland" and characterized its intellectuals as "hollow men." Robert Frost complained that "life went so unterribly" in America, and hence there could be no great literature.

Among the younger participants in the general chorus of gloom and sterility of the Twenties, one might recall Ernest Hemingway, Scott Fitzgerald, John Dos Passos and Edmund Wilson. They and their friends who had come out of the war into a decade of bourgeois prosperity and disillusionment were called the "lost generation" by Gertrude Stein. They were a little proud of that label, and with Archibald MacLeish, who wrote a long, whiny poem of self-pity, "The Hamlet of Archibald MacLeish," each fancied himself a solitary and tragic Hamlet lost in a vulgar world.

But it was Thornton Wilder, I believe, who most adequately represents the Twenties. His novel, *The Bridge of San Luis Rey*, was a best-selling sensation of the publishing season of 1929–30. With his other novels, it offers a good synthetic pastiche of the tastes of the bourgeois decade.

This analysis of the literary 1930s was Gold's address to the Fourth Congress of American Writers in 1941. Like most of the papers of that congress, it was never published and appears here in print for the first time. It is edited from the original manuscript which is now in the League of American Writers Collection in the library of the University of California at Berkeley. The manuscript is untitled, but Gold liked the one adopted here.

It isn't sporting to slug a corpse, and I am not going to reassault Mr. Wilder at this late date. He remains useful as a landmark, however. He was the perfect flower of the "New Capitalism," that wave of post-war prosperity which dazzled so many liberals and Socialists into believing that Marxism was outmoded, and that the capitalist system could go on expanding indefinitely.

A new parvenu class had risen in America, swollen with quick profit and as anxious as the old mining camp millionaires to acquire culture in a hurry. Thorstein Veblen, in 1899, had described almost exactly in his *Theory of the Leisure Class* the face of this group. Veblen was a grim and sourpuss St. John the Baptist who foretold the coming of the genteel, country club Christ incarnated in Thornton Wilder.

Wilder contained all the virtues Veblen had prophesied a parvenu leisure class would demand: the air of good breeding, the decorum, priestliness, glossy high finish; as against the intrinsic qualities: conspicuous inutility, caste feeling, love of the archaic, etc., etc.

All these virtues were needed to help the parvenu class forget its lowly origins in American industrialism. It yielded them a short-cut to the aristocratic emotions. It disguised the barbaric sources of their incomes, the millions wrung from American workers and foreign coolies. It permitted them to feel spiritually worthy of that income.

But ten years after Thornton Wilder occupied our literary sky, a different sort of star appeared there. The success of John Steinbeck's *Grapes of Wrath* is a sensation too recent to need much description. The novel won the Pulitzer Prize; it was made into a popular movie; the book itself sold almost half a million copies; and the story of the Joads, the family of Oklahoma farmers turned into migratory workers by the bankers and the dust storms, has passed into the American folklore.

Only two other novels in America's literary history have had the same social effect as the *Grapes of Wrath*. They were Upton Sinclair's *The Jungle* and Mrs. Stowe's *Uncle Tom's Cabin*. Less than a year after *Grapes of Wrath,* another novel made a success as phenomenal. This was Richard Wright's *Native Son*.

It is not conceivable that two such novels, based on such proletarian themes as the travail of a family of poor farmers, and the psychology and murder of a Negro boy in the slums of Chicago, could have won the same amazing success ten years earlier in the parvenu epoch.

What had happened in the ten years lying between Wilder and Steinbeck was a revolution of taste, morals, aspirations and social consciousness. American literature and the audience that read it had reached a certain maturity. A people's culture and hundreds of fine novels, plays and poems impregnated with proletarian spirit had battered down the barricades set up by the bourgeois monopolists of literature.

The individual talents of Steinbeck and Wright fused and synthesized what had become a new tradition. In their work can be traced the influence of scores of experiments, of agitprop plays, of critical essays, of southern novels, of plays about migratories, of the new America revealed by hundreds of proletarian writers.

If the gentility of Wilder, the snobbism of T. S. Eliot and the beer-garden aristocracy of H. L. Mencken had their origin in the boom decade of capitalism, the democratic renaissance of the Thirties was born out of the great depression. The depression stripped the American literary world of its most cherished philosophies. Freudism, Bohemianism, Humanism, Menckenism, Joyceism, even the fuzzy democracy of the mid-west school—all proved inadequate.

Alike did the disciplines of Mencken and Eliot find themselves going through the bankruptcy wringer, jumping out of penthouse windows and hunting for jobs with the rest of the American people. Being sophisticated, snobbish or skeptical was no more help now that it would have been on a shipwreck. It was a handicap, in fact, to remain aloof. If you wanted to live, you had to learn how to cooperate with other victims in a disciplined manner, how to organize.

So, from 1930 to 1940, our literature set forth on a second discovery of America. As in a famous decade in czarist Russia, the inverted, book-proud intellectuals "went to the people." Whole new areas of American life were opened up—the deep South, the daily life in factories, mills and mines, the struggle of the farmer, the souls of black folk, the problems of the recent immigrant and his children.

Now, at last, American literature came to grips with its own enormous and wonderful continent. Scores of gifted young "depression" authors appeared during each publishing season. There appeared a host of little magazines no longer filled with the usual poetic dewdrops, but proletarian in tone. The older writers were affected, too; many tried to come out of their introspective skins or warm little nests of sophisticated comfort. Some failed, but all were shaken and changed.

A sign of the renaissance was the furious literary controversies that set in. Literature was alive and dangerous, a social factor in the national life such as it had not been since the days of the Civil War. The Federal Arts Projects were created, a veritable revolution in popular culture such as America had never known.

Yes, it was a great and fruitful decade, one that burned much of the shoddy opportunism and adolescent fear and hesitation out of our literature. It taught American authors to be proud of their craft, because through it they could lead the people to great goals. It taught them to act and write like men and citizens, not like mere entertainers or perpetual Harvard boys or mystic outcasts from the national life. No longer was the writer an alien; he had rooted himself in the soil of the American people.

To describe this renaissance in detail is, of course, impossible in a brief paper. Future historians will devote books to it, as we now do to the movement of abolitionist, transcendentalist and socialist writers since the Civil War. We are too close, anyway, to the renaissance of the Thirties to judge it with sufficient objectivity. What impresses one, however, is its breadth and sweep —its vitality and genius in a dozen directions.

Great people's movements seem to have the miraculous ability to influence the national culture in unexpected ways. The Mexican Revolution began as a peasant movement for land, but before many years it had also created the finest school of mural painters in the modern world. The Russian Revolution, among other achievements, made a great art form of the hitherto degraded and commercialized moving picture. The Popular Front in France, during its brief life, rejuvenated the French cinema and revived the folk ballads of the Middle Ages. The Chinese Communist movement created the art of the woodcut, and introduced the short story and choral music into China. The Japanese revolutionary movement brought the realistic novel and an epic spirit into Japanese fiction, which had gone no further than a domestic and trivial autobiographical sketch form in the hands of the bourgeoisie.

In America, our people's movement of the Thirties was felt in many directions. The proletarian seed sown in a few first novels about strikes and unemployment grew by a hundred branches until it brought new dignity even to Hollywood. Pictures like *The Informer, Emile Zola, Mr. Deeds Goes to Town* were not being made in Hollywood before 1930. Folklore, the dance, painting, the theater—all felt the impact of a new spirit. The humanity of the Southern masses, both black and white, was restored by this renaissance. Do we not remember the time when William Faulkner's morons and their symbolic corncobs were supposed to represent the white manhood of the South, while Carl Van Vechen's flashy pimp was lionized as the "New Negro"?

The South had been marked off as a solid block of reaction, as the reservoir of American fascism. We were assured by politician and author alike that the race conflict was insoluble, and the South could not be changed. But the Gastonia textile strike, led by the Communist Party, smashed through all the paralyzing cliches of reaction. Out of this strike, and the miners' strike in Harlan, Kentucky, and the unemployment demonstrations and new sharecroppers' unions, white and black solidarity became a fact, and a new South was born.

Dozens of books began to appear about this new South. The southern textile worker, a primitive mountaineer still speaking Elizabethan English who in one generation was plunged into modern industrialism, appeared as a new American hero in such a lyrical novel as Fielding Burke's *A Stone Came Rolling*. There were also *Strike* by Mary Heaton Vorse, *Gathering Storm* by Myra Page, and *To Make My Bread* by Grace Lumpkin, among the signs of the new revelation that came with the strikes in the Carolinas.

A prolific Southern literature arrived, deeply progressive in tone. Faulkner's picture had been only an upper class truth; it described only the demoralized and defeated feudalism still lingering among the ruins of the Civil War. A new class, the discovery of new social hopes, was needed to rejuvenate this region of broken Attic columns and moldering customs and prejudices. It was the great wind of communism, pure and harsh as the storm that breaks up a month of midsummer drought, that scattered seeds of a new life in the South.

In 1935, midway in the decade and therefore incomplete, an anthology was published with the title, *Proletarian Literature in the United States* [International Publishers]. In it one may find a short story by Robert Cantwell about a lumber town in the state of Washington, scene of his childhood. Jack Conroy has a deeply moving autobiographical sketch about the midwest coal mining camp where he was raised. Ben Field contributes a highly original story, "Cow," its scene laid on an upstate New York farm; Albert Halper has a story of striking taxi drivers in New York; Albert Maltz contributes his famous "Man on a Road," a story of workers' silicosis in West Virginia.

William Rollins writes about a New England textile mill; Josephine Herbst about the social changes in a middle-class Pennsylvania family; Meridel Le Sueur writes of Minnesota; John L. Spivak's "Letter to the President" is a memorable little tragedy of the Mexican beetfield workers in Colorado; John Mullen sketches an incident in a Pittsburgh steel mill; John Dos Passos reports Hoover's pogrom against the unemployed veterans at Anacostia Flats.

As you will notice, this is not only proletarian material; it is also a regional exploration such as American writing had not known. Judged by such an anthology, the American people had simply never been described before.

But more than the discovery of new material and new regions distinguishes a proletarian literature. It is really the rise of a new philosophy of life, a new way of looking at the material and the region. Marxism is the name of the philosophy that gave a pattern and point of view to the poets, critics and fictionalists of the democratic renaissance.

I cannot hope to describe at this point the battle over Marxism which raged in all the literary journals of America, pro or con; it would need a bibliographer to trace. I cannot refrain, however, from recalling one amusing tactic of the enemy critics. Whenever a new proletarian novel or play appeared, possessing enough quality and virtuosity not to be ignored, these critics would hail it as "an exception to the Marxist rule." Their dogmatic prejudice assured them all proletarian literature was schematic, monotonous, coarsely materialist, obviously didactic and narrow. But here was a novel rich in human nature, dramatic and not didactic, and broad and free as life itself. So what? So they hailed it as a delightful revolt against Marxism, as a welcome exception to the rule of the Moscow literary dictatorship, etc., etc. Thus, in time, the exceptions grew and grew until there was a new exceptional literature; proletarian literature itself, not an exception or accident, but the thing itself.

But now that the dangerous word Moscow has been mentioned, I must stop for a brief look at those theoreticians who claim that this whole movement of the Thirties was, in the words of the late V. F. Calverton, "only an artificial, Moscow-imposed proletarian literature." There are quite a few schools of historical theory. In Hollywood, there is one school of thinkers who believe that history is made at night in an immense bed with silken sheets. Certain psychoanalysts affirm that Karl Marx wrote *Das Kapital* only because he was constipated, and that the Russian Revolution was the result of a national Oedipus complex. But the most stupid of all the schools is the one that traces every calamity and social change of our times to one monistic source—the famous plot in Moscow.

Marx, however, lived and wrote over a hundred years ago; and Marxism grew out of the German revolution of 1848, not the Russian Revolution of 1917. It is a synthesis of traditions and a scientific continuation of the political ideas of France, the economics of the British school and the philosophy of Germany. Marxism is the heir of all the democratic traditions of mankind, and was intended to arm the people with modern weapons against the new and terrible weapons of modern finance capitalism.

If it was able to influence American writers so widely during the depression, this can only mean that Marxism was really able to help them in such a situation. And the fact that there was present a living core of Marxist thought in America, ready to shape the thought of the intellectuals, is due to the presence of a mature and firm Communist movement—itself no Moscow plot, but the legitimate child of American parents and grandparents such as Horce Greeley, Albert Brisbane, Eugene V. Debs, Bill Haywood, Jack London and Walt Whitman.

What if it had been otherwise—and Marxism had not been ready to meet the depression decade? What if the Humanists had been stronger and readier than the Marxists—the Humanists and their pre-Nazi thinking? What if they and the Menckenites had had as much understanding of mass demagogy as Hitler? Might not the bewildered masses of intellectuals have followed them, and helped bring fascism to America?

For democracy was dead in our literature in the Twenties. It was Marxism that revived it, and that saved the intellectuals from fascism by giving a democratic form and method for their inchoate protests. And if this was a Moscow plot, then every American might well be grateful to Moscow.

But it was not, of course, any more than Jack London was the tool of a Moscow conspiracy. It is the development of class conflicts in society that produces a proletarian literature during the various crises, just as in turn such literature plays a large part in hastening, crystallizing and shaping the outcome of these crises.

One might venture to outline roughly the steps by which the decade of the Thirties unfolded:

1. The economic crisis and the Wall Street crash.

2. The misery grows of twenty million disinherited and unemployed Americans. Norman Thomas, Herbert Hoover and William Green have no better solution to offer than the famous apple-peddling inspiration.

3. On March 6, 1930, a million unemployed American men and women, led by the Communist Party, demonstrate in all the cities, demanding not the wretched bones of private charity, but unemployment insurance as the democratic right of every citizen and worker.

4. This mighty demonstration set the tone of the decade. It became a decade of social struggle, instead of defeatism and despair, in literature a Maxim Gorky decade, instead of a T. S. Eliot or lost generation decade.

5. Thousands of professionals, intellectuals and other middle-class people found themselves attracted to Marxism and communism as an adequate answer to their own problems and despairs.

6. Many writers changed rapidly in the furnace fires of these first bewildering years of the depression. A Congress of such writers was called by an organizing committee in 1935.

7. Other congresses took place among artists, dancers, musicians, the various arts and professions. By this time many trade unions and guilds had been formed among the professionals. And out of all these organizations, in which a progressive ideology was the shaping force, the nucleus of a cultural renaissance is born.

8. It is a pioneering movement, comparatively small yet able to join its pressure with that of the economic problems of unemployment upon the government, until the great Federal Arts Projects are forced upon Washington, just as works projects and home relief were similarly won for the American masses.

9. Now the pioneering left-wing groups merge into a great national movement, they become the core of a cultural renaissance, which lasted until 1940, when Roosevelt died to us as a liberal president.

Thus, it will be noted that the decade divides into halves: first comes the Communist and leftwing pioneering; then this movement broadens into a national, united front period.

Our wild west was won that way: a few hardy settlers fought off the Indians, cleared the virgin forest, built their shanties and tilled the earth. Towns and cities formed about them. Some of the pioneers then moved on to other virgin soil; others were swallowed up in the new civilization. Many were crowded out, and even forgotten. But still, they had planted something; it was enough of a reward for a pioneer. The Communist pioneer felt sufficiently rewarded when toward the end of this decade of the Thirties he saw that democracy had conquered in our literature, he saw hundreds of theaters, books, dance recitals, concerts, moving pictures, appear each few months, bearing, however faintly, grotesquely, even opportunistically, the shape of proletarian ideas.

"Did you, too, O friend, suppose democracy was only for elections, for politics, for a party name?" wrote Walt Whitman in his *Democratic Vistas:*

> I say democracy is only of use there that it may pass on and come to its flower and fruits in manners, in the highest forms of interaction between men, and their beliefs—in religion, literature, colleges, and schools—democracy in all public and private life, and in the army and navy.
>
> I should demand a program of culture, drawn out, not for a single class alone, or for the parlors or lecture-rooms, but with an eye to practical life, the west, the workingmen, the facts of farms and jack-planes and engineers, and of the broad range of the women also of the middle and working strata, and with reference to the perfect equality of women.
>
> Democracy—it still sleeps, quite unawakened, a great word whose history remains unwritten because that history has yet to be enacted.

The complete history of the Federal Arts Projects also must remain unwritten, because they were choked off just as they had begun to be vital. "What the government's experiments in music, painting and the theatre actually did, even in their first year, was to work a sort of cultural revolution in America," confessed the

Wall Street magazine, *Fortune,* edited by Archibald MacLeish, in a survey of the WPA projects made in May 1937.

Yes, if America was ever on the way to finding its democratic soul, it was through these projects. How is one to describe in statistics the wealth of murals that came to life on the walls of schoolhouses, courthouses, post offices and other buildings up and down America? The millions of people who attended a theater performance for the first time? The thousands of art galleries, music classes, symphony orchestras, children's theaters and the like that first appeared in such unlikely places as Big Stone Gap, Virginia; Laramie, Wyoming; and Ocala, Florida? The state guides, the various histories of the Negro and immigrant stocks, the research groups that uncovered our vast unknown treasuries of American folklore?

The story is stupendous, like the story of democracy itself. But from the beginning, these cultural projects were bitterly attacked and sabotaged by all the Wall Street Philistines and fascists, who also smelled a "Moscow plot" here. Well, it was true that all this vast preoccupation for the people, all this huge non-profit making war on backwardness and poverty, all this renaissance of national education, health, recreation and public building, had happened, if on a vaster and more conscious scale, in the Soviet Union. It had also begun to happen in Republican Spain, during a war against the heaviest odds, when the Spanish people were being betrayed by democratic friend and fascist foe. During its war against the Japanese fascists, the Chinese people are also building schools, hospitals, and a new national culture. Wherever the people are released, they burst into such great movements. The will, the energy, the ideals are always there, like the fires of a slumbering volcano. A WPA or people's war uncaps the volcano, and one beholds democracy in action at last, moving in the manner visioned by Walt Whitman.

So the American monopolists were right in fearing and suppressing the cultural projects; here was the democratic enemy they must always fear and suppress. But is it not paradoxical that a war for democracy against fascism gave Roosevelt his cue for ending the projects? Might he not rather have found this democratic renaissance usable if he wanted to fight a democratic war?

There is something significant in the fact that the projects were the first war casualties in America. Every liberal, at one time or another in the anti-Nazi battle since 1933, has repeated that famous Nazi line: "When I hear the word Culture, I cock my automatic." For years the Wall Street monopolists had cocked their revolvers at this WPA cultural movement, and the war gave them their chance for the killing.

It is significant, too, that the Waldo Franks, Lewis Mumfords, Archibald MacLeishes, and other liberals now recruiting for the Roosevelt war find it necessary to launch a simultaneous campaign against the literary tendency of the Thirties. Social realism is being attacked, and a suspension of democracy in our literature is demanded. The call goes out for a reaction in literature, a return to faith without works, a return to the old, stale, mystic nationalism that has served Czar, Kaiser and Fuehrer equally well.

Said Mussolini in one of his numerous speeches, "Fascism denies the materialistic conception of history outlined by Marx. Fascism repudiates the concept of economic happiness whereby the sufferings and sorrows of the humblest can be alleviated. Fascism believes in heroism and holiness."

It is this same humbug heroism and holiness, this same repudiation of economic happiness for the masses that the MacLeishes and Mumfords wish to substitute for the democratic ideals and achievements of the decade just ended.

But I should not, at this late point, begin any discussion of the war. Let me, however, before concluding repeat that the proletarian decade of the Thirties was no misunderstanding or accident, no foreign plot, no feeble esthetic cult that a few critics had artificially created and now can as easily destroy. It was a great movement out of the heart of the American people. It can no more be erased from our national history than can the public school system or trade union movement. It is fascistic to want to destroy the trade unions of America. It is just as fascistic to try to destroy this people's culture and literature of the Thirties. The Roosevelt-intellectuals surround their holy war with a mighty smell of fascistic corruption when they launch such a campaign.

The Thirties compares favorably with the Civil War decade, the greatest single chapter in the history of American culture. Its importance lies in its mass character. Therefore, no single Emerson or Walt Whitman stands out, though thousands of potential Emersons and Whitmans were formed. They are still young. Many will be drafted into the army. They will not surrender their souls to the army sergeant or to the literary Fuehrers now on the scene. Democracy still has a future in America—as it has all over the struggling world. The present war interrupts the democratic renaissance of the Thirties. But that renaissance and its literature will in turn end the system of war and profit.

Let us persist.

Renegades: A Warning of the End

IT TAKES years to make a Marxist out of a bourgeois intellectual. He was fashioned in the womb of the middle class; his every fiber absorbed its traditional fears, loves, and "eternal" values; to bring all these deeply hidden fears and dogmas to light, is almost the task of a psychoanalyst; and the relatively high percentage of renegades among intellectuals, as contrasted with workers, is only the ultimate demonstration of this truth.

Begin, for example, with the simple dogma named "individualism." It is the core of bourgeois life and thought. The capitalist system of economics is based on individual enterprise and the competition of one against all. But the worker has already been removed from much of this world by the very technique of modern industry. He works in large factories, with thousands of other workers, in a cooperative process. To earn a raise in wages, he finds he must still cooperate with his fellows in a trade union. Out of this difference in the manner of making a living, psychological differences take place between the worker and the middle class.

What the unbridled individualism of capitalism has made out of the middle class can be traced in a hundred different directions. Let us look at but one trait—the lack of human feeling, the absence of love for people, that is such a major strain in

This polemic marks the decisive end of Gold's twenty-five year association with major figures in twentieth-century American letters. Some of the men Gold attacked here, like Lewis Mumford, had once been warm friends; others, like Sherwood Anderson and Ernest Hemingway, had been cordial acquaintances. In the late 1920s, Gold had even carried on an amicable debate in letters and articles with, of all poets, Ezra Pound. Life was simpler then. Through the disasters of the late 1930s, the 1940s and 1950s, Communists and fashionable men of letters in America had very little friendly to say to each other. As chapter three of The Hollow Men [*International Publishers*], *this piece appeared in early 1941, just before the Nazi invasion of the Soviet Union. Further commentary on this difficult piece is offered in the Introduction.*

modern bourgeois literature—in Nietzche, in Mencken, in T. S. Eliot, in James Joyce, Ezra Pound, Dos Passos, James Farrell, Celine, etc.

> I lacked something essential to a Socialist—love of mankind, perhaps. I have known many Socialists like that, people to whom Socialism is really alien. They are like calculating machines: it does not matter what figures you give them to add, the result is always right—but there is no soul in it, it is sheer arithmetic.

Thus speaks Karazin, the renegade in a tale of Maxim Gorky's named "Karamora." And Gorky adds,

> Thought alone, unfertilized by feeling, plays with a man like a prostitute, but is quite unable to change him in any way. Of course, even a prostitute is sometimes loved sincerely; but it is more natural to treat her with caution, otherwise she'll steal something from you, and infect you with disease into the bargain. I observed that people are strongly governed by a favorite idea because it has thoroughly gripped their feelings. . . .

So the revolution is loved by some bourgeois intellectuals as one loves a prostitute—without feeling, with caution that something may be stolen from one, or an infection set in. Their communism is apt to become an abstract idea—the inescapable realization that the world is dividing into two camps, and perhaps the workers may win eventually in the great class struggle. But the idea is not fertilized by true feeling, or any contact with the masses of workers.

Maxim Gorky never heard of Vincent Sheean when he drew his portrait of an intellectual renegade, and yet the truth of his picture is corroborated by an illuminating passage in Sheean's well-known *Personal History*.

If you remember the story, it revolves around the conflict in the mind of Sheean as to whether he is to become a Bolshevik. For months, in revolutionary China and in Moscow, he has been in love with an American Bolshevik Girl, Rayna Prohme. In an atmosphere of revolutionary events, the two have been debating furiously.

Sheean has seen revolution, masses of workers, the tragedies and heroisms of Chinese communism; he has brushed against the great dream that sent millions of humble men forth to fight and die; and Rayna, already firm in her convictions, has tried to make him understand the great ideas behind these events.

But he goes for a breathing spell to England. Sheean left believing Rayna had won, and that he was a Bolshevik, too; but London changed him very swiftly.

I was angry and alarmed, on arriving in London, to discover that the old world of comfort, pleasure, taste, diversion and amusement still powerfully appealed to me, that the misery of nine-tenths of the human race could seem distant and dim when considered from the midst of a well-supplied bourgeois drawing room; that the things that a Bolshevik had to give up—a working Bolshevik, like Rayna or Borodin—were things I valued. . . .

I felt convinced that the issue of revolution was the only genuine issue (the only "live option," as William James would have said), in the world I lived in, but my own position in respect to the revolutionary struggle was more dubious than ever. The effect of England on me was like that of a brake applied to a wheel. It slowed me up, made me ask questions. The questions England suggested were personal ones. They went something like this:

Why should you, leading an externally agreeable life under the bourgeois system of society, try to do anything to change it? What does it matter to you if Chinese coolies starve to death, if boys go into the coal mines of Lancashire at the age of twelve, if girls in Germany die by the hundreds from tuberculosis and occupational diseases in the chemical factories? What do you care if the steel workers in Pennsylvania are maintained in conditions of life equivalent to slavery?

Can't you forget about all that? You'll probably never starve; you can earn enough money from your silly little stories to lead a pleasant life; why not do so? You think revolution is inevitable—or say you do—and why not, then, leave it to other people, workmen, soldiers, Bolsheviks? It's their business, not yours; what have you got to do with it?

Are you prepared to give up all the pleasures of modern Western culture, everything from good food and sexual liberty to Bach and Stravinsky, to work for the welfare of other people's grandchildren in a world you will never see?

The answer was, decidedly no. That was what England had done to me in the short space of twenty-one days.

But Gorky has said it more simply than Sheean through the mouth of his self-analyzing renegade: "I lacked something essential to a Socialist—love of mankind, perhaps."

What one must notice in this confession is that Sheean has made a choice not between two political parties, but between communism and cynicism. In this choice, he had begun that

MIKE GOLD: A LITERARY ANTHOLOGY

process of stripping his nature of the ordinary humanitarian social feeling that exists above and outside parties. By this same
reasoning a man can justify himself in peddling cocaine, in refus-
ing to take the risk of saving a child from drowning, or in any inhuman choice.

However, it is interesting to contrast this decision by Sheean,
made in one of those crucial hours in a man's life when he is
alone with himself and naked reality, and the decision made by
John Reed in a similar hour. This was in the spring of 1917.
John Reed was twenty-nine years old, and the energy and faith
that had carried him through the preceding decade had seemed
to vanish.

A serious operation—the removal of his left kidney—had
been followed by the termination of his three years' employment
by the *Metropolitan Magazine,* with whose editors he had quarreled over war policy. He had been one of America's best paid
ace reporters, but his fight against America's entry into the war
stripped him of some of his bourgeois career, of his income and
even his faith in the Workers' Revolution.

Woodrow Wilson, whom Reed had supported, had betrayed
America into the war, and a stampede of Socialist and liberal
renegades to the war bandwagon was on. It was the darkest hour
in Reed's life when he wrote this essay, "Almost Thirty," a sort
of private accounting to himself as to where he stood.

> All I have witnessed only confirms my first idea of the class struggle
> and its inevitability. I wish with all my heart that the proletariat
> would rise and take their rights—I don't see how else they can get
> them. Political relief is so slow to come, and year by year the op-
> portunities of peaceful protest and lawful action are curtailed.
>
> But I am not sure any more that the working class is capable of
> revolution, peace or otherwise; the workers are so divided and bit-
> terly hostile to each other, so badly led, so blind to their class in-
> terest. The War has been a terrible shatterer of faith in economic and
> political idealism.
>
> And yet I cannot give up the idea that out of democracy will
> be born the new world—richer, braver, freer, more beautiful. As for
> me, I don't know what I can do to help—I don't know yet.
>
> All I know is that my happiness is built on the misery of other
> people, that I eat because others go hungry, that I am clothed when
> other people go almost naked through the frozen cities in winter;
> and that fact poisons me, disturbs my serenity, makes me write
> propaganda when I would rather play—though not so much as it
> once did.

So here are two young middle-class writers, faced with the same monstrous fact of capitalism: that one class' comfort is built on another's hunger and misery. Sheean cynically accepts the bloodstained luxuries, and decides to shut his eyes to the misery. But John Reed cannot give up the dogged "idea that out of democracy will be born the new world."

Thus there is obvious a profound psychological difference between a revolutionary John Reed and a renegade Vincent Sheean, something at the roots of their characters, even though both came from the same middle-class milieu.

I believe the difference was one of fear. I do not mean physical fear or physical courage; but a moral fear of becoming proletarianized. It is not comfort alone that Sheean was afraid of losing. Many members of the middle class give up their comfort cheerfully and go to war. But it has to be a respectable war, run by the right bourgeois authorities. But any revolutionary action terrifies them with strange and irrational forebodings, as Sheean himself again testifies.

Rayna Prohme was about to join the Communist Party. "This is the end of Rayna Prohme!" he went about muttering to himself. He regarded it as an "immolation"; he spent weeks frantically trying to argue her out of this course; he "took refuge in vodka." "No decision in life could be more final," he says of Communist membership.

> The vows of a nun, the oaths of matrimony, the resolution of a soldier giving battle, had not the irrevocable character of this decision. . . . I struggled to bring her back from the certainty in which she dwelt to the easier world where men did not die for their beliefs—where they did not, in fact, have any beliefs if they could help it. She would be lost to me and my world; in the sense of a bourgeois individuality she would be lost altogether, for her intentions were, even for a Communist, extreme.

This, of course, is a purely hysterical and bourgeois "leftist" account of a simple fact of life. Millions of people have joined the Communist Party, in America, and in other lands. It is a mass movement, and you find in it the same species of humanity that you find outside. Feeling must be part of the choice, but millions of ordinary people suddenly do not desire to become "nuns" or "soldiers." Nor do they experience any sudden desire to "immolate" themselves.

No, despite all the frightened little bourgeois bystanders, here is a political, rather than a religious movement. The chief reason for which millions of human beings join the Communist Party is that they have reached the end of all the bourgeois promises, liberalisms, parties and political plans. Nothing remains but to struggle for a new system of society. The choice, indeed, is between this struggle for a new society, or suicide within the old. Thus, people enter the Communist Party with hope, with courage, and a sudden widening of horizons. That sacrifices may be demanded for one's new faith they fully expect, since they already know the brutality of the desperate and dying bourgeois regime. But since millions of young men, drafted by capitalism to fight in wars in which they do not believe, often fight as bravely as volunteers, why should one not expect the same humanity to be ready to fight for what it does believe?

Furthermore, Communists know that capitalism is a dying order, and cannot long survive. Fascism, which is the last stand of capitalism, has served no purpose but to further weaken and disorganize the old system. Thus, the predominating emotion in a Communist is a strong belief in victory. But the Sheeans never have such feelings or such perceptions. They are organically wedded in every fiber to the bourgeois system. They cannot conceive of a Soviet Europe, or a Soviet world. This always seems to them the most forlorn of lost causes, even when they go along with it for a while.

And this explains why "Jimmy" Sheean was so frantic when the girl he adored seemed ready to cast off her "bourgeois individuality" and to take "the Communist veil." As it happens, I met Rayna Prohme on several occasions some years back in Chicago. She was a lovely, gay and warm human being, with none of the morbidity that makes the nun. Furthermore, she seemed to me extremely well-balanced and objective, the student type—no adventuress, or Bohemian. It is interesting to note that in his book Sheean truthfully paints her as the well-balanced and objective partner in their debates, while he assigns all the hysterics to himself. She joined the Communist Party after deep thought, soberly and calmly, because she was ready. But Sheean was never ready to quit the bourgeois world, not even after what he had seen in China, Russia, and Spain. He touched the fringes of the people's struggle, was even moved for a time to partisanship. But the fear never left him. He did not want to be proletarianized.

This same fear, I believe, is one of the strongest emotions of the middle class in our epoch. Caught as they are between the hammer and the anvil, between the big monopolists and the working class, they vacillate from one side to the other. In prosperous times, they want to be rich; hence they fawn on the Rockefellers and du Ponts. In bad times, they approach the working class in search of help against the monopolists who squeeze them. But here they do not fawn. They are arrogant, often. They assume that they are to be the leaders in the partnership. And fear, fear of the workers, is always in their bones.

The worst tragedy in bourgeois life is to lose one's money. During the panic hundreds of bankrupt stockbrokers and businessmen committed suicide. They were still in good health, but they feared poverty more than death. One of the most difficult things during the depression decade was to organize the so-called white collar people. There was a profound psychological hurdle in the way. Not only newspapermen, engineers, technicians and other professionals facing sure starvation, but even your lowliest $12-a-week clerks and typists could not bring themselves to acknowledge that they were "workers."

Many were frightened by the very word. Calling oneself a "worker" meant, to the middle-class subconscious, the surrender of the class dream of being a millionaire some day, of giving up one's individual chances in the great capitalist lottery.

This crude desire for wealth is naturally translated into more "spiritual" terms and conflicts in the minds of the bourgeois intellectuals. It becomes an obscure and complex fear of being regimented, coarsened, robbed of freedom, of being told "what to think" by Communist or trade union "dictators," of being reduced to cogs in an organization, after having experienced the large freedom of a bourgeois superman, etc., etc. . . .

So here are two psychological elements that go into the makeup of a renegade: his deep fear of proletarianization, from which he has never freed himself, and his lack of love for people, a trait arising out of the inhuman competitiveness of bourgeois society.

At certain great crises, such bourgeois intellectuals have enough brains to understand that there is a class conflict, and that the workers may even win it. So they hasten to jump on what looks like a bandwagon. But it is really with fear, doubt, and hatred of their new associates. They are never at home. It is opportunism that sends them to the workers, not deeply felt convictions and loves. When the tide turns, and the workers must temporarily retreat, the same opportunism makes them jump off the bandwagon as hastily as they jumped on.

The revolutionary current of the Thirties was bound to affect the older generation. Sinclair Lewis spent several years, for example, making researches for a big labor novel, which his whole shallow past inhibited him from ever writing. On the other hand, Theodore Dreiser became a staunch fighter for the rights of the people and in his own grand and massive manner has remained loyal to that position even during the present time of testing.

Waldo Frank attempted a revolutionary novel, *David Markand,* in which he grafted his own pathology, the ugly masochism, the egotistic Messianic complex, the sexual confusion of his whole life's pattern onto the working-class movement. The result was bound to be failure, as impossible as to bring forth offspring from the mating of a lion and a jittery, hairless little Chihuahua, that most subjective of all dogdom.

Edmund Wilson ascended the proletarian "bandwagon" with the arrogance of a myopic, high-bosomed Beacon Hill matron entering a common streetcar.

Ernest Hemingway wrote a transition novel, *To Have and Have Not,* probably his poorest technical job, because it was a painful experiment in new values, a desperate attempt to escape from the "lost generation."

One could name many others. Some day literary historians will delve deep into the Thirties, and many books will be written to trace the revolutionary upheaval that then changed the whole course of American literature. But here I am attempting only a first rapid sketch of the decade, and must pass on, only pointing out in transit that even Robinson Jeffers was fanned for a moment by the revolutionary gale. In his stone tower on the Carmel coast, Mr. Jeffers pondered and pondered, and finally brought forth a poem in extenuation of the famous renegade, Judas.

Was Judas really a traitor? No, said Mr. Jeffers. Judas loved Christ. But he loved law and order more. Christ, the proletarian agitator, was leading the people into a social revolution. After wrestling with his conscience, Judas saved them from this "terrible" fate by selling out his adored leader and best friend.

Poor Judas, poor Robinson Jeffers, poor little bourgeois neurotic, living safe as a bug in a rug on your little income, self-pent
in a self-made prison, fearful of sunlight, of women, of love of
children, fleeing the common fate of mankind, shrinking from
the common give-and-take, the friendships, rivalries, coopera-
tions of daily life, all the passions, great and small, that produce
Beethovens and Shakespeares, as well as Mayor Hagues. Poor
sick man, poor hollow poet, are you not, like Nietzsche, merely
another unfortunate guinea pig into which an extra large dose of
bourgeois individualism has been injected to prove that it is the
most deadly mental poison?

But let us look at Sherwood Anderson for a moment. Without
doubt, Anderson was a fine pioneering artist in his beginnings
around the time of the last world war. His first book of tales,
Winesburg, Ohio, which still remains his best, was a picture of
the frustrations and tragedies under the surface of a small American town. It was not, as critics at the time believed, a geo-
graphic study of the Middle West, but was a social portrait of the
American petty-bourgeois and his family: the lack of large vision, of joy of life, of healthy sex and family relations, of the
eternal economic and social anxieties that afflict this group, constantly pressed downward by the monopolists.

The naive style, deeply childlike and blundering, in which Anderson couched his tales, was a fitting vehicle for the confusions
and vacillation that mark that group in its political adventures.

But see what happens to Anderson, after he has "arrived,"
and has grown fat and saucy in the boom period. Here, too, he
reflects faithfully his class; in adversity—humble, confused, democratic, frustrated and semireligious; in prosperity—when
enough crumbs fall from the rich table of the monopolists, suddenly arrogant and aristocratic, the Beggar on Horseback.

In a little article appearing in *Vanity Fair* at the peak of the
flush years, 1929, Mr. Anderson tells us that a foreign radical
magazine had asked him some questions about his attitude toward proletarian art.

> How confusing that is [he comments]. Laborers working are often
> beautiful to me. The banker who sits in his banking house making
> money, is not likely to be beautiful. But the banker has money to
> buy rich, beautiful things. Money—that is a beautiful idea. It excites
> me. I rarely look at the banker without wishing to thump him on
> the head, grab and run, but I have never done it yet. I lack nerve

perhaps. My own class, the artists' class, is supported by the rich. If money were not accumulated by the few, how would anything beautiful ever be present in this world?

You will notice the same pre-fascist note here, this hate of bankers and love of money, which love must mean, in turn, a fear of proletarianization and a secret hatred of workers. "I see no reason," goes on the fat and temporarily prosperous petty-bourgeois poet,

> why the underdog should be given the upper hand of things. Why should I set myself up against anyone—any thief, any prostitute, any man who has got rich by lying, cheating, stealing—if he has got rich that way?
> You see, I am ready to brush all downtrodden people aside. Let them go, let them suffer. If they became slaves, let them be slaves. I am now as aristocratic as any man in the world can be. I am as cruel and heartless, too. I am, as Mr. Bernard Shaw once said of a character in one of his plays, "a very simple man, perfectly satisfied with the best of everything."

A few years later, caught in the crash, seeing the downfall of the glittering bankers he had flunkeyed to ("My own class, the artists' class, is supported by the rich"), Sherwood Anderson also jumped for a time on the great proletarian "bandwagon."

He wrote *Beyond Desire,* a novel of Southern textile workers and a strike. It was a sincere attempt to make himself over, no doubt, but the social confusion, the lack of any real will-to-democracy, the dreary sex obsession, and all the mystical hangovers of his past could not help spoiling the experiment. The operation was a failure. You certainly can change human nature, even the human nature of a cockroach aristocrat, but not in one year or one book. Sherwood Anderson hadn't the heroic will or the truly humble patience, and, after his book flopped, he returned where he came from, to *Vanity Fair* and Raymond Moley's *Today.*

I have cited Sherwood Anderson for the reason that his case did not happen yesterday, as a result of the anti-war stand of the Communists, of the USSR-German pact, or even the different Trotskyite traitor trials.

At each of these political turns in the world strategy of communism, made necessary by rapid changes in the fevered decay of capitalism, a group of petty-bourgeois fellow-travelers have leaped off the proletarian "bandwagon," uttering complaints, sighs and curses, and inventing remarkable political alibis for their desertions.

But the case of Sherwood Anderson proves that these are only theatrical masks concealing a deep and more permanent truth: a class truth.

Mr. Anderson needed no alibis. He was merely following his class instincts, as simply as a bird heading south at the first frost. He didn't need, like Professor Sidney Hook, to search the whole library of Marxism to rig up his own private structure of treason. He didn't pretend, like the ad writer, James Rorty, to become "more Communist than the Communists." He didn't need, like John Dos Passos, a "wronged" leader like Trotsky to guide him. He didn't need a war, a pact, or anything. He just got out in a hurry. It was the wrong address. This was no complicated and moralistic renegade like Granville Hicks, Max Eastman or Waldo Frank. This was a simple, barefoot businessman, who found he had moved his store into an unprofitable neighborhood, and quickly moved it to a better one. Does such a man have to apologize or invent intellectual alibis?

Yes, the war has merely proven to be another opportunity for renegadism, a continuation of the process that commenced when the first fellow-travelers began to leap on and off the proletarian "bandwagon."

Around 1936, Trotskyism and the Moscow trials served as the pretext. Along this line, permit me to quote from a piece I wrote for the *New Masses* in the winter of 1937. It may help us grasp the psychological continuity of the renegade type, whatever the political events of the moment.

> They are a small band, working in a small milieu, but what energy, what remarkable ingenuity and persistence they display! Some of them called themselves "Communists" two or three years ago; but they were faint-hearted then, passive fellow-travelers with little passion. Now they overflow with enthusiasm against the People's Front, against the Communist Party, against the Soviet Union, against Loyalist Spain, and China, and proletarian literature, the emerging labor party, the CIO, virtually all the manifestations of Gulliver, the awakening people. . . .

> Intellectuals are peculiarly susceptible to Trotskyism, a nay-saying trend. The intellectual under capitalism is not a full man, since

capitalism has little use for a culture that brings no immediate dollar profit. The intellectual is rather like a stepchild at the capitalist feast. The great and small fiction of the western intellectuals during the latter part of the nineteenth century and up to the present is permeated with the bitter poison of frustration, and the malice and pessimism that accompany it. Suspicion of life reached a point among them, until, as Nietzsche pointed out, it became almost a form of biological inferiority.

We can therefore discard all the new "Marxist" jargon these people have picked up in the past few years, and pierce to the malice of the frustrated intellectual, hating life. Iago has merely found a new mask to assume in a new situation.

Recently, the *Saturday Review of Literature* has conducted a veritable campaign against proletarian literature and Marxist ideas. The *Nation*, as Granville Hicks has pointed out in a documented study, has been second in the campaign, and from time to time, *Scribner's, Harper's* and other slick-paper magazines join the literary Red-hunt.

Why do these magazines need to conduct such campaigns? The answer is obvious. The depression drove thousands of the American middle class into the leftist camp, and it has become necessary to bring them back. Tory authors would not be effective for this, only Trotskyite authors, renegades who have learned the left phraseology, are effective. In Chicago, the head of the police department's Red Squad claims to have been a 1905 revolutionist. This Lieutenant "Make" Mills has built his police career on his "Marxist" knowledge of the revolutionary movement. In the American literary world, similar careers are now being made by a group of Trotskyite authors.

Even though I pointed out the police character of many of these Trotskyite authors in 1937, I must confess that it never ceased troubling me for some deeper psychological explanation.

What, for example, was the original germ of evil in the soul of a Ben Stolberg, a former radical, who for years now has served in the capitalist press as a literary stool pigeon against the CIO indistinguishable from a Lieutenant "Make" Mills?

How does one account for the malicious satisfaction that the editors of the *Nation* take in listing Communists with Nazis as "subversive," secret agents, and sabotagers of munition plants, when Freda Kirchwey ate, drank, talked, and cooperated with Communists for enough years to know better?

What brings out this ugly lust in liberals and renegades to point out to the police, to slander and betray the Communist and labor movement?

There has never been, as I have said, any literature on this theme in America, any psychological novels revealing the soul of this "new social type." But in going through some Russian literature I found the following curious passage in Dostoyevsky's *Winter Notes:* "Why are there so many *lackeys among the bourgeoisie,*" wrote Dostoyevsky, underscoring the phrase,

> and what is more, lackeys with a liberal and benevolent exterior? The lackey spirit is progressively corroding the nature of the bourgeois and is being increasingly regarded as a virtue. It must be so under the present order of things, of which it is a natural consequence. And the most important of all is that the nature of the bourgeois encourages it. Apart from the fact that there is a good deal of the born spy in the bourgeois, it is my opinion that the extraordinary craft of spying, spying as a profession, carried to a fine art and employing scientific methods, is due to their innate lackey spirit.

Dostoyevsky often throws off such sparks of intuitive insight, but leaves the reader to develop them for himself. But as I pondered over his use of the word "lackey," it began to illuminate our whole epoch. Yes, the social status of the petty bourgeoisie is that of a lackey to the monopolists. If one takes as a parallel the feudal order based on chattel slavery, one might say that the petty bourgeoisie are the house servants of capitalism, while the working classes are the hard driven field slaves.

From the petty bourgeoisie come the overseers, the administrators and executives for capitalism. They are also the artists, musicians, entertainers, as well as the engineers, doctors, preachers and teachers. It is a favored status, and some of them are willing to pay for it by being faithful to their masters, and arrogant to the lower classes whom they supervise.

In a slight book named *Everybody's Autobiography,* Miss Gertrude Stein once calmly informed her worshipful audience that,

> what distinguishes men from animals is money. Money is purely a human conception and that is very important to know, very, very important. The trouble with Communists is that they try to live without money and become animals.

Miss Stein also confessed with disarming candor that her chief passion was avarice—love of money. As for the working class, "it is not at all interesting to take working men so seriously if by working men one means only those who work in a factory."

Here is a frank and amusing lackeyism—because Miss Stein is
too politically naive and personally arrogant to hide behind hypocrisy.

Her chief passion is not literature, as most of her followers
had believed, but avarice. She wants money—lots of money.

Is this same hunger not the chief motive of the petty bourgeoisie, which, by definition, is a class on the make, educated to all
the modern desires, yet prevented from satisfying them by the
high wall thrown around "money" by the monopolists and big
capitalists?

The man who wants money badly will do anything for money;
and this accounts for the huge number of professionals and literary men in America who can be hired to do anything.

You can get journalists to write on any subject; Father Coughlin, for example, merely advertised and got enough writers willing to dress up his foul ideas in language and to work for his fascist paper. Advertising men can be procured in regiments to put
together prose poems in praise of practically nothing—or something vile and harmful. The tobacco trust can step out any day
and hire whole medical colleges to testify on the therapeutic effects of chain-smoking, just as any murderer with cash can always hire as many scientific experts as he can pay for to testify
that ballistically he could not have committed the crime, that
psychologically, he was insane if he did do it, and that legally,
the witnesses were incompetent.

But it is needless to recount all the various manners in which a
commercial system has demoralized the integrity of the arts, sciences and professions; the tale is too familiar to thoughtful
Americans. What it all adds up to is Dostoyevsky's flash of insight of seventy years ago: "The lackey spirit is progressively
corroding the nature of the bourgeoisie. It must be so under the
present order of things, of which it is a natural consequence."

As I have said before, these sudden changes of the renegade
go beyond the superficial logic and political reasoning with which
they construct their alibis.

It is a deeply rooted and irrational psychological process, a
throwback to childhood conditioning, like that of the profane
and atheistic sailor who suddenly begins to pray when he thinks
the boat is sinking.

If it were a logical process, a man like Granville Hicks could
not have been so stupid as to present in a *Nation* article nearly

all the banal slanders against Marxism that he himself had answered over and over again in his ten years of polemics. It is useless to go through all of them now, but here is one revealing psychological item. Mr. Hicks asks with the mock naiveté of a Sherwood Anderson:

> How do you build a revolutionary party? Since the motive obviously cannot be self-interest, the orthodox Marxist would say it was class loyalty. But why, then, should a man be loyal to his class— or, since Socialists have so often come from the bourgeoisie, to somebody else's class? No one expects a simple solution to a psychological problem of this kind, but Marxism offers no solution at all.

As it happens, Marxism has always offered such a solution, and if I had the time for research, I am sure I might find it stated even in the former writings of Hicks himself.

The compelling reason why a Communist of bourgeois origin can remain loyal to the workers, is that he has at last understood that when the working class makes its revolution, it will free not only itself from capitalist bondage, but all humanity—the oppressed races, the women, the youth, and even the petty bourgeoisie itself.

This is the historic task of the proletarian revolution, and you will find it stated in every Marxist book and pamphlet since the *Communist Manifesto* first proclaimed the great truth a hundred years ago.

So one is certain that Granville Hicks knew the answer, and that his naiveté was a fraud. However, if you have an ear for psychological nuances, you can hear something deeper beneath this naive "political" question. Something "Dostoyevskyian" has happened to Mr. Hicks. When he was an active Communist he was not probing himself in this fashion, or asking, "Why am I willing to incur sacrifices? Why am I really a Communist?" But now the personality has begun to split and the man really wants to know, not merely "why is one a Communist"—but "why must one do anything at all for humanity?"

It is the same question, you will remember, that Vincent Sheean asked himself in London, and answered, "I prefer my comfort." It was the same question Sherwood Anderson propounded and answered: "Let them go, let them suffer, they were born to be slaves, but I am an aristocrat." It was the same problem, in another form, that Lewis Mumford faced all his life, and consistently answered as he did in a personal confession appearing some years ago in the old *Caravan:* "I hate the capitalists for oppressing the workers, but I hate the workers more for allowing themselves to be oppressed."

Dostoyevsky probed to the depths of this lack of humanity, this absence of solidarity so necessary to a healthy people or a healthy, complete personality, which the capitalist system of ruthless competition had destroyed in the psyches of so many people.

Some of these writers, I am sure, will never rob a neighbor's hen roost, but the egocentric principle underlying their activity is the same that Dostoyevsky works out to its dark and terrible conclusion in the persons of Raskolnikov, hero of *Crime and Punishment,* in Smerdyakov of the *Brothers Karamazov,* and in other figures.

At one point Raskolnikov dissociates himself from the Socialists. "No," he says, "I have but one life, and I have no desire to wait for what they call the 'common weal.' "

From this conviction the next psychological step is inevitable. If you have begun to lose your normal contact with humanity, if the social tie has weakened, and you begin to question yourself, "Why should I do anything for humanity?" this can only mean that you have also begun to despise humanity, to feel it unworthy of your love and sacrifice.

So the next step is a feeling of superiority to this "herd," and the arrogance of Sherwood Anderson, or the contempt of Mencken. Raskolnikov's main idea, as he confessed to the police inspector, was that "nature had divided men into two categories: the first, the inferiors, the ordinary men whose function is merely to reproduce specimens like themselves; the second, the superiors. . . ."

Hence Raskolnikov made his moral experiment as to whether he belonged to the master or to the slave class by murdering an old woman who lent out money at interest. It was because, as he told Sonya later, he wanted money, power, and to discover if he was vermin, like the majority of mankind, or a true "Man," a Napoleon who could transgress all the human laws.

Edmund Wilson accidentally opened a curtain on the renegade psyche, in the course of a review of Hemingway's latest novel in a recent *New Republic.*

There is, furthermore, in *For Whom the Bell Tolls* something missing that we still look for in Hemingway. Where the semi-religious exaltation of Communism has failed a writer who had once gained from it a new impetus, a vacuum is created which was not there before and which for the moment has to be filled. In Hemingway's case, there has poured in a certain amount of conventional romance.

Edmund Wilson is mistaken in two facts; communism is not a religious movement, but the most completely humanist movement on the face of the earth; and second, since ratting on communism generally means that the humanity in oneself must first be amputated, this cannot prove merely a temporary vacuum. What is to fill it? How is the man to go on? Here is always the problem that faces the renegade.

The defeat of the first Russian Revolution in 1905 created thousands of such intellectuals. Former "revolutionists" joined the Orthodox Church, became mystics like Mereshkovsky. The suicidal pessimism of Andreyev comes out of this period. Others plunged into a systematic cult of Bohemianism—of vodka and sex orgies, blessed by the morality of Max Stirner's *The Ego and His Own*. Michael Artzibashev's novel, *Sanine,* is a good picture of the period. His hero Sanine was a self-made Superman, radiating the health of an egotistic animal who refuses to make any "sacrifices for the herd." He preaches Nietzscheanism, has given up work, sponges on his old mother cheerfully, seduces a young girl and quite cheerfully drives her to suicide, all out of supermanly principle. And Artzibashev as cheerfully presents this monstrous egocentric Sanine as a model for the temporarily defeated Russian youth. "Give up your revolution. Give up your humanity. Let the slaves go, they were born to be slaves. Live for good food, sexual liberty, and Bach and Stravinsky!"

But let me quote briefly on this from an authoritative source, *The History of the Communist Party of the Soviet Union.*

The defeat of the Revolution of 1905 started a process of disintegration and degeneration in the ranks of the fellow-travelers of the revolution. Degenerate and decadent tendencies grew particularly marked among the intelligentsia. The fellow-travelers who came from the bourgeois camp to join the movement during the upsurge of the revolution deserted the Party in the days of reaction. Some of them joined the camp of the open enemies of the revolution, others entrenched themselves in such legally functioning working-class societies as still survived, and endeavored to divert the proletariat from the path of revolution and to discredit the revolutionary party of the proletariat. Deserting the revolution the fellow-travelers tried to win the good graces of the reactionaries and to live in peace with tsardom.

The tsarist government took advantage of the defeat of the revolution to enlist the more cowardly and self-seeking fellow-travelers of the revolution as agents-provocateurs. These vile Judases were sent by the tsarist *Okhrana* into the working class and Party organizations, where they spied from within and betrayed revolutionaries.

The offensive of the counter-revolution was waged on the ideological front as well. There appeared a whole horde of fashionable writers who "criticized" Marxism, and "demolished" it, mocked and scoffed at the revolution, extolled treachery, and lauded sexual depravity under the guise of the "cult of individuality."

In the realm of philosophy increasing attempts were made to "criticize" and revise Marxism; and there also appeared all sorts of religious trends camouflaged by pseudo-scientific theories.

"Criticizing" Marxism became fashionable.

All these gentlemen, despite their multifarious colouring, pursued one common aim: to divert the masses from the revolution.

Decadence and skepticism also affected a section of the Party intelligentsia, those who considered themselves Marxists but had never held firmly to the Marxist position. . . . They launched their "criticism" simultaneously against the philosophical foundations of Marxist theory, *i.e.*, against dialectical materialism, and against the fundamental Marxist principles of historical science, *i.e.*, against historical materialism. This criticism differed from the usual criticism in that it was not conducted openly and squarely, but in a veiled and hypocritical form under the guise of "defending" the fundamental positions of Marxism. . . . And the more hypocritical grew this criticism . . . the more dangerous it was to the Party, against the revolution. Some of the intellectuals who had deserted Marxism went so far as to advocate the founding of a new religion (these were known as "god-seekers" and "god-builders").

Remember that all this happened in far off Russia, around 1905, a whole generation ago, and under a backward and semi-feudal form of state, tsardom. The whole scene would seem as remote from America in 1940 as if it were laid on the planet Mars. And yet the same capitalist forces were at work there as here, the same fundamental classes were engaged in daily social battle. So it isn't strange that the same psychological type of the renegade who had appeared in Russia in such numbers around

1905, also appeared like some epidemic of miscarriages in America, 1940.

We too are experiencing a "horde of fashionable writers" who "criticize" Marxism, "demolish" it every week. Here with us today they also "extol treachery."

But there are national differences that one must note: I doubt, for example, that you will see any repetition of the strong religious tendency that accompanied the 1905 decadence in Russia.

We have never had a feudal state church here; it has been a country of pragmatism, business and machinery. When our renegades drift back to reactionism, the most natural thing is to outdo the Babbitts in worshipping the crude materialistic side of America.

One saw that in the boom period, when the hero of the liberal intellectuals was Henry Ford; when poets and artists became mystical about skyscrapers, bridges, and the mere noise, smoke and dirt of factory towns. The slavery on which those towns were founded they ignored; humanity was absent from their sterile cult of steel and smoke; they were the awed flunkeys of mere power, of the brutal and seemingly eternal power of American capitalism.

Kowtowing to capitalism, defense of it despite its obvious oppressions and mutilations of humanity, is also imposed on the intellectuals by the necessities of their war propaganda.

Mysticism in defense of the du Ponts and Fords is a strange hash, but is it stranger than the mysticism once concocted in defense of the Tsar and his landlord generals and bureaucrats?

All such mysticism, all such "patriotism" that willfully suppresses the fundamental needs of the people, all this agitation for a "national unity" in which the poor can only become poorer and the rich richer, must lead, as the world stands today, only toward fascism.

"Let us take Communism away from the Communists," was the first instinctive reaction of Edmund Wilson when he encountered the movement. That this was not an accidental cry but came out of the deepest of class instincts, is shown by the fact that Maxim Gorky put the same slogan into the mouth of his Klim Samghin, in a novel written around 1920, which is the study of such a renegade.

"A rebel from fear of revolution," Gorky calls him and Samghin himself formulates his aspirations as follows: "We need a revolution in order to annihilate the revolutionaries."

May I conclude this sketch by adding that the bitterest enemies of the Negro people can often be found among the social climbers who are trying to forget that they are Negroes, and that some of the world's bloodiest and most brutal anti-Semites have themselves been Jews? The venom of the apostate is an old horror in the soul of man. It is a psychological compulsion that comes after the betrayal has left that certain "vacuum" to which Edmund Wilson has testified. There is a disintegration of personality and the renegade loses much of his humanity, and can no longer distinguish good from evil.

When a whole class is being affected by the great political and social changes of our time, individual traits such as these coalesce into political movements like that of social-democracy and fascism. Distrust of the working class and lackeyism to capitalism are thus found to be the causes for the betrayal of the German Republic and the rise of Hitler as well as the reason why in some eccentric little Chicago studio some promising young "proletarian" poet of the Thirties may now be voicing his obsessive hate of communism in poisonous little verses praising practically nothing.

There is a direct link between the two, even though the poet is not aware of it. The little house cat stalking a tiny mouse does not know she is related to the tigers in the jungle. One watches her with a certain amusement, as one does the anti-Communist rage of insignificant poets, like the poor little homosexual who once said in a poemlet published in the "little" magazine, Blues: "As for me, I spit on the proletariat."

But in 1937, about the time this little cat was spitting his venom at the rising sun, really dangerous tigers of treason were being placed on trial in Moscow before the workers of the world. They were the Zinoviev-Bukharin-Trotskyite gang of wreckers, assassins, saboteurs and Fifth Columnists.

These were his true leaders, these were the men who carried the logic of renegadism to its most horrible limits, and paid with their heads for the crime.

As one re-reads the evidence at those trials, it is extraordinary how Dostoyevsky's flash of inspired psychological intuition lights up the infernal shadows. These men became traitors only be-

cause they were lackeys. The same point recurs again and again
in their confessions: they believed capitalism was stronger, and
would remain stronger, than the workers and peasants of the Soviet Union. Trotsky's theory that it was impossible to build socialism in one country was only the fundamental statement of
this petty-bourgeois lackey's creed.

Trotsky proposed leasing out the Russian industries to western
capitalists. Bukharin wanted "freedom" for the kulak farmers, so
that they might enrich themselves. Neither could completely believe that Ivan the worker, Ivan the farmer, could build enormous socialist factories and collective farms. Only the Fords, the
Deterdings and Kreugers knew the secret laws of production, and
one must call them in to help poor Ivan, the illiterate, backward,
inferior man.

One reaches the climax of this lackeyism that changed to treason in the letter of directives sent by Trotzky to his agents within
the Soviet Union sometime in 1936.

"The main point in this letter," confessed Radek, "was the international perspective. It was that the victory of German fascism had ushered in a period of the fascization of Europe and
the victory of fascism in other countries, the defeat of the working class and the absence of revolutionary perspectives . . . until
some radical changes caused by an international war. . . ."

The lackeys were certain that the Soviet Union would be defeated in such a war. Hence there would arise "the inevitability
of making territorial concessions, and he specifically mentioned
the Ukraine." Hence, it would mean "the granting of concessions
on industrial enterprises to capitalist estates," and the breaking
up of the collective farms.

"It was an attempt to preserve the principal gains of the revolution," says Radek, not with irony, but with the seriousness of a
lunatic who tells you he murdered his wife because he wanted to
cure her toothache. Only Trotsky and his bloc could "preserve
what would be preserved of the revolution," because only lackeys of fascism could successfully rule Russia in a fascist world.

Fortunately, the Soviet Union was led by Communists who
believed in the creative genius of the people, and the possibility
of socialism. Stalin, like Lenin before him, never quailed before
the titanic difficulties of building a new world in the shell of the
old. Neither did Stalin and the Communists overestimate capitalism, and tremble before fascism.

The Soviet people rooted out and destroyed the Fifth Column. Then, it is now obvious, Hitler flinched before this new perspective of an exhausting and uncertain war against the united Soviet. He turned, therefore, to the west, where the Quislings, Henri de Mans and Lavals, his Fifth Column lackeys, were running governments, directing the armies, and following his blueprints for the "new order."

Radek, Trotsky, Bukharin, and their fellow-traitors forgot one "minor" factor—the comparative strength of the capitalist and socialist forces in the world today. They despised the people and bowed before the masters. This is the central core of all their vile and enormous treason; and it is also the heart of all petty-bourgeois renegadism, from the Granville Hickses and Edmund Wilsons down to the mangiest yellow dog who ever peddled his honor and his "Confessions of an Ex-Communist" to Hearst and the Dies Committee for thirty silver dollars.

Ernest Hemingway is another example of this same historic process.

There is no better story teller in America than Ernest Hemingway. A great artist, but limited, narrow, and mutilated by his class egotism, the very brilliance of Hemingway's talents has only served to illuminate the poverty of his mind.

It is poor because its owner has for years lived the limited life of a rich sportsman and tourist. Hemingway's novels so often express this spectator without responsibilities, who holds a box seat at the crucifixion of humanity, and is a connoisseur of the agony and sweat of others.

You go through the Hemingway country and find it a world of cafés; bullfighters; big game hunting; scotch, more scotch, absinthe; long-limbed, gallant, "aristocratic," women who succumb easily; and expensive pleasure fishing; and expensive traveling hither and yon; and bootleggers; prize fighters—a colorful if sterile world and one completely divorced from the experience of the great majority of mankind.

It is interesting to search through Hemingway's writings for a single portrait of a man at work. There is never such a hero. The bondholder lives by coupon clipping or other abstract financial means. He can be very philanthropic and even as "pure in heart" as a lean, ironic, hard-drinking, Hemingway hero. But he knows nothing about the factories and fields where men must work and where the sources of his income arise.

All these traits account for the strange distortion that affects Hemingway's recent novel of the Spanish Civil War, *For Whom the Bell Tolls.*

The hero, Robert Jordan, is the same lean, ironic, hard-drinking, very, very noble Gary Cooper-Ernest Hemingway hero. He meets the same long-limbed, gallant Hemingway-Greta Garbo girl (this time a Spanish maiden). Against the backdrop of the civil war, they go through the same old gallant, skillfully arranged death. (The Hemingway pattern of love, by the way, is as juvenile as the Hemingway picture of society. Just as money comes from somewhere, by magic, and not from the most fundamental fact of life: which is labor; just so does love never become marriage, and babies, and common domesticity. Just as he has never been able to portray a worker, so has be been unable to draw the figure of a single mother.)

Robert Jordan, former Spanish instructor at an American university, now a volunteer in the International Brigade, had been doing guerrilla work back of the fascist lines. Hemingway's story is concerned with the last four days of his life when Jordan is assigned to blow up a certain bridge in enemy country.

The inner life of this young volunteer, however, is not that of any loyal member of the International Brigade, so far as one can judge from the letters, writings, speeches and other public records of the majority of them.

It is obviously Hemingway's inner life, intimately resembling the philosophy, or lack of philosophy, of the autobiographical heroes in his other books. It is interesting to note, first, that this Hemingway-Jordan cannot work up any real hate of the fascists. He is forever searching for excuses for them; he wants to find the "humanity" in these people.

He is so anxious to be "fair" to them, that he goes to the length of spending more time telling of Republican cruelty than of fascist cruelty.

That there must have been, in a merciless civil war, some typical peasant excesses against landlords, cannot be doubted. But Hemingway is unable to see, what even the aged Miguel Unamuno saw, that peasant terror is sporadic and individual, but fascist terror is organized in cold blood, on a mass scale. "All these crimes are committed in cold blood," wrote the heartbroken old philosopher,

> all these brutalities result from collective orders by the General Staff, which calls itself national. The horrors reported to me as having been committed by the "reds"—and in which I by no means believe—are pale trifles compared to the cruelty, the systematic and organized sadism which every day here accompanies the execution of the most honest and innocent people, irrespective of their party label, simply because they are liberal and Republican.

And the old philosopher ends: "All this in response to the cry of this insane general called Millan Astray: 'Death to Intelligence! Long live Death!' " Yes, even Unamuno, a vacillator between fascism and democracy, could read at least some of the class lineaments of fascism, that made it so different from democracy.

But from Hemingway's book, it is obvious that he cannot see the class difference. The war to him is exciting, terrible, dangerous: really a bullfight on a vast scale. If one takes sides in it, it is for this very personal reason:

> He fought now in this war because it had started in a country that he loved and he believed in the Republic and that if it were destroyed life would be unbearable for all those people who believed in it.

But the majority of the Spanish people fought not only for the forms of a republic. They also fought for bread, against feudal taxes, against the great estates. They were fighting against the fascists so fiercely because they hated the landlords, usurers, and bloated hierarchs and generals who had oppressed them for centuries.

Regarding these class lines, or the enormous central fact of hunger in Spain, Hemingway has not a sentence. Not a word. Not a hint. He doesn't know it exists. The war is some sort of vague battle over words, without roots in man's earth. It is like every other war. It is a thrill.

It is an accident, into which Jordan-Hemingway has been accidentally placed, "because he loved Spain." When it is over, Jordan-Hemingway means to lose all further interest in the people.

People should be left alone and you should interfere with no one. So he believed that, did he? Yes, he believed that. And how about a planned society and the rest of it? That was for the others to do. He had something else to do after this war. What were his politics then? He had none now, he told himself. But do not tell anyone else that, he thought. Don't ever admit that. And what are you going to do afterwards? I am going back and earn my living teaching Spanish as before and I am going to write a true book.

But can the man "who has no politics" and hence no loyalty to democracy or the people write a true book about the Spanish Civil War, which was a political war, made by the people in defense of democracy and their right to bread? Of course not, and Hemingway's novel, despite its narrative genius, is a false picture of the war.

"He was under Communist discipline for the duration of the war," Hemingway-Jordan soliloquizes.

Here in Spain the Communists offered the best discipline and the soundest and sanest for the prosecution of the war. He accepted their discipline for the duration of the war because, in the conduct of the war, they were the only party whose program and whose discipline he could respect.

Very good. Maybe, at last, the boy has grown up. Maybe he has at last matured enough to understand "Communist discipline," which is not the strange and sinister thing it seems to philistine bourgeois minds, but is merely the organized responsibility of men and women who are in deadly earnest about the fate and victory of the people.

But only a paragraph later, the tourist Hemingway is back where he started from.

Enemies of the people. That was a catch phrase he could skip. He had gotten to be bigoted as a hard-shelled Baptist about his politics and phrases like enemies of the people came into his mind without much criticism. . . . But since last night his mind was much clearer and cleaner on that business. . . .

And why clearer? He had slept last night with Maria! "That was one thing sleeping with Maria had done." It had made him doubt the "party line" and to question phrases like this one: "enemies of the people." No wonder, the bullfighter, bartender hero reflects, "the Communists were always cracking down on Bohemianism. When you were drunk or when you committed either

fornication or adultery you recognized your own personal falli-
bility of that so mutable substitute for the apostles' creed, the
party line."

One of the tricks of the Hemingway style consists of its short,
positive, declarative sentences, each of them a final and authoritative judgment on everything. This rhetorical device never admits modifying clauses, or doubt, or, let us add, the painful proc-
esses of thought.

Thus, with the usual swagger, Hemingway-Jordan explains all
there is to be known about that little subject, communism. What
is communism? It is bigotry, he dogmatizes airily. And what is
bigotry? Bigotry is something that happens to you when you
have not slept for a long time with a woman. "Maria was very
hard on his bigotry." After he slept with this long-limbed, gallant
dream-girl, he tells us, his bigotry and his "communism" left
him. But drunkenness would have served just as well. A drunkard is as little "bigoted" as an adulterer, he says.

Based on this piffling barroom philosophy, this class persiflage
of the rentier, is it any wonder that Hemingway-Jordan, after re-
specting "Communist discipline, because it is the soundest and
sanest for the prosecution of the war," immediately repeats the
filthiest slanders that appeared in the Spanish fascist press during
the war? He employs and even adorns their slanders of André
Marty, a man who has lived for twenty-five years the life of a heroic leader of the people, a man who was the brains of a great
naval revolt, who was the first Communist deputy of France,
who spent years in prison for his beliefs, and who has led great
strikes. No rich tourist can ever understand the mind or heart of
such a man. It must always remain a mystery to him; since, if
understood, it might shatter his own smug universe. He is fatally
compelled to slander all the ethical and moral values forming
such a mind, lest they destroy him. He must slander the Russian
technicians and officers he met in Madrid. He must even slander
La Pasionaria.

Here again one meets the opportunist strain that corrupts the
intellectual under capitalism. If the Spanish Civil War had been
won by the people, Hemingway would not have thus slandered
the Communists, and been so painfully fair to fascists and "enemies of the people." But the people lost. One of the obvious reasons for their losing was that the Soviets could not afford to in-

tervene on a major scale. That was exactly what the British and French statesmen of Munich wanted. It would have opened the war of a united capitalism against the Soviets for which they had been plotting with Hitler and Mussolini. The Soviets evaded the trap. Yet they did risk the security of their own great Socialist land and stretched the diplomatic limits to help the Spanish people. They were the only nation other than Mexico that helped. The French and British ruling class conspired with the fascists. They gave no help. They assisted in the treacherous murder of Spain. But you will not find a harsh word or even a little "slander" against them in Hemingway's book. He is too busy kicking La Pasionaria around, the "gallant" soldier!

How different is the pattern of the overwhelming majority of the Americans who fought in the Lincoln Battalion in Spain! In the New York post of their organization you can find men like Irving Goff and Bill Aalto who actually did the dangerous guerrilla fighting behind the fascist lines which is the theme of Hemingway's book. Perhaps from their stories he may have even collected his material. He has retailed their physical adventures brilliantly in his novel, but has he captured the soul of these men?

That was a bigger story than the actual fighting. Fascists can fight bravely, too. Bullfighters and prize fighters are often brave, too. But it is how and why you fight that separates a Stork Club brawl from the battles of a Garibaldi or Lincoln. It was not for adventure or because they "had lived in Spain and loved it" that the young Goffs and Aaltos left their jobs, their sweethearts, their security. It was because they had a profound principle inside them.

For years before the Spanish conflict many of them had been fighting the same battle for democracy in America. The Spanish trenches were but an extension of the home front, a spot that most needed reserves. From the heart of the American democracy went its bravest and truest sons to aid the sister democracy of Spain. When that battle was lost, such men were not left hanging in the vacuum, nor did they succumb to what Gorky called the "anarchism of the defeated." They came back to work, to their people, to their comrades. They fell back into the familiar ranks of the American democracy. The war was still going on here, and they were still in it.

Hemingway-Jordan tells himself that after the Spanish war, he will return to his old job of teaching Spanish at an American uni-

282 MIKE GOLD: A LITERARY ANTHOLOGY

versity. It is a sign of how ignorant of social reality Hemingway is that he can make this sound like some sort of cushy peace for a former Lincoln brigader. There were actually a number of university teachers in the Brigade. But when they came home, they found no such peace. They found boycott, persecution and blacklist. Can one conceive of that furious red-baiter, the president of Brooklyn College, returning his job to David McKelvey White, a former professor who fought in Spain? Of course not; for to the reactionaries of America, the Spanish veterans are poison. It is a black mark against any young American conscripted in the present "war for democracy" that he has previously fought for democracy in Spain.

For Whom the Bell Tolls is only the story of Hemingway in Spain. It is a minor story. It is not the great story, the new story, the hopeful and epic story of our time, the story of Brooklyn clogdancers, and Bronx machinists, and Iowa farm boys, and California university instructors, and Alabama sharecroppers. They were not military men. They were not supermen or "lean, ironic" adventurers. They were just people. And with little training, and almost no arms, they went out against the professionals of fascism—the Moors, the army generals, the planes of Mussolini and Hitler, all the trained killers of capitalism. They stopped the Goliath dead in his tracks for three years. They actually did this—these rank-and-filers of the American democracy. They will do it again. And when the breaks finally come, they will win. Not only in Spain, but over the world.

Yes, it is the story of democracy itself that Hemingway has missed.

The Storm Over Maltz

THE ROAD TO RETREAT

ALBERT MALTZ, who wrote some powerful political and proletarian novels in the past, seems about ready to repudiate that past, and to be preparing for a retreat into the stale old Ivory Tower of the art-for-art-sakers.

If you can extract any other message out of his piece in the current *New Masses,* you are a better mind reader than this columnist.

His thesis is the familiar one, viz: that much "wasted writing and bad art has," for the past fifteen years, "been induced in American writers by the intellectual atmosphere of the left wing," and that this bad influence has its central source in "our vulgarized slogan: 'art is a weapon.' "

"It has been understood to mean that unless art is a weapon like a leaflet, serving immediate political ends, necessities and programs, it is worthless or escapist or vicious," he says.

Another charge is we tend to judge works of art solely from the standpoint of the politics of the author.

"Writers must be judged by their work and not by the committees they join."

As an example of our "narrow and vulgar" tendency, Albert says, "The best case in point—although there are many—is James T. Farrell . . . one of the outstanding writers of Amer-

---

This title is adopted to cover four columns which Gold contributed to the Daily Worker *in early 1946 in response to a* New Masses *article by Albert Maltz and in rebuttal to attacks on his criticisms of Maltz. Maltz had appealed for a relaxation of political demands on radical writers, and Gold was among the most vigorous to disagree. It was just after Earl Browder had been removed as head of the Communist Party, and Gold was enthusiastic in favor of returning to a more uncompromising revolutionary position. Maltz's original article appeared in the* New Masses, *February 12, 1946; Gold's columns appeared in the* Daily Worker, *February 12 and 23, March 2 and 16, 1946.*

ica. I have not liked all of his work equally, and I don't like the committees he belongs to. But he wrote a superb trilogy and more than a few short stories of great quality, and he is not through writing, yet. . . ."

There's a lot more of such theorizing, but I believe I have given a fair sample of the whole.

It has a familiar smell. I remember hearing all this sort of artistic moralizing before. The criticism of James T. Farrell, Max Eastman, Granville Hicks and other renegades always attacked the same literary "sins of the Communists," and even quoted Lenin, Engels and Marx to profusion.

One can refuse to answer Maltz on esthetic grounds, however. The fact remains that for fifteen years, while Maltz was in the Communist literary movement, he managed to escape with his talents and get his novels written.

This Communist literary movement in the United States was the school that nurtured an Albert Maltz and gave him a philosophic basis. It gave him his only inspiration up to date. It also inspired and created a Richard Wright, who was born and reared in a humble John Reed Club.

The best American writers of the past fifteen years received their inspiration, their stock of ideas, from their contact, however brief or ungrateful, with the left-wing working class and this Marxist philosophy.

Maltz's coy reference to the "political committees" on which James Farrell serves is a bad sign. Farrell is no mere little committee-server, but a vicious, voluble Trotskyite with many years of activity. Maltz knows this. Maltz knows that Farrell has long been a colleague of Max Eastman, Eugene Lyons and similar rats who have been campaigning with endless lies and slanders for war on the Soviet Union.

It is a sign of Maltz's new personality that he hadn't the honesty to name Farrell's Trotskyism for what it is; but to pass it off as a mere peccadilo. By such reasoning, Nazi rats like Ezra Pound and Knut Hamsun, both superior writers to Farrell, must also be treated respectfully and even forgiven for their horrible politics because they are "artists."

There is a lot more one could say, and maybe I'll say it in a later column. Meanwhile, let me express my sorrow that Albert Maltz seems to have let the luxury and phony atmosphere of Hollywood at last to poison him.

It has to be constantly resisted, or a writer loses his soul. Albert's soul was strong when it touched Mother Earth—the American working class. Now he is embracing abstractions that will lead him nowhere.

We are entering the greatest crisis of American history. The capitalists are plotting (and the big strikes are a first sample) to establish an American fascism as a prelude to an American conquest of the world.

Literary evasions of this reality can afford no inspiration to the young soldiers and trade unionists, the Negroes and all the rest of the toiling humanity who must fight. The Ivory Tower may produce a little piece of art now and then, but it can never serve the writer who means to fight and destroy the Hitlers of this world.

ALBERT MALTZ AND PLAIN SPEAKING

Albert Maltz has written a letter answering my column discussing his *New Masses* piece. Albert is angry. He says I have slandered him. His letter is long, but I give the gist of it in this limited space:

> I was prepared to find in your column a searching analysis of what I had to say. But what did I find? No analysis—a few words devoted to mis-statement of my position—and then the conclusion that I was about to join Max Eastman and Eugene Lyons.
>
> What follows now? Don't you see that the result of this personal attack on me can only stultify all discussion, frighten off people who have come to any conclusion (not necessarily mine) that disagrees with accepted tenets?
>
> It is easy for me to reject your scarecrow image of me, for I am firm in my beliefs and in my loyalties to the progressive movement. What I was—I am. The beliefs I held—I hold, and will continue to hold, despite your unfriendly haste.
>
> The real victims of your column are the younger writers . . . those new to the movement . . . who witness this ferocity, this unbecoming descent to personality slander—all directed against someone who raises a question and advances a thesis—possibly an unpopular question and unsound thesis.

Out of one omitted paragraph let me stop to pick this epithet —"political blackmail." Albert says I am using a "blackmail" club and forbidding anyone to discuss the points he raises.

This is very rich arguefying, indeed. Free speech to Maltz means that he can freely write a piece in the *New Masses* in which the Communist movement is accused of enforcing a vulgar, coarse, anti-artistic, narrow dictatorship over writers, a dictatorship that has hampered our literature and falsified our critical standards.

Albert can say this, in 2,000 words or so, but I am not supposed to take 750 words in a column to answer him. Which is not free speech, Albert. People have a right to defend the "left literary movement," as well as to defame it.

As to your charges of personal slander, I can't believe you are thin-skinned. You are not a little boy, a literary novice just coming into this movement, but a veteran of some fifteen years. It doesn't matter whether my manners are good or bad. That's not the main issue here. There are bigger things, one of them is the future of the Communist movement in this country. Over that we must fight like tigers for the Marxist line. Browderism is what happens when we don't.

Maltz shows by his letter that he still doesn't understand how dangerously anti-Marxian his whole way of thinking has become.

I might have been "personal, slanderous and crude," but Samuel Sillen, *Daily Worker* literary critic, took the Maltz contraption to pieces with skill, reason and good manners. Not a harsh epithet was used. Not a personality was uttered. Sam gave the "searching analysis" Maltz demands in his letter to me.

Maltz ignores all this, however, to concentrate on my lack of manners. I would rather hear him make some detailed answer to the case made by Sillen—that Maltz's thesis is a retreat from Marxism, that it is a denial of the social role of the artist, that it is a veiled attack on the Communist movement and lays a new basis for conciliating Trotskyism, that it defends the liquidators of left-wing literature, etc., etc.

And Sillen is not slandering—he is arguing for the basic truths and principles that alone can build a labor literature and lead the American people on the road to socialism.

As a veteran Maltz knows that the Communist movement is coming out of no decade of narrow, stifling sectarianism, but out of a period of Browderism, when Marxism was being liquidated. We grew so broad we lost our own shape and standard. All that was truly Communist and rooted in the masses was being skillfully wrecked by the champions of "breadth" and Browderism.

Now that is over, and we are painfully trying to get back on the Marxist rails of history. The young writers Maltz worries about will never be misled by this return to Marxism. But they would be derailed and damaged if they learned to tolerate Trotskyites and to be as nonpolitical as Albert Maltz tells them they can be.

That way lies the Ivory Tower, the floundering in the marsh, the negative and passive literature of the cafés and esthetic cliques. Albert is preaching a terrible confusion. It makes me mad to think of him doing it so "naively," after fifteen years in the movement. I have a right to fight such stuff and shall never surrender that right. Furthermore, the time has come to restore the fighting Marxian heart into our literature—fascism is strong now, we must become stronger, not weaker, Albert.

MARXISM DEMANDS A FULL LEFT-WING CULTURE

Weeks before "the Storm Over Maltz" broke out, on February 5, to be exact, I received a letter from an Indiana author which I put aside and intended to print at the first possible opening.

Other letters piled deep over it and only yesterday it bobbed to the surface again. But the letter is still timely; indeed, a live contribution to the current literary debate for it touches the important point: that under Browderism, we had almost destroyed our left-wing literature. Please read this letter, this typical letter, of a loyal left-wing author, who pleads for guidance, a literary movement, a home in America to replace the one that bourgeois Browderism tore down:

Dear Mike Gold:

Being well able to imagine the many requests that reach your desk, I am adding to their number with the greatest reluctance. I can only plead that in more than 10 years I have never done this before, and will not be put out if you fail to answer me.

But I believe my problem is shared by most of our aspiring Marxist writers at this time, in that we have almost no literary centers, no magazine, no advisors, no theoretical help, nothing.

In addition to the general poverty, I have a special reason for asking your advice.

About three years ago I finished a novel—a novel of 567 pages, and I don't want to minimize the task of reading it—dealing with the progressive labor and progressive movement of the years 1936–39.

Loyalist Spain, the General Motors strike of 1936, the movement for anti-fascist collective security form the background of events. The central character is no hero, but a wavering petty-bourgeois youth, in the words of Marx "fumbling at those above, and trembling at those below."

I have tried to approach the subject with utmost fidelity to life, and to show people of the movement and their opponents as they were. At the time I finished the work, I was living in New York. I submitted it to four or five publishers, just through the front window, and they rejected it. I did not submit it to International Publishers or any of the people that might have best been able to judge it. To tell the truth, I was somewhat afraid of my own brain-child. At any rate, I put it aside.

Recently I had occasion to look at the book again, and was again plunged into the problem of what to do with it. I can conceive of it being a weapon in a struggle, but who will judge it or publish it?

I would appreciate any suggestion you can make; if not, perhaps this letter can add to the evidence on the plight of the left-wing writer in America.

I still read dozens of manuscripts each year, novels, plays, poetry collections where formerly, I used to read hundreds. Out of a hundred such specimens of the raw material of literature, one or two talents can be found, and the work is worthwhile, if one has the time.

Yes, it is worthwhile, if one believes that through its people American culture can be rejuvenated, given a great purpose, a great meaning. Only a people's culture can free America from the coarse, soul-deadening influence of commercialism.

Browderism was a denial of the Marxian truth that there are only two great fundamental classes in modern society—Big Capital and Big Labor and that the one spells feudalism and fascism —the other leads to progress and democracy.

Writers and artists who recognized this, and who wish to work out labor's own cultural forms, were rejected and dissolved in the Browder reign.

They were told that labor had no independent role to play, since monopoly capitalism was objectively a progressive force in the world, and sufficient leader for all of us.

In France, in the underground, the Left managed to find paper and courage to print literary magazines and books of poetry and fiction and belles-lettres. This was during the Nazi occupation. It is to our shame in the rich United States that we now haven't a single literary magazine or publishing house to furnish guidance and a home for our left-wing artists and writers.

This, I believe, is the main problem at the moment, and not merely a theoretical question. Our left-wing cultural movement has to start to rebuild its shattered house. We must again learn to believe in ourselves, and in the independent role of the American working class and its culture.

We must set to work to create magazines, theoretical debates, groups of people who care passionately and work tirelessly for a people's culture. We must have a publishing house for authors like this Indiana youth.

"We must not be afraid of stating what we are aiming at, and why and how," to quote the great speech of the French Communist, Roger Garaudy. "The worst of errors is the fear of taking a stand." In culture, as in politics.

HOW CAN THEY FORGET THE RECORD OF TROTSKYIST BETRAYALS?

I am still receiving letters from writers, college teachers and other professionals who believe I was rude to Albert Maltz.

Rarely in recent years has one encountered such violent feelings. These people are mighty angry and it has set me to wondering.

How can they be so angry against me who attacked Maltz, when they haven't one speck of emotion to spare against the vicious Soviet-hater, James T. Farrell?

I am ashamed to realize that many left-wing intellectuals seem to have forgotten what Trotskyism is—or the part that people like Farrell played in the Moscow trials, the Spanish conflict, the elections of Roosevelt, and similar crises. No, the correspondents never mention this issue at all.

Maltz's peculiar discovery (after fifteen years in the left wing) was that art and politics lived in two separate air tight compartments, and that Farrell the author could be tenderly regarded, while Farrell the anti-Soviet warmonger was ignored.

We are living in a dangerous hour for such ivory-tower exercises. Monopoly capitalism in this country seems ready to shoot the works.

Trotskyites have been among the most active intellectuals serving monopoly capitalism in the war against the Soviet Union.

For decades the Eastmans, Lyonses, Chamberlains and Farrells have been a principal source of anti-Soviet atrocity material in this country. A third World War, using the atom bomb, and directed toward the destruction of the Soviet Union and the emerging social democracies of Europe and Asia, sounds in our ears, like some sinister drumming of a cosmic rattlesnake.

But it's a long story that I cannot go into here. Anyone who can remember the war in Spain should remember the disruption, in spying, the armed revolt raised by Trotskyites—not against Franco, but against the people's government of Spain.

Farrell was in on that. He was in on the movement to vindicate the traitors who sold out to Hitler and were tried at Moscow. He backed Chiang Kai-shek in China, against the Yenan people's movement. He has written books and numerous articles to contribute to the reign of terror against Marxist ideas that prevails in the American publishing field. He is ranged beside Winston Churchill and other warmongers today.

Anyone who could grant esthetic immunity to this obvious enemy has lost sight of the Communist polar star.

Let me repeat to the abusive letter-writers: I would respect your criticism, if I could detect in you also some feeling of aversion to Trotskyism and its conciliators. But you do not show such feelings. And there is something rotten in such a situation, I say.

I agree with Lawrence Emery and other correspondents that Trotskyism is not the central issue, however. Maltz led us off the main point.

The big thing just now is to shake off the dead hand of Browderism. During the Browder dictatorship the great structure of Marxist-Leninist philosophy was submerged. Our party's entire publishing apparatus was turned into a giant promotion scheme for an author named Earl Browder—a man infinitely smaller than those he had supplanted.

Thus, the Marxist philosophy which compares in the social sciences to Darwin and Einstein in other fields, was lost for a time to American culture.

We had no guidance from Marx, and therefore could offer no guidance for the bewildered literary forces seeking a way out of capitalist demoralization and breakdown.

Marxism flourished however, during the first half of the 1930's, during the economic breakdown and unemployment crisis. The Communist Party organized and led the unemployed, it was a period of vast suffering and epic struggle.

Marxism penetrated all the ivory towers; there were debates in the literary journals, pro and con.

Many books of Marxist critical theory appeared. New writers wrote "proletarian" novels, plays and poems and became a main stream in our national culture, that formed the finest literary epoch our country has known since the Golden Age of Whitman, Emerson and Melville.

It was a fighting art, a Marxist art and frankly a weapon in the class struggle then raging so openly. I was ashamed to note that certain latter-day Marxist literary critics have developed a tendency to patronize the Thirties as our period of crude and primitive beginnings. This is not so. The literature of that period is above anything produced since, in the years of Browderism and sophistication. The Forties are still nothing to brag about in America's literature.

To repeat: We must find our way back to the main highway, to join the people as they march to truth and socialism. We must rebuild the Marxist cultural front, with its literary magazines, theaters, music and art.

Let's not get bogged down in any cafeteria argument over little theoretical abstractions. Let us look at the world again, and plunge literature and art into life and the social realities.

A Jewish Childhood in the New York Slums

BY SEVENTEEN already a veteran of the alarm clock, I had gone through jobs with the Adams Express, worked in some factories and little nervous shops of the great city.

New York, my city, O stony cradle! O dirty fatherland! Place of my deepest, oldest friendships, in whose earth sleep my father, mother, brother and dear friends, you were never to me the tourist's gaudy postcard! I lived in another New York than the rich playboys and their famous nightclubs and call girls. Only a mile from those fabulous money mills, the skyscrapers of Wall Street, lay the country of the poor, the East Side slums, amid whose hungry tenements and boiling streets I was born and grew. Its people woke to the alarm clock every morning, as did most New Yorkers. They were out of the house before seven on the way to bread labor.

By seventeen I had been a soda jerk, errand boy, shipping clerk in clothing factories, in a print shop. My initiation had been into a hellish gas mantle factory on the bowery when I was twelve.

Gold called this series of articles, which appeared in his column in the San Francisco People's World *in 1959, a "sequel" to* Jews Without Money *(1930). These pieces demonstrate two things about Gold's career: (1) that, even as he approached old age, he lost none of his special power with words—his wit and dour humanity—but (2) that that power was best reserved for the recall of his youth, before he got tangled in the life of literature and politics. It is fair to say that nothing else Gold wrote after* Jews Without Money *so well matches the standard of that book. Properly speaking, these articles are not a* sequel *to the early semi-fictional reminiscences, but rather a* complement. *They add to the story of Gold's adolescence, but, like the earlier book, they do not go beyond. Such was Gold's indelible style that this late material might be interpolated into* Jews Without Money *without anyone noticing it.* People's World, *April 11, 25; May 9, 23; June 20; July 4, 18; August 1, 15, 29; September 26, and October 17, 1959.*

Now I was the helper on a high Adams Express truck, pulled by two powerful percherons, named Brownie and Queenie. I loved them for their wondering eyes and innocence. It was in the last years of the Horse Age in America and I grew up among truck horses and fire horses, loved horses as much as any country boy.

My driver's name was "Curley" Ryan, a tough, little, belligerent bantam with a bushy mustache. It was his bald head, of course, that won him the nickname of "Curley." He had four small kids at home, but pursued the habits of a jolly bachelor, sloshed beer all day and stopped to have a go with the prostitutes.

The Adams branch from which we operated was at 250 Grand Street, a block from the dark, tragic Bowery, half a block from my tenement. Since childhood I had known this neighborhood landmark, its busy drivers and beautiful big horses, the sidewalk always heaped with immense cases and trunks.

If I have had any trade other than journalism, it may be that of teamster. Half my youth was spent working for the Adams Express. I started when I was thirteen, would quite in a fit of ambition, try for a better job outside, come back when desperate again. I served at different times as errand boy, receiving clerk, wagon helper, tracer and for almost two years as night porter at the West 45th Street depot. Twelve hours a night stacking, hauling, lifting the heavy freight, till the sweat poured down in rivers.

I carried in my skull then many hundreds of names of cities and towns, and knew their freight rates from New York. The company provided us with a thick rate book, but in the daily rush drivers and clerks had to rely on memory. Later if the tracers found an error, it was deducted from your pay envelope. There was much grumbling over this. Also the hours—we worked from seven until the last hunk of freight was cleared from the depot—nine, ten o'clock, even midnight, without a cent of overtime.

It was a poor, common sort of job, but my boss often made it seem romantic. He was John Reynolds, an old Irish New Yorker with bristling brows and keen fearless blue eyes, the most extravagant cusser I ever knew. My Reynolds had worked under the great John Hoey, and was convinced that our company, the Adams Express, won the Civil War.

The alarm clock rasped its mean top-sergeant reveille. Dawn, like dirty bilgewater, spread in our basement home. My poor mother, always slaving, was first to get out of bed. She fed wood to the stove for breakfast, then tried to wake me, shook me, pleaded, even yelled in her final despair. The tumult woke my father and brothers. The Rumanian house painter, once so jolly a father, had long since begun his career as an invalid. While I washed at the sink, dressed, gulped my breakfast, he lamented over me, prophesied like a Jeremiah my ruin:

"So you are off again, woe to us all! To work on the wagon again with the Irishers! It was the only dream of my life in America that my sons would be educated people! In Rumania a Jewish child was not permitted to reach an education, but here it is free! Here the poorest Jewish children can become rabbis, doctors, lawyers! But my son spits on education. He is a basketball bum, a fighter, he comes back from that dirty Irish gym with a black eye, a broken nose, every night, like a bloody wolf!

"Oy, Mechel. You will yet wind up in the electric chair with your basketball! When you graduated from Public School 20, the teachers told me you were the smartest boy in the class! They gave you a prize, that beautiful American book with pictures. What have you done with it, my son? You have torn that beautiful book into little pieces! O God of the suffering Jews, help my son change foolish ways! Cut my throat! Mechel! Drink my heart's blood! but only go back to school!"

And so on and so forth. It always filled my blood with melancholy and defeat. How could I tell him it was his sickness that forced me to become a family breadwinner before my time?

I kissed him on the mouth and left for the job. If I did not show him some affection in the morning, my father brooded on it miserably all the lonesome day of an invalid.

THE PASSION FOR SPORT

How often did my father say in utter gloom: "Baseball makes gangsters of our children." He hated my baseball, my basketball, worst of all the boxing I did in the basement gym of a nearby Catholic church.

"It is crazy," he mourned, "that Jewish children raised by God-fearing, hard-working Jewish parents, should go into a Christian church, take off their clothes and in their underwear start beating each other like drunken peasants."

The ordinary gulf of misunderstanding between generations had terribly widened in the new country. Many of the East Side young cast off like rusty shackles the old ways, the religion of the fathers, the respect for parents and elders, the love of learning and even the *Mama Loshen,* Yiddish, Mother-Tongue so loved by Jews, the family speech so warm and tender, so rich with humble poetry and humor of the folk.

But worst of all was the athletics. A craze for sports swept the East Side. The parents could not understand. In the old ghetto prison sport was as unthinkable as in the slave barracks of America. Crippled by the ghetto life, the Jew had forgotten the beauty of earth, the joys of the body.

My parents loathed and feared the thing. My father wanted me to strive for education, not for basketball. Yet he had been a powerful swimmer in his youth, a diver and water athlete in the Danube. When the family spent a Sunday at Coney Island, he frightened us by swimming beyond the life lines.

An invalid loses courage, loses faith in the body, and my father now expected me to be killed at my sports. He was horrified, but not surprised when because of baseball I was arrested and put in jail. It happened one hot July Sunday when my "bunch" and I had traveled to Van Cortlandt Park and played a long argumentative game against a Forsythe street "bunch."

Hungry, bone-tired, a little fevered with sun, we started giggling and rough-housing in the crowded subway train going home. I was yelling and doing acrobatics from two subway straps when a heavy fist knocked me to the floor. I looked into the round, red, snarling face of a middle-aged detective disguised in a fireman's blue shirt and teamster's cap. With his other fist he held my pal, Abe Lastis. Another heavy dick with a pimp's fancy little moustache held Maxie Pearl, usually so snotty, now so pale and scared, and Louie Winecor, my best friend in the "bunch," a dark, warm-hearted, impulsive kid whose father was a consumptive tailor dying slowly and painfully like mine.

On a deserted factory street the dicks stopped to beat us up. They kicked us in the belly, the shins and tail, socked our faces until the blood came, spat on us, cursed like madmen: "Yuh little rats, dis'll loin yuh sometin'. It's the only way yuh can understand!" But we hated them then and forever; we learned hate for the bully. I later wrote an indigant letter to the New York *Globe,* regretting our guilt, but protesting the beat-up. It was my first political writing, but lost to history, for it never got printed.

Next morning an old Tammany judge with the cunning face of an old dock rat sentenced us to five days in foul, notorious Raymond Street jail. Our parents were not informed. There were gloomy alcoholics in the jail, perverts and peddlers. Our parents mourned for us and finally went to the police. When I eventually slunk into the door, my mother sobbed with joy but my father cursed the game of baseball that made gangsters of the youth.

Yet, as I have said, my father had been a free joyous athlete in the old country, who loved the sport of swimming. And my grandfather had been quite a strong man. He owned a pottery in the city of Jassy, in far-off Rumania. My father told us children many tales of his legendary father, described him as a tall powerful giant with red cheeks and great flowing white beard across his great chest, like Moses and the prophets.

"So one day my father was walking down the street in his big sheepskin coat and fur hat," my father used to begin, impressively. "And a strong drunken peasant grabbed him by the beard. When drunk, the Christians liked to torture and beat up Jews. The police often joined them so my father lifted his heavy cane and hit the drunken peasant on the head. He split it open. They arrested him and he had to bribe the police capitain. But my father did not fear. He was past eighty when this happened. He was very strong."

"Tell us about the synagogue wall."

"Yes, that time when a big wind swept through Rumania. My father saw that one of the walls of the synagogue was bending. The wind would surely smash our synagogue. Your grandfather put his back against the wall. He yelled for help. He saved the synagogue, but had to yell so long it cracked his throat. He had to wear a silver pipe for the rest of his life. He was 84 years old, and still strong."

"I only want to be as strong as my grandfather," I sometimes pleaded in those days of the battle over athletics.

"Your grandfather did not make a religion out of strength like you boys. It came to him naturally. It was a gift from God. He didn't play games with it, he used it to work for his father, to save the synagogue, to be a man, not an idle basketball player. Look at the horse. Any horse is stronger than a man. But it is

man who commands the horse. Why? Because man has a soul."
I failed to understand his logic. If I had a soul, it was now on
fire with passion for sports. Like so many East Side kids at that
time, I wanted to be a prize fighter, a hero like Champion Abe
Attell or Terrible Terry McGovern, whom I once had followed
with a group of cheering, worshipping kids.

ADOLESCENT FEVER

O magic, wild and dirty East Side night of young friendships,
the "bunch," you were my high school, my college! My bunch
contained some twenty boys, most of them working kids. All day
we drudged at meaningless jobs, harnessed like the truck horse.
At night we were free for the poetry of being a human.

Our "hangout" was at Orchard and Rivington Streets, near
the genteel little house of the College Settlement and Fuchs'
brawling beer saloon, the public library, the public school, the
yellow-bricked Rumanian synagogue with its Moorish dome
where my parents worshipped.

From this street corner we scattered to box in the gym, to
shoot pool at the Dropper's or go to a burlesque show on the
Bowery. Often it was enough just to mope together quietly, just
stand there in a bunch. In other moods we sang soulfully far into
the night, feeling all of love's mystery in "Sweet Adeline," or the
old American yearning in "Swanee River."

Our parents blamed the "bunch" for everything that went
wrong with us. But it was really an island of young innocence,
upon which beat the vast ocean of social corruption.

It wasn't our "sinfulness," for example, that made this barter
of human flesh that poisoned the East Side far and wide. Every
slum has always been used by the respectable as the convenient
hiding place for a city's vice. If the hard-working immigrant parents had to raise honorable families in the middle of a running
sewer it wasn't the fault of the families.

I had seen the cribs along my street since I was a babe,
watched the lines of half-nude girls in loud kimonos as they
lured every passing man and boy. I had only been a fascinated
observer, but now the fever of sex was in my blood, too. Shame
and fascination colored my face red when one of the women
tried to drag me into her crib.

It's strange but true that at seventeen, though every detail of the ugly sex commerce had taken place under my eyes, I had never yet kissed a girl, or even held a girl's hand. I mean the sincere kiss of a good girl, a guarded Jewish daughter of good parents on our block, or the girls we met at settlement house dances. And I am sure none of my bunch had ever talked intimately with a girl. But we dreamed about it, exchanged gossip and misinformation, often suffered in solitude from the immortal fever. Worst of all was the kidding and other pressure on us to become "initiated."

One winter night a few of us went to the Dropper's basement for a game of pool. It was a slow night there, with just a few Eldridge Streeters at one of the two pool tables. The Dropper was behind the cloth curtain at the back, he was fixing up with caramel coloring some of the untaxed rotgut he sold to Bowery saloons. A cheap gangster and pimp named Little Stuss was lying half-boozed on a bench near the red-hot coal stove. Stuss hated my bunch, as he hated and scared everyone else. Any one of us could have beaten him in a fair fight. But he used a gun, and as the Dropper said: "Stuss is so brave because he's so stupid he don't know he can get killed."

He was small, mangy and suspicious as a mongrel dog roving the gutters. He had a low forehead and the fixed, staring eyes of one hypnotized. He was always bothering the decent girls of the neighborhood. The pimp method was to seduce one, then spread the tale, and her parents heard, and a decent life and marriage seemed forever lost. Then she might in despair become one of his women. The iron virtue of the parents thus was made to work for the pimps.

He spat when he saw us and grabbed my coat and snarled: "Come here, yuh little punk!" I pulled away from him and he snarled: "Stinkin' mamma boys, go home and suck mudder's tiddy!"

"Hey don't bother my richest customers!" the Dropper kidded him from behind the curtain.

"These little punks, they don't never come to one of my girls, too stuck-up to give me a tumble, get the hell outa here before I cut yuh to pieces!"

We left in a hurry. Stuss and others were always taunting and pressuring us on sex. It was made to seem so shameful to be a scared virgin. Curley Ryan, the driver on my Adams truck, was always sadistically kidding me. Quite a few times, full of beer generosity, he offered to pay for my initiation.

There was smell and heat of sex all around, like steaming rot of a jungle. It dazed and confused the mind of a boy, in whose blood already burned the fever of the new hormones. I knew many miserable hours with the sickness that asked questions I didn't know how to answer. And no older friend and counsellor, a teacher, doctor or father, was there to help the young. The thing was kept a sewer thing, hidden from the clear sunlight. It was considered vile and taboo, but isn't it also the sacred fountain of human life on the earth?

THE YOUNG HOODLUMS

The East Side nickname, "Dropper," was given those heroes who could drop an opponent with a single punch. Moe Barkis, our neighborhood "dropper," once laid out five enemies who had caught him alone in his poolroom. There were numerous such legends. Once he knocked out the eye of a man with his mighty punch. He was paid $100 for the job. His friends and fellow-workers talked about the big fee with awe. It was rare then.

Moe thought of himself as a businessman, not a gangster. He was a pioneer of that change from the amateur to the professional gangster that has gone on in America. It was little business; now it is big business.

He took a businessman's pride in his poolroom, though it was dismal enough with its flickering gas jets, and the stink of putrid gall from the chicken dealer next door.

The East Side young were crazy about pool. But even more fascinating was the aura of danger around Moe's place. It was the hangout of a different bunch than ours, the tough ones who'd lost their innocence, who'd passed through courts and jails, stabbed, robbed, shot people. None of them worked at a job. Work was for suckers, they sneered. Lefty Louie was one of this bunch. He'd been my classmate at Public School 20, a black-haired boy with big eyes and the shy, averted smile of a troubled innocent. In a few years he would die in the electric chair for a famous underworld killing.

None of them felt like gangsters. None of them felt abnormal. The horror of the whole thing was that there was no horror.

They were only a few years older than us, but treated us like punks and inferiors. Only Moe the Dropper always had a paternal attitude toward me. I think it began that time when he saved me from the Italians.

I was twelve years old, and working on my first job, that nightmare job in the gas-mantle factory. Sick with fatigue, slogging home in the bowery gloom, suddenly I was surrounded by a band of Italian kids. Whooping like joyful fiends, they fell on me with sticks, fists, feet. The East Side was always at war, just like the great nations.

I tasted blood on my mouth, sweat of fear, and pain and believed the pack was out to kill me. Suddenly, a god stepped out of the machine, a skinny kid with blazing eyes and a white face. He threw himself on the enemy like a whirlwind. In a minute or two all six were in flight, I helped a little. My rescuer was Moe Barkis, son of the butcher on the street.

He stared at me and said, coldly: "Yuh stood there like a dummy! Why didn't yuh fight? Yuh should have kicked them in the balls, bit off their noses. Yuh get hurt less if yuh fight!"

We never knew, really, the business secrets of Moe's poolroom. He sold chocolate bars and cigarets, of course, also manufactured cheap bootleg that he sold untaxed to the Bowery saloons. What else? He must have been receiving stolen goods. Once the Dropper disappeared for several days. I was shooting a game with Big Maxie Korn when he stumbled down the steps. He lay down on a bench, breathing hard. His face was like a raw, bloody hamburger, a sickening sight. The cops had been beating him for three days trying to make him stool on some thief or other.

All he now said was: "Get me a coke and a salami sandwich." He didn't complain or curse, just burbled his coke and chewed his sandwich. Later he washed the gore off his face. Moe also "owned" two young prize fighters, whom he trained at our gym. He did a little money lending too; thus began the usury racket that has made him one of the most successful underworld usurers today, the friend of Mayors, Judges, Tammany brass and society folk and other celebrities. If some poor slob who borrows money doesn't pay on time they break his arm or legs as a warning.

It was a mean, slushy night, and not many customers in the poolroom. I sat by Dropper near the stove. He said, thoughtfully:

"Look, I been thinking about yuh, Mike. You're a smart kid, not no Adams Express donkey. You should be a lawyer."

"I gotta work, Moe. My old man. . . ."

"Yair, your sick old man and everyone else's sick old man. I know, but to hell with that! You gotta be a lawyer. I'll fix it for yuh, I'll get yuh a new job you'll have time to study. It'll pay five times more than you get now. O.K.?"

"What sort of job is it?" I mumbled, stupidly.

"How do I know?" he snapped. "Let's wait and see, O.K.?"

"O.K., Moe."

A raggedy kid with a face flushed by running tumbled down the stairs and handed Moe a note. He read it slowly. "Come back here," he said and I followed him behind the curtain at the back. He handed me a loaded revolver. "I got a thing to do," he said. "Carry this and walk behind me. When we get to the place follow me into the hall and gimme the gun." It was a familiar trick with the professionals. If a cop stopped them he would find no gun. I was nervous, looked behind me often, yet felt confident. The great man always made me feel safe around him.

He did his mysterious "thing" in the tenement, then we came back in the same fashion. As I returned his gun, Moe resumed our conversation. "Yair, Mike," he mused, "it's a good thing, law. If I could read good like you I'd try it myself. A smart lawyer goes places. Yair, Mike, you be a lawyer. I'll fix up that job for yuh. Trust your Foxy Grandpa."

WHY I'M NOT A LAWYER

Why did I avoid the Dropper all those days? Why did I gloom with nameless worries? One sultry summer night the Dropper found me in the Catholic gym. I was boxing with one of his young fighters, "Kid O'Reilly," a gaunt printer's apprentice with a wicked punch whose real name was Aaron Cohen. (The Irish had dominated the prize ring for a century, an Irish ring name was then a necessity for the "lesser breeds.")

The Dropper took my gloves, but didn't strip, just in his street pants and shoes, gave the Kid a ruthless lesson in legalized slaughter. He told me to walk him home. He bought an orange from a pushcart and ate it. "Where ya been?" he said harshly. "Don't ye like the deal?"

"Gee, I like it, Dropper."

"O.K., so ya gotta keep in touch wit me. Dis is a business deal, not no ring around da rosy. Unnerstand?"

"Yep."

"O.K. then. I saw Bennie yesterday. In a week or so he'll have a route set up for ya. How much do yuh pull down at the Adams?"

"Thirty bucks a month."

"Big stuff," the Dropper drily commented. "Wit Benny yuh'll knock down at least fifty bucks a week. A week. And no sweatin and hustlin freight. And time to study like for a lawyer. Ya wanna be a lawyer, donchya?"

"Yes, I guess so."

"Don't guess—know! I'm going places, Mike! In five years I can use a smart young private lawyer of my own. The big shots all have their private lawyers. I'll make money on ya! This is a business investment, like I got wit Aaron and the other kids I manage. Get it, Mike?"

"I got it."

"Then cheer up, fer God's sake! I hate a guy can't make up his lousy mind! How ya expect to win sometin if ya won't gamble?" The Dropper always knew what he wanted. I think this is why we admired him so much.

How the news spread I don't know, but the next night "Horney" Fleishman was telling my bunch all the inside facts. He was an envious, inquisitive slob with a foolish grin and loads of stupid ambition. Once "Horney" bought a revolver to make himself out a tough guy, and surprised us one night, pointing it at our feet and saying, like in cowboy stories, "Dance, yuh buggers, dance!" So Maxie Korn took the gun from him, and slapped him around, and we all pushed him around. "Mike'll be making fifty bucks a week!" he now yelped, with his hot envy. And I could see their faces fall, and envy in their eyes.

Big Maxie said, in his slow, honest way, "Nah, dem jobs have got no future, Mike, like regular work has got. Duh cops is always on your tail." So there was a hot discussion, yet I could feel their envy, and it's wrong to flaunt fifty dollars in the face of nine dollars a week. I was ashamed.

I had no will power, nor any craving for success. I don't know what I wanted, I was formless, and the Dropper could have molded me in any shape he desired. Except for one obstacle. I was a romantic. In me the will woke only when the heart was on fire. I needed something more inspiring than the Dropper's dollar flag.

Bone-tired, I came from work one night to find my home sunk again in tragedy. My father had suffered one of his worst attacks —liver, kidneys, blood vessels—that horror and crucifixion, the painter's lead poisoning. My mother wiped the cold corpse sweat from his gray face. She whispered, her strong dark face smeared with tears: "He wants to die! Tell him something good, Mechel. Make him live!" So desperate I invented a quick fable, a Horatio Alger fairy tale about how I'd met a rich, kindly lawyer who gave me a job at fifty dollars a week and offered to make me a lawyer, and so forth. They listened like small, trustful children. My father's sad, fading eyes gleamed again with hope. All of them were suddenly happy. For the next few days, my heart warmly urged me to became a lawyer, to keep them happy.

That Sunday, I was shooting a quiet game of pool at Dropper's place, and Al the Bastard came hustling in, a young, mean gangster punk. He excitedly whispered something in the Dropper's ear. The Dropper smiled, grimly, signalled to me, "Come along."

Al led us up dirty stairs till we came out on a roof. It was always glorious to come there from the street. The sun setting in red and gold on the Jersey shore! The skyscrapers flaming in the sunset! The vast endless pure sky above! Clotheslines flapped like colored flags in the Atlantic breeze, and on some Sunday newspapers lay a girl with her skirts rolled up to her waist. She was "Woogie," a sort of half-wit of the neighborhood. She munched a chocolate bar and stared calmly at the sky. Around her buzzed a dozen young products of the Thing, like dirty flies around a carrion, cruelly gloating, snickering, wise-cracking nervously. It was that slum horror, a "line-up," or "shag party," as the West Side Irish called it.

I caught a look from the Dropper. He grinned at me cruelly, it was the same cruel, gloating look of the others. He was part of the Thing, too. I ran away. Down the steps into the street, where old-world Jews were moving to the synagogue for evening prayers.

Maybe this experience on the roof was the reason I never have become a great lawyer, the Dropper's own.

THE VOICE OF THE PEOPLE

Amid all its dirt, violence and poverty, the East Side yet sang. My father loved to sing and he and his friends often argued fervently over the merits of their favorite folk singers and synagogue cantors. Poetry and music were important to these paupers.

My mother hummed or sang in the kitchen; at dawn the pensive music of the housewives began to flow down the airshaft walls. From every floor there came also the Biblical lamentation of the grandfathers, rapt in their endless synagogue passions. It was the outcry of the Arabian desert, heard 3,000 years ago in Babylon and Egypt, when the Jews were slaves. Now that ancient music penetrated the blood of the young American Jews, as with George Gershwin, born and reared in a tenement only a few blocks from my own.

The pushcart peddlers in the street often chanted raucous little ditties of their own composition, praising their bananas, tinware, gloves, potatoes. And in the gloomy shadows of the sweatshops, above the tyrannous roar and humming of the machines, the workers sang and relieved their hearts.

Song broke out softly and spontaneously there, as in a prison at dusk, or with soldiers on a painful march. The low bitter voices of the men mingled with the silver sorrow of the girls, and on my Adams Express rounds, I would often stop to listen, and wonder why God had chosen the Jews for so much suffering.

At night in my sleep I would hear the bakers sing, the bearded, tubercular young bakers toiling in the rat-infested cellar next door.

Even the prostitutes often sang the old songs of the folk. They sat before their cribs, night and day waiting for customers and sang to help them forget America.

It was from my father that we learned the old songs; it was he who sang the lullabies to us when we were small. His favorite was "Raisins and Almonds," by Goldfaden. That pure, lovely melody still is sung and when I hear it my heart is touched and I remember my poor father.

Once, as we walked in the tumultuous street, he pressed my hand and pointed to a passerby who wore a cloth cap and an old yellow coat with large buttons. He had burning black eyes and the pale, tense face of a sweatshop slave.

"Look and remember him!" my father whispered. "That is Morris Rosenfeld, the poet." He recited for me a little lyric in which the poet laments that he rarely sees his beloved child, because he leaves at dawn for the sweatshop, when the child is

sleeping, and returns late at night when the child has returned to
sleep.

There was a group of these sweatshop poets. They knew the
same life and suffering as the people, and what they wrote of
themselves was true of the people. They dwelt on no special, remote planet of fine letters, but in the world of the people. Their
poetry was realist as a photograph, all the homely details of truth
were there, yet ennobled with the rebellion and hope of man.

The East Side Jews knew and loved their poets as warmly as
the Scottish folk have loved their peasant-bard, Bobby Burns.

And another time my father took me to see the great Eliakum
Zunzer in his printing shop on East Broadway. That street was
broad as a boulevard, and one of the last where there were trees.
My father pointed out the coffee houses where the Jewish intellectuals with long hair and pince-nez glasses played chess day
and night, drank tea and argued over God, socialism, and the
acting of Jacob P. Adler.

"It must be a wonderful thing to be an actor," my father
sighed. "Or a poet like Eliakum. I could die for one of his
songs." He tried to show me the greatness of the old bards, but I
guess I was too young to understand. Only later, after reading
Sol Liptzin's biography and the collected songs in translation, did
I understand his magnitude.

In his youth, Eliakum had become the most famous *Badchan*
in all Lithuania and Poland. These bards presided over the wedding feasts and improvised witty, sentimental, often philosophic
verses. Then he began to write his ballads and songs, a veritable
history in rhyme and music of the Jewish struggle for survival.
Every great movement and crisis that confronted the Jew through
the nineteenth century is there—beginning with the coming of
the railroads and the economic problems they made for Jewish
innkeepers on the old highways. The great Enlightenment, a
thrust to modernism, then the disillusionment, the anti-Semitic
horrors and pogroms. The Zionism that followed as an answer to
anti-Semitism, then the flight to America. Eliakum shared every
experience of his flock and put it into his poems, which he sang
like Homer.

The gentle old grandfather, around whom his family and
friends were always gathered, had a trim white beard and twin-
kling eyes. He patted my head and said kindly: "Your boychik is
strong. He probably wants to be a baseball player." He impro-

vised a funny little song about baseball for me. He was all human. If Jewish children liked baseball, he would learn to like it, too.

On his gravestone in a Brooklyn cemetery there is inscribed this epitaph: "O Passerby, pause in reverence. Here, silent in the dust, lies the faithful voice of his people."

TWAIN IN THE SLUMS

Though surrounded by it for decades, my father never dared to speak English. He was subjective. But English wasn't really needed on the old East Side, that Jewish metropolis where one could work and love, live and die only with Yiddish.

At home our parents talked to us in Yiddish, and we answered in English. It is a custom among all immigrant families in America. A young Mohawk bridge worker once told me it is just as common among Indians, where the older generation is often un-American and can't speak English.

Language is important. You can get to feel lost and inferior not to understand the speech of the people around you. But I think my father envied me only for the story books in English I brought from the public library. Above everything, he loved a good, flowing yarn. He himself used to hold groups of his friends with wonderful tales from the Arabian Nights that he'd learned in youth from the Rumanian peasants.

Now it was the epoch of Mark Twain in America. That great story-teller was almost as famous as Jim Jeffries, the heavyweight champion. He was perhaps the last of our national writers, loved by the whole people. The East Side kids knew him and loved him as well as did other Americans. My father watched my fascination, heard my chuckles, as I devoured *Huckleberry Finn* under the gaslight.

He offered me a nickel an hour if I'd read it to him. A nickel was big money then, but he was a lusty young house painter, free with his nickels.

So I read him the history of free-hearted Huck Finn and the noble slave, Jim, and their escape from injustice on the broad Mississippi, with its starlight, rafts and mystery. "It's like when I was a boy on our own Danube," said my father, fondly.

How he laughed when I read about those brassy swindlers, the self-styled "Dauphin" and the crummy old "Duke." He compared them to a certain Count in Rumania who tried to swindle his father, the potter, but was exposed as a forger and the bigamous husband of fifteen wives. "Your Mark Twain, he understands the aristocrats!" my father chuckled. "He spits on them, he has a heart of gold! Like our own Sholem Aleichem he wants to help people to laugh. Laughter is healthy, all the doctors prescribe it, says Sholem Aleichem. But I think he also feels the tears of the people. Mark Twain has no tears."

"I love Mark Twain better. And I wish I could live on a raft like *Huckleberry Finn*."

"We would all like to live on a raft," smiled my father. "But God wants us to live in these tenements. And cats and dogs do their business in the halls."

Mark Twain often visited the East Side. He liked to talk in the old-world cafés where the writers, actors, doctors and other Jewish intellectuals all day drank tea and philosophized. Mark Twain showed a deep concern for the Jews, would issue frequent protests against their slaughter by the ugly Russian tsardom. The East Side loved him the more deeply for such passionate friendship.

I was eleven years old when at the school assembly one morning our bearded old Civil War principal, Colonel Smith, announced there'd be a free performance of *The Prince and the Pauper* at the Educational Alliance, a big settlement house.

That Saturday morning in spring, while engulfed on the sidewalk by the waiting mob of howling, pushing, wrestling, excited young East Siders in knee pants, an open carriage with two horses drove up. Out stepped a magnificent figure all in white. He smoked a big black cigar and wore a pirate's big moustache. His noble white hair was like the battle plume of one of Henty's kings. All of us recognized him. "Hooray, it's Mark Twain!" rose the battle cheer. The great man seemed pleased. He patted our heads as he passed among us. My head he also touched.

Now an event later when I was seventeen. It'd been a long day for me, up at six. I'd sweated on the Adams truck till about eight at night, then hung around with my "bunch" until about one. So I was dead tired and grateful for bed, but at three in the morning I was shocked out of sleep by a frightened call from my mother. I lit the gas, and saw a terrible sight. My father, white as a

groaning corpse, with wild, staring eyes, was smeared with blood.
He'd had another of his fits of accumulated despair, grabbed a
kitchen knife and slashed his wrist. It had happened once before.
"Talk to him, Mechel!" pleaded my mother. "Tell him he
must go on living!" I tried as best I could, but he was trapped in
his fury. "Only let me die!" he muttered monotonously. In my
heart I agreed with him. A chronic invalid is like a running sore
in the family that cripples your living. It tears your heart out and
fills you with poison. I even found myself hating my father at
times, then hating myself more with the guilt of having such evil
thoughts.

I trembled, didn't know what to say next in pleading. Then by a
miracle I remembered Mark Twain. Carefully, I started to read
the beloved book aloud. Gradually my father began to listen, to
forget his suffering, his career of an invalid.

A JEWISH FATHER

My father had been the soul of our home. Now it was hard to
accept this stranger as my father, this suffering invalid with the
shrunken face and gloomy eyes. What justice could there be in a
universe that punished so? And there had been no crime—he
was innocent, innocent!

I could remember how handsome he'd been as a young father,
a tall, rangy figure with a smiling, clean-cut face, high forehead,
a red moustache and long sideburns. His eyes sparkled, he had
that quality only the French regard seriously as an important virtue—he was gay.

He liked to dress well—on the holidays this house painter
dressed in a stiff white shirt and collar, with an elegant bow tie,
a big gold watch chain, a suit with long tails like an actor's or
rabbi's. He loved friends and family, loved wine and food, feasts
and parades, and above all, the theater. My father was one of
those fanatic theater patriots of the old East Side, an audience of
illiterate sweatshop workers who adored the classics, and most
resembled the working folk of London in whose sun of warm
comprehension Shakespeare was able to flourish.

I was the first of three sons—he made me his companion,
showed me his world, talked to me seriously as to a grown-up, answered all my questions, as with a respected friend.

One summer day my brother, Manny, a braggart of four, was run over by a horse car. The cruel metal wheel was deeply imbedded in his ankle. A crowd of emotional East Side neighbors agreed that the car would have to be pushed over my brother's foot to release him.

But suddenly my father flung himself under the car, his head under the wheel beside my brother's foot. "Lift the car! I won't let you cut off his foot! Cut first my head!" They pleaded and argued with him; finally, straining and groaning, they managed to lift the horse car, thus saved my brother's foot.

I was four years old, it was the time of Christmas. My father and I were walking through the frozen slush on Houston Street and passed the huge brown church of the Germans. Through the open doors I saw a fairy vision, a sudden glory that ravished my heart, green, red and silver balls and gleaming candles, my first Christmas tree!

"Papa, I want to go in there," I said, trembling. "No, no," he said kindly, and tried to explain what a great sin it was for a Jew to enter the church of his enemies. He related terrible anecdotes of things he'd seen in Christian Rumania, he told of pogroms and centuries of persecution.

"Only once, Pappa, just let me touch that tree once," I pleaded. When I started to cry, he shuddered and with a grim face led me to the tree. When we came out into the street again, I began to feel sorry for the thing I'd made him do. "Papa, don't worry. It wasn't your fault—God will punish mè not you."

He shrugged humorously and said: "It's finished! The sins of a Jewish boy until he is thirteen and a man, must rest on his father. But it was really a beautiful tree! What a good thing for the children!" And we remembered with joy all the way home that beautiful tree.

He was drinking wine and reading his Yiddish newspaper one night after supper. Suddenly he exploded: "Great news, Katie! The twentieth century is coming next Thursday night!"

"Whatever it is, it probably means more trouble for the Jews," sniffed my mother, ever the peasant skeptic.

"They promise us telephones, Katie, electric lamps, wagons without horses, flying machines and wonderful new battleships."

"All I ask is they should leave us alone," said my mother. "And Goldfaden is also coming to New York, they say," my father exulted. This was Abraham Goldfaden, father of the Yiddish theater, an exquisite genius who composed words and music of numerous folk operas. My father had known him in Jassy, Rumania, their common home.

There was to be a welcome to the new century on the Brooklyn Bridge. My mother refused to go, so my father and I trudged through the damp snowfall and at midnight, heard the great city welcome the mysterious stranger with full exuberant voice. All the tugboats and ocean liners boomed deeply. Hundreds of thousands of people packed on the immense tall bridge sounded their holiday horns, we heard from miles around all the street cars clanging their bells and the fireworks banged and splashed the sullen sky.

My father clutched my hand and said, joyfully: "And to think Goldfaden is also coming here!" This delighted him more than all the promised telephones and battleships of the new century.

GLORIOUS YIDDISH STAGE

Boris Thomasheffsky, of the younger generation of East Side tragedians, was tall and imposing, with a cap of black curly hair, large mournful Neapolitan eyes and a most tremendous belly. What Anglo-Saxon star would dare to play Hamlet with such a Falstaffian stomach? But the East Side paid no heed to such petty details. The play and the acting were the thing. The Elizabethan audience had the same indifference to the fact that Shakespeare's women were played by boys. The play was the thing.

The stage door of Thomasheffsky's theater faced our tenement. One summer night I was shooting marbles on the sidewalk with some friends when there loomed over us a fat young man with painted cheeks and a little beard, dressed in the long alpaca coat, skull cap and fringed white Tzizas of a Talmud student.

"Come children!" he commanded. "I will give you candy." It was Thomasheffsky. He led us down the long, narrow alley into the center of a blazing stage. We could see nothing, we heard only the mysterious groans and shuffling of an invisible audience.

"Stand in line!" our captor commanded, giving each of us a

peppermint drop. "And rub your eyes and try to cry! You are orphans, your papa and mama have just been killed by the gentiles. Do you understand? Cry, cry!"

It was impossible, somehow. We just stood there dumbly on exhibition in our torn, ragged, realistic shirts and pants and dirty street faces, but couldn't produce a tear. Then Thomasheffsky spoke a long loud speech that set the audience off into a storm of sobs and wails as though someone had dropped a bomb. We caught the contagion, and now how we cried! Then suddenly the tall actor with the big belly herded us off the stage, then hurriedly into the drab, ordinary street.

Jacob Gordin was the East Side's great playwright. Every season half a dozen of his works were produced. Some were originals, others translations and adaptations from world literature, including Shakespeare. Gordin was a man of the widest culture and fluent in most of the languages of Europe.

One of his devices was to reshape such classics as Goethe's *Faust* into the tale of a poor Talmud scholar whom the Devil tempts and turns into a rich, unhappy, alcoholic millionaire. *The Jewish King Lear* told of a wealthy dry goods merchant whose American children betray him.

Many of the plays of Gordin and other playwrights seemed to concern themselves with the tragic gulf that had opened up between the old-world immigrants and their American-born children. The authors were always on the side of the parents and the offspring were often portrayed as coarse, heartless social climbers, in a shameless hurry to cast off the old Jewish God, the old family love, the Yiddish speech, anything that reminded them of their humble origins.

The vast, generous spirit of Shakespeare hung over this theater of the immigrant Jews. The tight "well-made" problem play was not to their liking. They demanded life in full abundance. The feelings had to be deep, the tragedy must be heroic and optimistic, and of course, there had to be the clowns of Shakespeare, and a cheerful wedding or drinking party. The banquet table was an important piece of furniture.

The actors ate and drank a great deal on and off stage. There were no pretty little shallow Hollywood teen-agers among them, they were hefty, solid, real men, real women, who had lived and suffered, therefore could interpret life. And they never grew old;

the East Side audience, like a fond husband, never could see the changes of time in the dear one. These grandmothers were forever Juliet.

My mother, foundation of our home, used to brag now and then, "I am strong like a horse. I wish I could be sick."

But in one of the periods when all our troubles piled up on us, she had the flu and was depressed and nervous. So my father insisted on taking the family to the theater, so my mother could have a good cry and be healed.

He took us to see *The Merchant of Venice,* with Adler or Kessler in the leading role; I don't remember which, I only remember the strong emotion of that theater night, the swelling sobs and outcries of that sensitized audience, as they suffered with Shylock, the poor little Jew typically alone in a land of lynchers, the butt of the wit and spittle of every ignorant yokel or young aristocratic punk, deprived of every means of defense, deprived by law of all livelihood except this miserable outlawed trade of usury.

Was he not a man, Shylock asked, who bled like other men when pricked? He felt like any man the heart pain when he was debased and tortured, and could utter no protest. Silence and humiliation were his daily portion and only one human thing was allowed him—his love of family. There was his only shelter in the world of Christian hate and racism. And now the fortress had been breached from within—his daughter, Jessica, had betrayed him to the cruel and murderous enemy. "Jessica, my daughter, what have you done?" Only a Jewish audience, could truly understand that cry of Shylock, the full depth of his tragedy.

Marvelous Shakespeare, who despite his own gentile prejudice, could yet register some of the deeps of the Jewish tragedy. My mother, who so rarely could weep, now had joined the theater collective of tears. Her heartfelt sighs and sobs unpacked her heart of our own family suffering. She leaned over and kissed me fervently, I felt the hot tears on my face. "It cuts the heart," she sobbed. "Do you understand, Mechel? That girl betrayed her father to the killers." So I began to sniffle, too, but my mother wiped the tears away and gave me another salami sandwich to eat and a pickle.

THE YIDDISH THEATER

The theater was almost a sacred institution on the East Side. Everyone and his old aunt was a theater patriot, argufier, addict. Fleeing for their lives in the 1880's from the bloody tsarist pogroms, in haste and trembling, the people yet remembered to pack their theater in the baggage.

How the great actors were worshipped! I have a memory after these sixty years of beholding Jacob P. Adler, dean of the tragedians, as he moved through the filth and confusion of our street. It was a drab wintry day. Tall, white-maned and hawk-nosed, how magnificent he seemed in his costume of the prospering East Side tragedian, the rich fur coat, the wide black sombrero, gold-headed cane and flowing Windsor tie! His ragged subjects and their noisy kids followed, applauding the haughty Bourbon king. He lit up the dirty street like a sudden ray of Utopia!

Since the time I had begun to walk and argue, my father had taken me at least once a week to some theater show. He was, like a child, eager for all life, all experience, omnivorous in his taste. He liked everything that glittered, the circus, the Yiddish vaudeville and comic operetta. Above all, he loved, as did most theater patriots, the classic tragedies and problem plays of the East Side stage.

There must have been at least ten theaters devoted to the serious repertoire. Before I was seven I had seen plays by Gorky, Hauptmann, Tolstoy, Jacob Gordin, and of course, the divine Shakespeare, playwright of all humanity. Every serious Jewish actor had to compete with his rivals in the Shakespearean drama, or lose status and following.

The Robbers by Schiller was one of my father's favorites. He could recite long passages of this romantic ode to freedom. In the play, one of the robbers named Franz kills his brother. When I got into some fierce domestic battle with my younger brother, Manny, and hurt him, my father would shriek at me, "Franz! you will die in the electric chair some day!"

My father's group of friends, among them housepainters, clothing workers, bearded pushcart peddlers, and some wanderers, were all theater fanatics. None had ever benefited by any good college course in the drama, but what passion, what fine-smelling finesse, they often showed in their esthetic disputations! In the wine celler or around our kitchen table, they were forever arguing just like intellectuals, about God and socialism and their favorite actors and plays.

I remember an argument one night between my father and "Tessie" Miller, a young sweatshop slave. Tessie's nickname came from the fact that in his shabby clothes he always managed to look elegant. He was slim and handsome, with large romantic brown eyes like some starved poet. He smiled shyly, maybe because he couldn't make up his mind as to which of my beautiful aunts who worked in his shop he loved the most. He courted both by frequently bringing them violets and cheese cake bought out of his starvation pay. Some of my father's friends were semi-Americanized and it was they who'd given him the nickname of an effeminate because he liked flowers so much. They supposed it was somehow un-American to like flowers!

Underneath, this Tessie was tough and obstinate, a hot partisan of David Kessler, that fiery dark young tragedian lately arrived from Rumania, who was pressing hard and winning followers of Jacob P. Adler. My father, poor, unfortunate conservative, clung to the great Adler, of course.

So, waving his glass of red Rumanian wine, my father was bragging in our kitchen of his hero. "When Jacob P. Adler walks on the stage, he just has to look at you, and your heart trembles like a bathtub full of running water. He doesn't have to speak a word!"

Tessie gaily sneered, "So a mad bull in a meadow could also make you tremble just by looking! But David Kessler is a man and a Jew, not just an actor! Kessler makes you think and feel and suffer! He is deeper than Adler! Adler is only an actor, always showing off!"

My father exploded with righteous indignation. "Adler not a man! Adler not a Jew! You have gone crazy!"

Tessie, calm and cruel, broke in quietly: "And they say Adler has a hundred wives and children scattered over the United States. Wherever he tours, there he leaves another family. Is that being a great actor of the Jews? Is that a man to act Shakespeare? David Kessler acts only Shakespeare, not himself. Adler exploits Shakespeare like he does his wives. You can tell he feels himself better than Shakespeare."

"Out of my home!" thundered my father in his most theatrical voice almost the voice of Adler. "You wolves, always trying to tear my King into pieces! Even in my own kitchen, drinking my wine! Out, out, lousy atheists, Epicureans, socialists, anarchists! Take your violets and cheese cake to hell! Spit on the sun, not on Jacob P. Adler! He will live long after your Kessler, your cheese cake, your Shakespeare are long forgotten!"

Tessie gasped, everyone looked horrified at my hot-headed father's blasphemy. The East Side had no parochial view of the divine Shakespeare, even if he was a gentile. And the next night my father apologized to Tessie and the other sweatshop theater patriots for his burst of ignorance. He loved the theater too much ever to belittle the divine Shakespeare.

NEW THOUGHTS, OLD FAITH, YOUTH'S TROUBLING TIME

I had to be up at 5:30 to make that Adams Express job by 7, when I had to be at the stables to help Curley, my driver, harness up the team. Curley Ryan was all louse. Once I was only five minutes late, but he pulled out without me, cost me a day's pay.

One Monday morning my mother just couldn't force me awake. There'd been too much excitement over the weekend, a burlesque show, a rough basketball game, some boxing, rambling, hardly any sleep. My bunch and I parted reluctantly on the corner, singing soulfully our last barbershop chords. Only three hours later here was my mother shaking me, begging me to get up. It was a real shock. She pulled off the bedclothes. Nothing helped. Her despairing cries woke only my father and two brothers. The middle brother, Manny, an obstinate one who regarded me as his chief obstacle on the road to life, poured water on my head. I chased him around the room, then dressed in a hurry, gulped a hunk of black bread and milk and started to go.

My father looked at me timidly. "You are not laying your phylacteries? You are not davvening your morning prayers?"

"No, papa, it's too late. I don't want to lose a day's pay."

"A day's pay," he sighed, and said no more. I kissed his unshaven cheek, smelled again that sour bed-smell, then hurried off into the fighting world of wage labor.

Curley and I and the big, patient, kindly truck horses made our familiar morning deliveries of supplies to the garment factories, the big wooden boxes of woolen and cotton yardage, the big bundles of buttons, thread, trimmings. In the afternoon we would cover the same route to collect the manufactured products.

I liked this hard work, really enjoyed using all my muscles and sweating freely in the open air, not pent up in some stifling factory or office. It was a fine spring day. A new sun was shining warmly on the hurry and worry of the most anxious city in the world. When we passed a little park I could smell growing grass and see buds on the skinny trees. Such moments and such days always moved me strangely, made me want to escape from the world. But today a dark, obscure guilt lay on my mind, a melancholy that clouded all other feeling.

What crime had I done? In the dusk, passing a wooden little synagogue shack, I saw the bearded Jews going in for the evening prayers. Then, suddenly, I remembered my crime. Since my thirteenth year, when by the ancient tribal rite I was made a man and a Jew, I had failed for the first time to say my morning prayers. That's why my conscience accused me all day, and clouded the young poetry of spring.

Religion is deep in all of us, because it is so close to fear. Strange pale flower of fear, religion has grown out of the crisis in man's history. An old man on his deathbed will call for his long-gone mother to come as in his childhood and kiss and comfort him. Religion is the old mother, strong in us and bearing the old irrational hope and fear.

Now at seventeen I was entering a painful time when religion was to begin to trouble me. It wasn't just a reflection of the sex delirium of the adolescent, though God knows I had that trouble, too. Religion was man's first questioning of the universe, the questions that separated man from the animals: What is life? Why are we here? Not how the world was made, but why, why?

Next morning my mother tried to wake me at the usual time but I groaned and turned away sharply. It was so wonderful to have that extra half-hour of sleep. But this morning my mother didn't plead or wring her hands; she just let me go on sleeping. And my father didn't say a word. I think they pitied me, and wanted me to have the sleep, because they knew how badly I needed it. At hard work twelve hours a day, then playing hard for another five hours, they often said I was crazy, all youth was insane, but they loved me anyway, I guess, so let me sleep.

My fear, my conscience, kept aching, I was cheating someone
up there, the old buried fears emerged, the angry God was
watching and waiting. Yet literally, those morning prayers had
meant nothing to me. I'd been taught just enough Hebrew to enable me to read the prayers, not enough Hebrew to understand a
single word.

Judaism was a ritual, an old, old folk memory, a frustration.
And my heart was with the folk and their old God. But mumbling through the twenty or thirty blackletter pages, sometimes I
would send out a private prayer into vast mysterious spaces. It
was in English, my native speech, a prayer for my father. There
is no place for the spontaneous private prayer in the old Judaism.

One night my father suffered another crisis, fever, vomiting,
the terrible bone-pain of lead poisoning. I was up half the night.
He liked to have me near. I wiped the cold sweat from his face.
His eyes stared at me hungrily. They seemed to be accusing me.
Next morning I woke early and resumed my morning prayers.
But in a few days, I again dropped the ritual, this time, forever.

I had had a taste of freedom. But the old Jewish God was not
dead in me—only transformed. Now I was searching for Him in
English. I hunted Him on the express truck, in the gym, on street
corners, not in the synagogue. Yes, at that time I was troubled
not only with my job, my sick father, boxing, basketball, and, of
course, my lost education, and mad explosions of the sex problem, but also I had to worry over God.

THE JEWISH SABBATH:
"OUR BEAUTIFUL BRIDE"

How sacred was the Sabbath to our fathers and mothers. The
old-world Jews called her their beautiful Bride, and welcomed
her with mystic song. We children welcomed her for her wonderful food.

It began early on Friday morning when from all over the tenement you heard a tireless drumfire, the housewives chop-chop-
ping the pike and the carp they would blend with spices into
that classic dish, "gefielte fish."

Flushed with the coal stove heat, my mother was busy as a
general on the battlefield. She cooked, she baked, she scoured
and cleaned the home in every crack and corner. She laid the
festal white tablecloth, and then, when the first star appeared in

the sky, she lit the Sabbath candles and blessed them. There was a candle for each of us, her strong, work-scarred hands blessed the family. A strange, withdrawn look came over her face as she prayed, it scared the children, the mother had abandoned them.

But soon she relented, the Sabbath feast began, how we ate like gluttons her home-baked Sabbath bread, her chicken soup with fine noodles, her stuffed fish and boiled chicken and potato or carrot pudding, the apple sauce, the cake, everything. Hurrah, another victory for the Jews! Papa had been working that week, there was food in the house!

(Don't turn up your nose, gentle reader. Food is quite important. Children need it, as learned doctors have often pointed out. Even a healthy man can die without food. So, friend, to stay alive, eat food.)

If you can find it. Yiddish literature often described as a typical hero a little village Jew who has traded all week and tramped the icy roads, but failed to earn enough money to provide a Sabbath eve supper for his family. What despair he feels. He can stand all of God's little jokes, but not this one. It's too humiliating.

The Jewish sabbath was stricter than even the notorious Scottish Sunday. The orthodox not only were forbidden to labor, but they could not smoke or handle money, or make a fire for cooking, or walk further than the synagogue, or read a newspaper or secular book, or ride in a streetcar or other transport, sing a popular tune, make love or war—and more besides. But the stern code was obeyed and many a faithful one would rather have died than smoke a cigaret on the sacred Sabbath.

My father had always worked on the East Side, thus had no Sabbath problem. Then he fell sick, and at twelve I left school and went to work. I could find a job only in a hellish factory that toiled on the Jewish Sabbath. My father was too sick to forbid me. My mother too desperate with the bigger problems of how to live. It just was never discussed. The three dollars a week I brought home was necessary to our survival. Living came first, as it did with many other East Siders. Little channels of change were undermining the ghetto walls. Often youth was carried off into the great river of American life by such necessities.

And at seventeen I first departed from the Mosaic code and ate non-kosher, gentile food. This was also an accident, not a rebellion. How many Jews through the ages had taken martyrdom rather than eat the forbidden pork. It sounds irrational, but how many non-Jews have also died for an idea, for an abstraction. In this case the pork was a symbol of tyranny, like the apple on the head of the Swiss patriot's son.

The Jews were my family, and I felt loyalty deep in my bones. The Irish or Polish Catholic will often have this same loyalty to the national church that has suffered with their folk. From the time I was Bar Mitzvah at thirteen, initiated into the tribal manhood, I prayed every morning with the phylacteries and shawl. And I refrained from the non-sanctified food of the gentile.

But one summer the drivers in my Adams Express branch organized a picnic on Staten Island. There were a few ragged trees in the dusty grounds, the sun blazed like a loud drunkard, the rowboats bobbed in Raritan Bay like happy drunks. We played baseball and drank barrels of beer. It was flowing like a fountain. Curley Reynolds, my driver, got to third base where there was a barrel for anyone who reached there. He refused to travel on and tried to empty the barrel. Charley Ryan laid him out with a calm hook to the jaw. Everyone laughed, Curley was unpopular. We dragged him out of the sun and sloshed him with cold beer.

Everyone seemed to want me to drink with him. I think it was because I never drank and I was a Jew. I supposed they wanted to see a drunken Jew. But the beer made me love everyone, and I sang barbershop harmonies with them and played baseball and drank the beer.

I was not on guard, therefore, when the dinner gong sounded and Ernie Bahnmuller, a stocky driver with eyeglasses, herded us to the eating shack for the shore dinner which was the feature of such picnics.

They passed a huge dish of some fried stuff and it tasted salty and good. "What are they?" I asked old Murph, a driver who looked like John L. Sullivan. "Clams!" he boomed, "Staten Island has the best!" I was shocked, I was thrilled. The clam is a shellfish. They, too, are forbidden my Moses. But I was young, and born in America and couldn't feel too guilty. The ghetto walls were thin in America.

Bibliography

BY MIKE GOLD

During fifty years as a working journalist, Gold contributed thousands of stories, poems, and articles to publications like the *Masses,* the *Liberator,* the *Daily* and *Sunday Worker,* the *National Guardian,* the *New Masses, Masses and Mainstream,* the *People's World,* and a number of commercial papers, among them the New York *Globe,* Boston *Journal,* Oakland *Post-Enquirer,* and San Francisco *Call.* In addition, he published the following principal works:

> *The Damned Agitator and Other Stories* (Chicago, no date [around 1924]), fiction.
>
> *Hoboken Blues,* a full-length play, in *American Caravan,* edited by Lewis Mumford, Paul Rosenfeld, and Alfred Kreymbourg (New York, 1926).
>
> *120 Million* (New York, 1929), anthology.
>
> "Money," in *One-act Plays,* edited by D. H. Clark and T. R. Cook (Boston, 1929).
>
> *Jews Without Money* (New York, 1930), fictional autobiography.
>
> *Change the World* (New York, 1935), anthology.
>
> *Battle Hymn,* with Michael Blankfort (New York, 1936), full-length play.
>
> *The Hollow Men* (New York, 1941), literary comment.
>
> *The Mike Gold Reader* (New York, 1954), anthology.

ABOUT MIKE GOLD

Although Gold is frequently referred to and briefly discussed in books about twentieth century American literature and politics, the most substantial published commentaries on his life and work to date are by the editor of this volume. These are an appreciation of *Jews Without Money* and a biographical study of Gold's early career (up to 1930):

> "The Book of Poverty," in the *Nation* (February 28, 1966), pages 242–45.
>
> "The Education of Michael Gold," in *Proletarian Writers of the Thirties,* edited by David Madden (Carbondale, Illinois, 1967), pages 222–51.

The latter should be read with caution, since it includes a number of errors in fact which subsequent research has brought to light.

One may wish to look also at Walter Rideout's article, " 'O Worker's Revolution . . . the True Messiah': The Jew as Author and Subject in the American Radical Novel," *American Jewish Archives* (October 1959), 157–75.

The editor of this volume is in the process of preparing Gold's memoirs for publication. At this writing (1971) at least three graduate students in the United States and Great Britain are at work on Ph.D. dissertations on various aspects of Gold's career.